GREENHOFF!

BY BRIAN GREENHOFF · FOREWORD BY TOMMY DOCHERTY · INTRODUCTION BY SAMMY McILROY

EMPIRE
PUBLICATIONS

EMPIRE PUBLICATIONS

1 Newton Street, Manchester M1 1HW

© Brian Greenhoff 2012

ISBN: 1901746 976 – 9781901746976

Printed and bound by CPI Group (UK) Ltd, Croydon, CR0 4YY

CONTENTS

This book is dedicated to my wife Maureen for all her support over the years and my sons Paul, Brian and Peter for being three great lads.

AUTHOR'S ACKNOWLEDGEMENTS

THANKS TO BRIAN and his family for their time and help. Thanks to the following people and resources for their assistance: Tommy Docherty, Sammy McIlroy, Gordon Hill, Arnie Sidebottom, Tony Park, AboutManUtd.com, mufcinfo.com, EnglandStats.com, Graham at LUFCTalk, Paul at WAFLL, and Iain McCartney.

Thanks to Ash and John at Empire for their work and support. Thanks also to Phil, Mikiel and Dan for their valuable help.

Finally, thanks to my beautiful wife, my mother and my family for their support and belief.

FOREWORD BY TOMMY DOCHERTY

THE FIRST TIME I heard of Brian was when I was manager of Rotherham United, and our scouting system covered the South Yorkshire area. Our chief scout came back and recommended two Greenhoffs, not just one; Brian and Jimmy who were Barnsley born and bred, along with Trevor Phillips, another lad who played at that time. I went to see them one Saturday morning and it didn't take us long to see that he was an outstanding prospect. I tried to sign him but I found out he'd already been earmarked for Old Trafford, so it kicked that one in to touch! They were nice lads, a bit quiet, and I was a bit disappointed not to have signed Brian.

Of course in 1972 I became manager of Manchester United and one of the first things I did when I saw him was say "Well, I've got you at last, a long road round to get you, but I got you at last!" He was a fringe player then, but you could see very quickly what a good player and what a lot of talent he had. He was skilful – I never imagined at the time he would go on to play centre half for me, because that is a position where you've got to be a bit rough and tough, and a little robust! If Brian had a weakness it's that he didn't frighten centre forwards but he was a footballing centre half and he was brilliant for me at Old Trafford.

From then on he began a fast acceleration into the first

team. It wasn't difficult to see what an outstanding talent he was for the future and I had always been a great believer in the saying "if you're good enough, you're old enough". People would say "Oh I don't know, he's not ready yet, he's too young", but I always said, "How do you know? How do you get experience?" I must admit that Brian played a lot for me at wing half but it was when we got one or two injuries we drifted him into centre half and purely by accident or instinct, he just took off. We had him and Buchan as centre defenders, both footballing defenders, not kick and rush merchants – they developed an outstanding partnership, one of the best. Brian brought a new dimension to the team because when he got the ball he would play a one-two with someone, or he would come out with the ball and go on or build up an attack. We started playing football from the goalkeeper forwards and it was fantastic. The closest I would say to Brian is another lad who played for United and then went to Barcelona, Pique, he was like the continental defenders who start attacks from the back and don't just lump it up to a centre forward.

Our whole team philosophy was built on that, and Brian was probably our most efficient player at coming out from the defence and playing with the ball. Martin was probably our least efficient! He was a tremendous defender, quick, aggressive, but when he got the ball, we'd say "Give it to a Manchester United player as quick as you can!" Brian and Buchan in a strange way got on very well, because Brian in his quiet way would tell Martin what he thought.

It was amazing how the transformation came about. Brian went from right side midfield to centre half! We were playing Wolverhampton in the FA Cup at Molineux and I think Lou

Macari got injured, and we had to switch things about. We put Brian into defence alongside Buchan and within half an hour we were thinking "what have we got here, why didn't I think of this before?" You could see, Wolverhampton didn't know what to do, there were two defenders coming at them and playing with the ball, one-twos, shots at goal... it was a new dimension to our football. But Brian could play any position, I think the only two positions where he didn't get a long run was at centre forward or goalkeeper of course, but he ended up playing both of those positions too at some point. I was always careful to play him where he wouldn't get whacked, because he'll be the first to tell you himself, he wasn't the bravest of players in terms of tackling! He could win the ball, but he wasn't a ferocious tackler like Tommy Smith at Liverpool... he would win the ball, come out with it, start attacks and have a few pops at goal as well. For me he was a great professional and what really amazed me is that he didn't play for England more.

I remember going to Tottenham and scoring a few and we were walking off the park at time up to go up the tunnel, Bill Nicholson says "Congratulations Tom, well done", I thanked him. Glenn Hoddle was right behind us and said, "But not very good defending!" - Bill said "How do you know? You never saw them defending!"

We played Leicester in the Cup and Tommy Cav was there as coach. I was sitting in the directors box as I would 9 times out of 10 because you can see everything that's going on. We had a corner kick maybe 20 minutes or quarter of an hour from half time, Brian came up for the corner and went up with the goalkeeper. Whack! He got the full force of the goalkeeper's fist and he was out like a light. I thought it looked very serious so thought I better nip downstairs, particularly as it was nearly half time. Tommy Cav went on to see if he was ok and as he was coming off Tommy was holding a sponge at the side of Brian's face, and I said "What's the matter, how's Greeno?" and Cav said "He's concussed, he doesn't know who he is." I said "Tell him he's George Best and put him back on the pitch!"

Brian and I shared highs and lows at Manchester United, relegation to Division Two and promotion as Champions, then the FA Cup Finals in 1976 and 1977. We were disappointed when we lost to Southampton because we didn't play as well as we knew we could. It wasn't a great game, not because we lost – we lost on the day to the better team, and Lawrie McMenemy was a smashing bloke. If you want to get beat, you at least want to get beat by a nice person! We just felt we didn't do ourselves justice, and that's why I said at the time (a little bit tongue in cheek) that we'd go back next year and win the Cup. And Brian was the same, of course, he said he didn't want his runners up medal!

That made winning the Cup the following year even more special for Brian in particular. It was nice to go back and win it. I remember making Brian captain on a couple of occasions where we faced Stoke and his brother Jimmy was the opposing captain – I was subject to making decisions like that, but he deserved it. I might have had a tendency to be ruthless but if I'd have stayed on at United there's no way Greeno would have left Old Trafford, he would have carried on playing the position he was playing. But different managers have different ideas.

He was a very quiet lad, Brian. If we had a bit of a shindig, or go out for a drink, he wouldn't be the life and soul of the party - and I don't mean that disrespectfully, he would just go and do his own thing, he didn't like all the fuss which goes with it. He was a model professional, you didn't have to say "do this" or "don't do that", he looked after himself well, played to the best of his ability, always trained hard, one of the first out and one of the last to go in. He was just a manager's dream as a player. I might have given him a rollicking once or twice and he maybe disagreed with one or two of the things I did - maybe going with the physio's wife was one of them! - but he was terrific, and I had a great relationship with him.

Tommy Cav always used to say, "If Greeno wasn't so soft he'd be a great player", and I'd always say, "He is a great player".

INTRODUCTION BY SAMMY MCILROY

I LEFT BELFAST IN 1969 and that's when I first met Brian, who had signed the year before me. We met at the training facilities at the old Cliff and we got on. Back in those days I was very, very homesick and I used to travel back to Belfast every three weeks. During that first year Brian and I started living together in digs in a place on Lonsdale Street in Stretford. Mr and Mrs Barber were our landlord and landlady, and it was in those digs where Brian and I really got to know one another. He even took me to Barnsley one weekend, and we got on really well.

We grew up together and then we roomed together when travelling with the first team. He was a fantastic player and I have fantastic memories of him. In any position, be it centre half or midfield, he did a fantastic job and he had a number of England caps as well – I think he should have had more, as he was a brilliant all round footballer. He wasn't a big lad but he competed very well in the air. He was a great passer of the ball – that for me was his strength, especially coming out of defence, he used to set many moves on. With his control, he never seemed to panic, he was very elegant on the ball and he had a really good understanding with Martin Buchan. Martin had the pace, but Brian read the game and his use of the ball was very good.

As a partnership they were absolutely one of the great

underrated defensive partnerships – if anyone thought "just get the ball in the air and either of these two will be easily beat", there was not a chance, they were great individually and had a wonderful understanding.

There's one game that stands out; Brian scored the equalising goal at Wolves in the FA Cup – I got the winning goal and we won 3-2. It was a quarter final replay – Brian did like scoring at Molineux, but that was a very important goal, as we were 2-0 down in a quarter final replay, enabling me to score the winner. Of the goals he scored and games he played, the Wolves game really sticks out. Brian could do that though, a lot of people just saw him as a defender, but he did very well in midfield. Sometimes if things weren't going well, Tommy Doc would change things and put Brian in midfield which he did very easily because he did it for England and his quality was very good.

We played against each other three times at international level – obviously England used to do really well and would beat Northern Ireland quite convincingly, but we still got on and would have a little snigger about certain things that might be going on in the teams. We never really had any fall outs at all, I respected him as a player and he respected me. I played against him when he played for Leeds after he left United, and he got a great reception when he came back.

Before we moved houses we would meet up at Christmas and have a Christmas drink as well over the years and bring his son Paul. I'll never forget how he helped me when I first came over from Belfast and he helped with my homesickness, it was one of the turnarounds for me being able to share digs with him in Manchester, and being able to go to Barnsley with him. As a player he was definitely under-rated, he could play in a number of positions and gave 100% wherever and whenever he played, giving great service for both England and Manchester United.

1. A BARNSLEY BOY

IT WAS A CUP FINAL AT WEMBLEY and all of the Greenhoff family were there. It was a proud day as both myself and my brother James graced the famous turf at the home of football. We held the cup aloft and celebrated in the dressing room with the rest of the team - and I wondered if this was as good as it might get. It was the 1968 League Cup Final and my elder brother James played for Leeds United against Arsenal. I was there, at pitchside, as a ball boy. Yet to sign for any club let alone the one I'd dreamed of playing for since I was a lad. Little did I know that less than a decade later we would be back, together, lifting another cup…

I was well on the way - having been earmarked for a career in the game before I even attended primary school. In my infant years I lived in the house I was born in on Dillington Road, Barnsley. It was a two-up, two-down, the bath on a nail outside, and the toilet across the back yard. When my sister Joan, who was 15 when I was born, and brother James who was 6, lived with us, I always wondered how we slept there when I was too young to remember!

Due to the big age gap between me and my brother and sister, it did feel at times like I was an only child. It was a tiny house, but my mother was very house proud. My dad was a bookie's runner, then he worked in the office as he was good with numbers. I can also remember him working down the pit; I can remember going to meet him when he would get off the bus and walk up the hill – I can still see the coal dust in his eyes. Many people used to talk about him as one of the best amateur footballers in Barnsley, a great inside forward but that he'd missed his chance.

As a family our holidays and days out always seemed to be to Blackpool. Highstone Road Working Men's Club would always run a trip, you'd be given a little brown envelope with your money in which your parents had saved up in the club for you. The coaches would be paid for, and they'd just give you the envelope when you got there. It was popular as there'd be anywhere between thirty and forty coaches going, so the earlier you got there for that first bus, the quicker you got to the seaside for your fish and chips!

My earliest memories, though, are my infant school days at Park Road Primary School, a school that was known in the area for being interested in football. The head teacher was a lady called Mrs Thacker who was mad keen on the game – they knew I was coming, and with my brother having already gone there and having done so well, they couldn't wait for me to go there too. They only had one football side, and I was barely into my second year when they put me into the team! Really, they wanted me in when I was in my first year, or so I was told by a friend called Raymond Smith but it wasn't allowed. The Smith family were local, they lived only thirty yards from us so we were really close and friendly. They were really good to us, to me and my mother. As soon as it was summer and the football season was over, the stumps came out in the playground, and you'd get the teachers and the supervisors coming out. If you bowled someone out, you batted! I got a lot of encouragement to play football but in those days we'd play on the corner of the street just to get a game and people wouldn't bother you. You might get the odd one that would say "come on, move along!" but it hardly happened where we lived. It wasn't a main road, and there were very few cars in those days. Our family never had a car, my mum and dad never owned or drove a car, so when I wanted to go and play football, it was shanks' pony! You'd put your ball under your arm, meet up with your mates and go and play.

Facing our front door was a back ginnel and at the top of that there was a wall that ran alongside a football pitch where Park Road used to play. Basically it'd be a game on a Saturday where the local working men's club would play their home games, until around the early sixties, when they found a bomb there! So they took the nets down, went and played elsewhere and that was our pitch gone! We didn't have our own football pitch at school and we didn't have our own cricket pitch either, so when we played football we'd go and play at Yorkshire Traction's Bus depot's pitch which was about 15 minutes walk. So we'd get changed at the school, walk down to the pitch, play the game and go back to the school to get changed. No showers, just a matter of playing the game. When we played cricket, we'd go and play in the local park, we'd just find a spot, put the stumps in and that was it.

Of the two, my love was always football. There were no replica shirts in those days, there were red and blue shirts we'd get from the army and navy store for Christmas, and I'd always get bought some new socks, shorts and a shirt. I'd get football boots when my parents could afford them, but they had to last a season, if not longer, sometimes until they didn't fit me! I was always encouraged to play by my mum and dad. My mum always made sure I had the cleanest kit, it was immaculate. We had to take the kits back to school after we washed them, and when I used to take mine back, they were always impressed. Before I'd go to play a match, my dad always used to make sure that my boots were clean, so whenever I played I had sparkling boots and a lovely clean kit.

My first position in the school team was on the right wing, because that's where they'd tend to stick you when you first went in as a young lad. Because I was the best player in the team, they'd always try and give me the ball, and they'd want me to be on the ball all the time. But that's how it was, not as organised as it would be these days. I don't think we ever practised, certainly not a practice match. All the practice we got was in the schoolyard. During the football season, the footballs would come out, we'd have two sets of nets, one drawn on one wall and one on another, and that'd be it. If the ball went over a fence then it'd go onto the main road and we'd hope that someone gave us the ball back before a lorry ran over it! Our team never won anything; we didn't have a particularly great side, but we always fulfilled our fixtures.

My sister tells me that my first hero was former Manchester United striker Tommy Taylor, and that must have been when I was about 3 or 4 years old. Tommy was sold by Barnsley to United for £29,999 because they didn't want him to become the first £30,000 player, and when I was a kid he was always someone I idolised. I always used to go and watch Barnsley. They used to have a trial match at the start of every season which was a real highlight, the reds v the blues. In those days, because we had no car, Barnsley were the team we'd go and watch, in any case my dad would not have allowed a young lad of my age to go to Old Trafford.

I have always been a red of course, I always wore a red kit. On a Christmas morning, the first thing we always used to do, a lad called Melvyn Hill and me would go up on the tips, and say we'd play 90 minutes, 45 minutes each way, and after about 10 minutes we'd be back in because there was no way 1 against 1 you were going to last for ninety minutes! When we'd go up to the working men's pitch and they'd put the nets up and marked out the pitch with sawdust, those were the times that you'd be dreaming of playing for real. The first player I pretended to be wasn't Tommy but Bobby Charlton, I always wanted to be him, because he could smack the ball. The footballs that we had were far too hard to bend, so it'd be head down, arse up and smack it (as Tommy Cavanagh would later say)! Sometimes they'd come and shoo us off because they didn't want the lines mucking up, but we weren't bothered, we just wanted to play.

I think that kind of attitude was instilled into us from our upbringing. Our parents were strict but fair. My dad could make me cry just by bollocking me, but I knew he was doing it for the right reasons. He'd never shout at me while I was playing, he'd just watch, and when we got home he'd say "sit down" and then he'd tell me what he thought. If I played well he'd tell me, if I had an area to improve he'd say so, as he was always very encouraging and supportive, and I'd always take that advice on board. He watched a lot of games that James and I played in. My dad had gone to Lincoln City and passed the trial but he couldn't play for them as they didn't pay enough – he knew the game and won trophies, so he knew what he was talking about.

I can remember James signing for Leeds. He was at Barnsley Grammar School and left early – in those days you couldn't leave until you were 16, but my parents bought him out for a fee of around £10 so he could go to Leeds. James played in a very successful Barnsley boys side that won the English trophy. Me and my dad used to go all over watching him – his school side were unbelievable, I don't think they ever lost a game. I think about ten of that school team got into the Barnsley boys squad, and for a team like that to win the trophy for a town like Barnsley was a big thing. I remember they beat Liverpool in the final 2-1 on aggregate. It's ironic that years later James would feature in another 2-1 final win against Liverpool! That side featured Alan Ogley who would go on and play for Stockport and Manchester City, and Alan Woodward, a right winger who went on to play for Sheffield United. Those were the three that stood out, although others went onto play league football. When James first signed for Leeds the plan was that he would travel there every day and come home, but in the end he went in digs. For a time he stopped with Norman Hunter – Norman's mother had moved down from the North East, so James stopped there so he didn't have to travel. My sister had already moved out because she'd got married, so I was the only one left, and I had my own bedroom.

James was fortunate in going to a grammar school, they played all sports and their facilities were fantastic. I failed my 11-plus and ended up going to Racecommon Road Secondary

School and all we had was a football pitch, because the cricket pitch was tarmac – and we still had to walk about three hundred yards to get to that! We never had anything at the school. We had a good gym-master there, Mr Carbutt, who always wanted to get us out playing football or cricket instead of just going in the gym. Again, our team won nothing at football. By that time we had Arnie Sidebottom on our team. That was it really, there was me and Arnie, and another lad called Harry Stott – the rest were making up the numbers and you'll never win anything with only three players. But at cricket, we won everything, I would bowl them out and Arnie would knock them off! Arnie was in the year below me – we only had two teams, the 1st and 2nd year team, and the 3rd and 4th year team. When I was a second year I played in both sides for both football and cricket, and Arnie was the same, though he later played in the older cricket teams when he was only in his second year – he was that good.

Although I had failed that 11 plus, academically I didn't do too badly. When I was in my next to last year, I was in the top class and finished second in exams. The following year however it was a different story. By then I knew I was going to be a footballer and the headmaster Mr Kay (who was absolutely fantastic with me) used to let me have any time off I wanted. If I had a game at night, or dinnertime, he just looked after me because he just knew what was going to happen. It was something the careers officer would later find out when he asked, "So what are you going to do?". I said "I'm going to play football", and he said "Oh yeah, have you had any interest from anybody?". I said "Well, Manchester United are after me". I remember him looking at me going

"Oh? Oh... so you're pretty sure with what you're going to do then." I suffered in class as I dropped from second to nineteenth, but only because I was never there. I was always top in maths and even though in the last year I did hardly any of the work that the others did, I still finished fourth. I've always been good with numbers and so it didn't take me long to pick it up. I'm still a fan of working things out, I love a game of Sudoku!

I was thirteen when I got my break in the Barnsley Boys squad, and played a few friendly games where I did alright. My first proper game was against Hull at Oakwell, I was on the left wing. I had an absolute nightmare, I hated the game and hated playing there. By that time, we'd moved out of our house on Dillington Road and into a pub called the Morning Star. It was a miners pub, which we took over for a few years from my auntie Hilda and uncle Hubert. We had a tap room, where the men tended to go, then there was the snug and the main room. The darts team played in the best room on a Tuesday, and I would score for the darts due to my good maths ability. In those days, no kids were allowed in pubs, but I'd be there adding the scores up, and the next thing you would hear the shout of "coppers!!" and I'd run into the ladies, which was next to the snug! Then when the coast was clear, I'd get a knock on the door, "tha can come out now", and there'd be a bit of mickey taking from the miners. I think living in the pub, it really did feel like I was an only child sometimes; I would have to go to bed before the pub closed and it was a bit scary sometimes as you could still hear what was going on downstairs. It probably didn't help that my bedroom was above the gents toilets! I used to make sure

I had the dog with me for company.

I walked home after that game against Hull, into the pub through the off-sales part and my mother asked me if I was ok, I said no and my dad noticed. He'd spoken to the coach and said to me, "I didn't think you played very well." He gave me both barrels! Nobody could hear him, but he went in, told me how bad I'd done, and tears were streaming down my face. I used to have to walk through the pub to be able to get in but seeing me, my mum said "Jump over the wall". She gave me a bag of crisps and a bottle of pop, and said, "Go and watch telly". My dad could do that to me. I've always been emotional, and I cared what he thought. He didn't tell me what I wanted to hear, although I knew it was coming. I have no doubt that he only did that to help me, that if I really was to become a professional footballer there were certain things that I had to improve and he was very quick to tell me. I don't think he was ever wrong, though I wouldn't have told him anyway!

Discipline was different then – even the schoolteachers wouldn't think twice about giving you a clip round the ear. You'd get the slipper and cane at school but again, I didn't really talk back as such then. I used to sit next to a lad called Les Cooper, and he was perfect. I'd just load the bullets and he'd fire them, then he'd get the hit from the teachers! But he'd get the laughs, I was just the scriptwriter! I think whenever I did get the slipper, it was Les' fault, and vice versa, so I got payback for all the whacks he got. I got the cane once and that was nothing to do with me, there was a big fight and I was sat watching it, the headmaster came in and caned us all! But I was a good boy, I was a prefect so I must have been good. I was always willing to help everybody. The school helped me out in my last year, I was barely there. Mr Carbutt, the games teacher, was off with a bad back, and Mr Harris, the maths teacher, used to organise the games, and I would pick the team and how we played. It was the only time we had a chance of winning the league but we lost it on the last day of the season. In those times, kids would leave school at Easter, and the team who won it had a few who actually came back and stayed on to play. If they hadn't have come back, we'd have won it.

After that terrible game on the wing against Hull, it took me all year to get back into the Barnsley Boys first team – I was substitute the entire season, though always in the squad, until the last game of the season. We played away at Chesterfield and I was back in the team, and we won 4-3. My dad wasn't there which was a shame because I had a blinding game, destroying them with a lad called Stewart Barraclough who went on to star for Newcastle. That really sowed the seeds for the next year. They had to pick two players to go up to an England schoolboys' run soccer camp in the North East, and I was picked with a lad called Steve Daley who later played for Wolves and Man City. We went up to Newcastle for five days and ended up picking four teams, and I got picked for the top team. That was quite a feat, because there were quite a few players in that team who played for England schoolboys, though unfortunately I didn't.

As soon as I went back home from that Newcastle trip, I was straight into the Barnsley Boys team and they made me captain. We didn't have a bad squad that next season – some of the players went on to have good careers in the game, there was a lad called Trevor Phillips who started at Rotherham and played for Stockport, a lad called Jeff English who played for Arsenal, who was the only one from our team to play for England schoolboys. I remember our first game, where we played Leeds who were always a strong side, and we beat them 4-0. So after that we thought "Aye aye, we've got something going on here", and we did really well. We got to around the 5th or 6th round in the Cup and we played at Sunderland. That was a great trip up for everybody - we went up early, had a little warm up, went and had something to eat, and then got to play on Roker Park. We lost 2-1 but had two goals disallowed in the first six minutes, and it wasn't a surprise that the three officials turned out to be locals! In the end, we got a penalty which I scored, but it was a little bit too late. We all felt a little bit cheated after that and then we fell apart as a team, the disappointment got to us and nothing really happened as the season just drifted away.

As for me, I continued to do well. I was selected for both the football team and cricket team for Yorkshire Boys, where I played alongside Arnie Sidebottom again. We played for the town team even though I was a year younger than the rest, and Arnie was two years younger. We had a decent team and got to the semi-final of the Yorkshire Cup, where we lost to East Riding, and the following year lost at the same stage to Rothwell and Stanley. In school cricket we never lost a game, we'd win everything with Arnie and me in the same team. I was the best bowler, he was the best batter. For representing the football team you'd get a badge, and for the cricket team you'd get a cap. I got a cap representing Yorkshire Boys and Arnie and myself got a bit of attention from the media, getting our picture in the paper walking out at the home ground at Shaw Lane with our caps. We weren't batting, it was just for the papers – you'd get your caps before the game, of course. I loved playing at Shaw Lane, it was a pleasure as they were such good wickets. Mainly, they were good batting wickets, and I was a bowler but I did alright. We played against South Helmsall once and they wanted seven to win in the last over with three wickets left, and I got a hat-trick. I can always remember that afterwards the umpire gave me sixpence – why he did that I don't know. I got a bottle of pop and a packet of crisps with it. Winning the cap was a special moment. As a proud Yorkshireman – it meant a lot to me. I still have the cap and the badges I won.

I was starting to get used to the attention. There was always going to be a bit of a spotlight on me with our James having already played and done well for Barnsley boys. It was always said that I was, "the brother of Jimmy". I was always in his shadow and it was hard to live up to as he was a good schoolboy player. I could never be Brian Greenhoff in my own right, and people would ask if it bothered me, but I would just say no because one day I would turn it around so it would say Jimmy was the brother of Brian. And when it eventually did, it gave me great pleasure the first time I saw it! At Racecommon Road I can remember the papers coming to take pictures of me, and all my mates were trying to get in the background of it, so they all knew I was getting the attention, but none of it was with any resentment, far from it. And of course they knew of James, and the attention I got from that.

If I wasn't playing my dad would take me to watch James.

Even if I had played in the morning, we'd always get someone to take us because we'd get tickets and give one to whoever had a car. In the 1968 League Cup Final, our James was in the Leeds team that played Arsenal. Strangely enough, I ended up as a ball boy. For every final two towns would get selected for schools to put boys forward to be ball boys. We got chosen, and about half a dozen of us went down. The other town was Islington in London, where Arsenal played – I recognised one of the boys from there, as he had been on the youth trip to Newcastle, and I think he actually signed for Tottenham. We went to Wembley on the train, accompanied by the teacher. At the stadium we were told to sort the tracksuits out and that our boots had to be sparkling – mine always were of course, so that was never a problem – and then they walked us out on the pitch, they told us what we had to do, which way we had to throw the ball back. Then we had something to eat and then it was show time!

I was behind the goal at the tunnel end and Leeds were kicking in that end in the first half. I can remember Jack Charlton chipping the ball into my hands – it might have been odd or surreal being a ball boy at Wembley with World Cup winners, but I knew Jack, with our kid having been at Leeds for about 6 or 7 years. I was comfortable with them, I was always hanging around with my autograph book as plenty of lads used to ask me to get autographs for them. Leeds went on to win the game and I had a great view of the goal which was scored at the other end, and was more or less behind Terry Cooper when he smacked it in. After the game we had to stand in the centre circle, and when they were running around with the cup, we were allowed to walk around the stadium. I was allowed to hold the Cup, and I even got in the dressing room with the Cup because I knew everybody. Leeds coach Les Cocker gave me the first new pair of boots I ever got. They were Bobby Collins' Stylo boots, but they didn't fit him and he gave them to me when I was 14. I always had boots, but they were the first "proper" boots I had. Mixing in such company I could have been forgiven for thinking that it might not get better than that.

In the early days of the 1967/68 campaign, the Yorkshire Boys team played a game at York. I played and some of the lads were playing in the next game. I went and had a shower, then came back to watch the lads play. Suddenly this little fella with an umbrella came and put it over me and said, "Hello, I'm Joe Armstrong, from Manchester United. Could I have your address? We'd like to come and speak to your parents". So I gave him the address, and the very next day, Johnny Aston senior turned up. I was out playing football. Johnny told my parents that they were interested in signing me on Joe's recommendation. Joe was a legendary scout at United, having 'discovered' the likes of Bobby Charlton, David Pegg and Eddie Colman. He was a lovely gentleman – he always had a daft joke and I can't think of anybody who disliked him, he was such a nice man. From that point on I was watched for the rest of the season. I wouldn't know they were there but my dad would tell me such and such was here, as somebody had had a word with him.

We also got a call from Chelsea, who wanted me to go down. The man at Chelsea was called Ron Suart, formerly of the famous Blackpool team that featured Stan Mortenson and Stanley Matthews. Ron had wanted our kid to go to

Blackpool some years ago, and then when I came along and he'd heard things, I don't think he even watched me, he just wanted me to go down for trials. My dad wouldn't let me go, he just said, "You're not going on trial anywhere, if they don't like what they see, you're not going". He told me to wait until the end of season, sit down and go through all the clubs, and then I could decide where I'd go and we'd take it from there.

I went over to United a couple of times and played in a couple of little matches, and luckily enough I must have done alright because they offered me a contract. It was close, though. Rotherham were watching me at the time and Tommy Docherty was manager. Tommy took us out for a meal – me, my dad, Jeff English and Trevor Phillips and their dads too – at the Brecks hotel on the road out of Rotherham into Maltby. He wanted to sign all three of us and offered us the money there and then and talked through what the deals would be. At that time the Doc was known for giving kids a chance but the only problem was that he never really stayed anywhere for a long time. It was very tempting as I could have lived at home and travelled in every day because it was only an hour on the bus. Barnsley wanted to sign me too and they'd looked after me, I'd been away with them a couple of times watching matches, and of course being local I knew them. It was a tough choice and I went on holiday to think it over with our neighbours Mr and Mrs Smith and my auntie and uncle to Calella De La Costa in Spain for ten days.

When we got back in early August my dad said "right, make your mind up!" Of course, my mind was already made up for United before I went. While I was away, that was the only thing I ever heard about, Manchester United this, Manchester United that, even the barman was talking about United! They had just won the European Cup but even so, it was incredible that their fame stretched as far as Spain (or at least it seemed so at the time). So dad rang Johnny Aston, who turned up that same afternoon. He arrived with a contract and we signed there and then, and my dad said, "Right, when do you want him to come?", to which Johnny replied, "Now!". I gathered all my stuff together and went back with Johnny and stayed at his house that night, in young John's old bedroom. The next day I was training at the Cliff!

It was difficult to get used to right away, I was used to having my mum look after me. It may have been a fairly difficult choice but I always thought, if I went to Rotherham or Barnsley and didn't make it, I could be working down the pit! But if I went to United and it didn't work out, I could always go back to Barnsley or Rotherham. So I thought by starting at the top with a team that had just won the European Cup was as good as it got. They were the very best but I think what swung it was the fact they gave my dad two tickets to a game. I couldn't go but my dad went with a friend who had a car!

It was a strange coincidence that Arnie eventually ended up joining me at United. He didn't get into the town football team because he mustn't have been good enough but after I'd been at United for a couple of years, Johnny Aston told me he'd been talking to a scout from Barnsley and asked me what I knew of Arnie. I said "Yeah I went to school with him, he's a good footballer". They took him on - not on my say so obviously - and he did well as he was talented at most sports, though it was cricket where he made his career.

While at United, I'd still go home often and it was strange to start playing for the biggest club in the world and return to the working class town I was from. I learned a lot from the miners in the pub, those same ones who had taken the mickey out of me when I was younger, particularly my sense of humour which had to be quick. I learned how to play cards, crib, dominoes and darts. When I signed my first contract at United it was for three years, and I'd tell people that I was on seven pounds a week and people would say, "That's twice as much as me, bloody hell I can't believe they gave you that much!"

One thing I learned, growing up in a town like Barnsley, was how to deal with money. Years later I went back when the miners strike was on, and all the same blokes were there. Some were working, some were not and some were on the sick and that was hard to see.

I made the mistake of criticising Arthur Scargill. He used to work under my brother in law Bill, who was a deputy at Woolley Edge pit, and Bill used to say he was the laziest sod ever. I remember asking my pal's dad, "Are you still on strike?", and he said "Aye", so I said "the quicker you get rid of that Scargill, the better!" Well, you should have heard him, it was if I'd blasphemed. "Tha' dunt know what tha' mean, he's our hero, he's our saviour! I can't believe tha's said that!"

Later that evening I went out with his son for a meal and he said, "You didn't mention Arthur Scargill did you?" It was incredible that nobody would hear a bad word about him.

2. A BUSBY BABE

TO MOVE SO QUICKLY - going from a holiday in Spain to training at the biggest club in the world alongside the European Champions - in the space of around seventy-two hours was a bit of a culture shock. On my first day of training there were a few familiar faces, not just because I'd been there a couple of times the previous season. I knew Kevin Lewis who I'd played for Yorkshire Boys with, I knew Eric Young and Bobby Lomas from the England trip I went on to Newcastle and England trials. The England trials would always finish up North v South - the North had such a good side that I ended up playing for the South as a substitute, which didn't impress me as I didn't know anybody. Eric and Kevin made me feel welcome, showed me around to where the lads used to go at night, to the bowling alley and that sort of thing.

I moved to Manchester with Johnny Aston Sr. and the next day we had to find some digs for me. I didn't want to find somewhere I would just stay for a couple of weeks and then move again, it was important to find the right digs. The first two I went to didn't work out. At the first one, which I moved into with Eric and Kevin, I didn't see eye to eye with the landlady, and the second one, we got on fine but I just didn't like the place. Finally a lad called Willie Carrick, an Irish lad who was a goalkeeper for the youth team, said there was a spare bed in his room. He asked his landlady, Mrs Barratt, who said I could move in. I went to Joe Armstrong and asked him and he said it was no problem, so I moved in and shared a room with Willie. In the back room, there was a single bedroom where a reporter from Sheffield by the name of Michael Morgan who worked for the *Daily Express* stayed. He wasn't there long before he left, and so Willie being Mrs Barratt's blue eyed boy moved in to that room and then Sammy McIlroy moved in and we shared a bedroom.

It was a good place to stay but we always used to say that the cat got fed better! It's not like it is now, we would get meat and potato pie, burger and chips... looking back at what we used to eat, it was ridiculous. Even at the Cliff, when we first went there, there'd be soup, sandwiches, pints of milk, and that was your diet - no-one was bothered. You'd come in pre-season and they'd weigh you, and then they wouldn't weigh you again! Some people got a little bit obsessed with it, which might not have been a bad thing for me as I did struggle with my weight but I usually managed to keep it under control.

The facilities at the Cliff were very poor. The changing rooms weren't very good, the upstairs weren't good, it was just a pleasure when the new changing rooms were opened, it felt like luxury! It was such a change from what we'd gone through where they'd just come in, throw the kit on the floor and you had to fight for the best gear. If you were playing in the gym, they used to have boots in a little room and you'd have to get a pair that fit you. It was a surprise to me how disorganised it was.

As apprentices we had to pick our kits up from Old

Trafford – the first team's would always be a lot better than ours – and we'd get all the rubbish thrown at us. There was no kit manager – as we learned later when the first, A or B team would be away, we used to have to do the skips, the apprentices would have to do it with Jack Crompton, Johnny Aston or Wilf McGuinness. We'd just have to fill it up and make sure everything was right. The A team would only get one set of shirts while the first team would get two sets so if they wanted to change, they could. Sometimes when we had to get the shirts, it was hard work getting them from the laundry ladies – it was as if they were precious, even the socks! It was a hard job for the laundry women but they only got so much kit for the entire year, it wasn't like today where there's new kits for every game.

At the time I was staying in Gorse Hill. If we were on earlies, where we'd have to go to the ground to pick the kit up, we could get a lift to the Cliff, with either Jack, Wilf or Johnny who would be doing it. If not, we had to get two buses – one to Victoria Station, and then another up to Broughton, until we learned that if the first team were playing we could hang around at the ground and someone like Denis Law or John Fitzpatrick would give us a lift up there. We'd pop in to have a cup of tea with Mrs Burgess in the morning but we had to make sure that we knew the first team were training, because if they were off, then we had to catch the bus.

I'd been scouted by Joe Armstrong and physically taken to United by Johnny Aston senior but the man in charge was of course Sir Matt Busby. I'd met Sir Matt the previous season when they'd invited us to a game against West Bromwich Albion, we were upstairs in the visiting directors box and afterwards they took me down to the changing rooms where I got to meet everybody. When I signed for the club, Matt always made sure he had time for me – he said hello to everybody, and made it his business to know people's names, and later on, the players' wives and children's names. He was noted for that. Many years after I'd left, actually, I went to watch a game at Old Trafford and I was in the grill room and he walked through, saw me and shook my hand and asked how my wife was – by name, of course. But that was him, he'd always say hello and he'd never just walk past you.

The first season at the club as a fifteen year old was difficult at times. I got left behind because, joining late, I'd missed the pre-season, and I was always about three weeks behind, and I struggled a bit. The fitter I got, the more training I'd do. At Barnsley Boys I'd train maybe once a week and play on a Saturday. At schools we'd just play games, and that was all we got. So to go to United and train every day – and not only train, we'd have to go back to Old Trafford and do the cleaning! And that was after we'd cleaned the Cliff! At Old Trafford we'd clean the boots, but also the floors, the drains, the toilets, the baths, showers, everything. There was no job that we didn't do. It was hard work but rewarding – some days we might not finish until five o'clock, and a footballer finishing at five o'clock after going in at nine just doesn't happen now! The only good thing was that we didn't have to clean the terraces, because some of the other trainees did that.

My first game for United was against Blackpool at home in the Youth Cup and we won 7-2 – I was still only fifteen, the youngest in the side. I think I did alright – I didn't pull up any trees but it's hard sometimes playing with lads that are two years older than you. As it was their last year, they were all thinking they should be in the side, but we had a decent side and some of the first year lads were in it. Kevin and Eric would have been in, as they were big strong lads – Eric was a tall, elegant player, Kevin was a typical tough Yorkshire lad. That first year when I signed, quite a few schoolboy internationals signed – a lad called Damien Ferguson came over from Ireland, a couple of players from Scotland – Tony Young and Tony Whelan were local, Bobby Lomas from Stockport, Eric from Stockton, Willie Carrick from Ireland of course. After that first game, I tended to be substitute for a few of the games right up to the semi-final, which was reminiscent of those days at Barnsley Boys. I'd always played in teams with older boys but while it might have been ok at school level because there wouldn't tend to be a lot of difference between the players, jumping up to the professional level where I would be playing with first year pros as a first year apprentice was a big difference. You got a three year apprenticeship contract and then it was up to the club whether to sign you to professional terms on your 17th birthday, or they'd let your contract run out and you could leave. United didn't tend to do that with many lads though – they'd either sign them professionally, or have a word and say they could find another club.

United were renowned for playing a 4-2-4 formation that evolved into a 4-3-3 around the time of them winning the European Cup, but at youth team level, although there was always a philosophy of playing with wingers, we didn't always play to mirror the first team. We were always told to express and enjoy ourselves, to work hard for each other, the basic beliefs. It wasn't until we played against Liverpool that you could notice the difference. Liverpool's youth side mirrored the first, and even the players looked similar! That was probably why they were successful over the years - when somebody came into their side, it was a natural progression, and it was uncanny watching and playing against them. Liverpool's method was regimental, but ours was always based on getting the best out of the player's ability - with a huge emphasis on working hard. If you were playing in central midfield and one of the pair moved, the other had to keep their discipline and stay. As a full back you were more of a supporting act, to keep the overlaps as a surprise - whereas today, some of the full backs are more advanced than the wide midfield players. But United always had a great belief and emphasis on attack, and in years to come when I got into the team it was clear that the supporters loved the way the team played.

Personally, I was given a pretty settled role in the youth team, I would usually play centre midfield, moving onto centre half later on. In the A and B teams I would play everywhere - right back, left back, centre forward, I got moved around quite a bit. I always found the left back spot a bit weird, but the coaches must have seen something in me to keep moving me around, and I'm not even sure it had anything to do with injuries. I even played in goal twice, once for the A team and once for the B team. I can remember being sub for the reserves and thinking "Great, I'm substitute for the reserves!" when suddenly I get a phone call asking me to go to Old Trafford to go with the B team. I asked "Why?" in disbelief, and they told me they hadn't got a goalkeeper and I was going in! We won 5-0 and it was good fun. Having the freedom to express ourselves was good, but I just wanted to play on the Saturday. That's how it was, everyone wanted to play on the Saturday and that's why you trained all week – nowadays, some players don't play for weeks or even months and I can't understand how they can be happy with that. Whether I was playing right back, left back, centre midfield, centre defence, up front or in goal, I was happy playing. After training, the four teams would go up and remember there was only one substitute, so that was forty eight players trying to get a game, the others were just reserves and didn't play. It must have been hard for many but fortunately, unless I was injured, I didn't miss a game.

At the end of the first season with the club there was the Blue Star tournament, an annual competition held in Switzerland that still runs to this day. Manchester United had, and still have, a proud record in the tournament and were holders in 1968, just before I had joined. Representing the club abroad was a very special thing. The first thing we were told is that we were representing Manchester United, we had to conduct ourselves in a proper manner. We stayed in the Hotel Stoller, which wasn't far from the ground. On the first day you played three games, twenty minutes each way, and if you qualified you played the next day but moved into the big stadium rather than on the pitches outside, where the games would all be played at the same time.

I hoped to play in every game. Unfortunately I didn't, but I played some part. In the final, I was lucky enough to come on as substitute, and I scored the winning goal – the ball just came to me at the edge of the box, I thumped it and it flew in the top corner. It was a great experience. To be picked to go on the tour at all was an honour – some of the apprentices didn't, so to be picked was to say that you'd done well that year. The day after we won it, we went out to do a bit of shopping, I was out with a lad called Tommy O'Neill, and it started to rain. We went into a bar, us being two sixteen year old lads – a bar called the Playboy but it was nothing like the name suggests! Tommy said, "Shall we have a pint", and I said "Aye, go on." So we had a couple and by the second, all the other lads had joined us. They were winding me up about scoring the goal, then said "Ey, you can break Carlo Sartori's record. He supped nine pints!" Little did I know they were spiking my drinks! When we got back to the Stoller, I fell and banged my head in the lift, and of course Johnny Aston found out, and they put me in bed.

Next day I woke up and Jimmy Murphy was there – he just beckoned me over and gave me the biggest rollicking of all time. I thought I'd had bad ones from my dad, but it was nothing compared to Jimmy! "You've let the club down son, you've let yourself down, you've let your team-mates down!", he reminded me, going through it all about the conduct expected from a Manchester United player. Yet afterwards he said that was the end of it, there was nothing else to be done. We had another game the next day and they named the team – I wasn't even on as a substitute. I just had to sit and watch – that was my punishment. The game after I was back playing, but I learned a valuable lesson. My relationship with Jimmy was more or less the same as with Sir Matt, they'd never walk past without saying hello. I used to go and get their sandwiches for them – there used to be a Dictaphone in the passageway by the changing rooms, they'd buzz through to tell us to go and get two salmon or two tuna, and we'd go up to the shop and put it on their bill. This was before there was a restaurant at Old Trafford, so we'd have to go up to the cafe on the corner.

The day we got back from Switzerland, I got the bus home to Barnsley from Manchester, and when I got in my dad was in bed, waiting for an ambulance to come. He'd had a heart attack, and they took him into the hospital that day. I just had time to show him my medal before the ambulancemen came and took him – trying to get a stretcher down the stairs in that house couldn't have been much fun. I'd try and see dad in hospital when I had the odd night off and mum would be there as much as she could be. Sometimes we'd get a lift, but the majority of times we'd have to get two buses. I was supposed to be going on holiday with the lads to Lloret de Mar, but I had to cancel it. I took the call on July 4th, 1969 when they informed us he had died. That happened while I would have been on holiday, so it was the right decision to stay at home.

When I went back to United, it was strange. Everyone was asking how my dad was, and then I told them and it was upsetting but Dad would have wanted me to carry on and do my best. I hope that he would have appreciated what I did do. In my first year, after tax I came out with £6 a week. I'd give my mum three pounds from that, and I'd live off the other three. Luckily enough work would pay for my travel home, either the bus from Mosley Street to Barnsley or the train from Piccadilly Station to Penistone, where I'd catch the bus.

I just carried on paying my mum the way I had, and even when I turned pro and had to start paying for my own digs, I always made sure I gave her something when I went home, anything I could afford.

That summer, Sammy McIlroy signed for United on his birthday, August 2nd. He moved into the digs at Mrs Barratt's, and we always got on well, immediately striking up a friendship. In the early days Sammy would get homesick but was only allowed to go home once a month. He found it difficult, but we used to rally round him. To unwind, we'd go to the discos, down to Brown's, where in 1970, we met the girls who would go on to become our wives. I met a girl named Maureen, and Sammy started seeing Cynthia. Near to where we lived there was a hairdresser where we'd go and have a bit of a laugh, always getting our hair done, having the hair blow dried if we were going out at night.

In my last year in the youth side, the legendary Bill Foulkes joined as youth team coach. I had my appendix out in the October of 1971 – I can remember in training, having a really hard session as Bill liked to get the lads fit, as he was a bit of a fitness fanatic. I sat down next to John Connaughton and said, "I've got a hell of a pain in my side", and he reckoned it was just a stitch. I said it wasn't, as I normally got that further round, so Laurie Brown, the physio, came in, checked me over and ordered me to see Doc McHugh. He was in Whalley Range, and he said I had a grumbling appendix, but I had to wait two weeks as the surgeon who did it was on holiday. I had it out at St. Joseph's Hospital at Whalley Range by Sidney Rose who was a director at Manchester City.

I had a great relationship with Bill. There was a big lad at centre half in the youth team called Bill Fairhurst, who, like Bill, was from St. Helens. He was honest as the day is long – he probably lacked a bit of confidence in himself but he could head the ball, tackle, he wasn't frightened. He wasn't the best passer of the ball, but that's why I played alongside him. I could pick the balls up off him – we had a good relationship as a defensive partnership. Bill worked hard with us, he'd get us back in the afternoon, and take us in the gym at the Cliff (if you could call it that – this was before they built the actual gym!) at the new building. We'd put one bench perched against another, put some rope on, and do sit ups. He used to make us work so hard on building ourselves up, but he would do it himself too – he would never ask you to do anything that he himself couldn't do.

Some might have said that Bill was hard – I never minded people being hard on me, so long as it was fair and constructive. I don't like to see people criticised for the sake of it. I didn't mind people being in my face as it got me going, as I found out years later with Tommy Cavanagh, who came in at half time during one game and said "Who the fucking hell do you think you are? Fucking Beckenbauer?" I didn't like what he said but I went out second half and played really well. At full time Tommy just looked at me and said, "Worked, didn't it?" That's what it was about – if someone has to be hard, then it has to be done for the right reaction and I felt Bill was fair like that.

Of course Bill is steeped in the history of the club and it was great to have him and another hero from the Munich Air Disaster, Harry Gregg, around helping and supporting us. It was something that encouraged me to do the same when I got to the first team, I would go and watch the youth team, because it gave the lads a lift. These are the people we wanted to impress, people like Bill, Harry, Sir Matt. Looking back at who actually ran the A and the B teams, there was Bert Fishbourne who had a club in Chorlton and Joe Travis who was the trainer for the B team, but we hardly saw them during the week. We had somebody looking after us called Jack Pauline, who would just come in rubbing his hands saying, "Alright lads! Are we right? Enjoy it yeah?" We used to wonder what was going on! Of course it wasn't as well run as it is now, in fact it was a million miles away. To think that Manchester United have produced so many great youth teams and so many great players, it made me wonder how! I think they were lucky to have great players to fetch through; there was no chance of splashing £20 million here or £15 million there. At United you always thought you'd get a chance because youth was so important to the club but how it panned out to be that way when I look back, it can't have been the facilities!

Compare the set-up there to one of the other clubs I considered signing for as a schoolboy. Burnley had a great youth set up and great facilities, far better than at United. When I got taken around there, you had to see it to believe it. They had four pitches – one that was set up to mirror Turf Moor, an all weather pitch, a big gym, and other facilities. They even had a gym at the ground. It was far better than the Cliff. We were brought up playing on poor pitches, I used to feel sorry for the groundsman when we just had the one pitch there. The pitches today are perfect, no bumps or divots, when back in our day we'd often play on mud.

The great thing though was United had a wonderful scouting network and they signed good players. A lot of lads came over from Northern Ireland where the great Bob Bishop worked, and Southern Ireland, where Billy Behan scouted. What we might have lacked in facilities we gained in values that were taught to us – we learned good habits. They knew what kind of players they were looking for and that came right from the top with Sir Matt Busby and Jimmy Murphy who would have identified what sort of player they wanted, and when you look at the number of players that Bob and Billy sent over, it certainly worked. You had players coming over from Ireland and moving from different areas of England at a time when transport wasn't so easy, all on the strength of United's name. Even travelling from Barnsley wasn't easy, it was a good hour and a half or two hours on the bus, if the weather was good. It was a nightmare in winter. Sometimes coaches used to go from Barnsley to Old Trafford to watch games and I'd cadge a lift back afterwards! It was an education and United were very good in helping the development of players as young men. That's why a lot of lads go on from United and make good careers elsewhere, even if they're not good enough to play for the first team, and I think that's a key reason that United have been so successful over the years. Today the academies are so well run that I can't even imagine what they're like.

I was one of the last to be brought through as a "Busby Babe". By this time, Jimmy Murphy was far more involved than Sir Matt who was coming to the end. He'd be the one training us, the one who'd be there playing in the five or ten a-sides. In the youth setup it was mainly Johnny Aston and

Wilf who looked after us and our development, and it was those two and Bill I thank for my personal development. In the days before Bill joined as a coach, we'd never go back in the afternoon to work on our skills, as we'd have to go to Old Trafford to do the cleaning.

On the senior managerial front there were a lot of changes. Even though everybody was disappointed to see Sir Matt retire because of what he'd done for the club, when they promoted Wilf (which was a little bit of a shock) we knew he would be for the youth, because he was trying to build a team around George Best and all the kids got excited because we thought we'd get a chance. By the summer of 1970, he'd started introducing one or two kids into friendly games to give them their opportunity - he was trying to do it the right way, keeping the team competitive as well. He did that by getting United to two semi-finals which unfortunately were both lost. I only went to see him once to see how I was getting on and he told me to keep doing what I was doing - all I wanted was a bit of encouragement to let me know I was doing ok. Perhaps it happens more frequently now, but getting personal encouragement didn't happen that often back then. Someone might come up to one of the players and say "You're playing in the reserves this weekend" - I'd played my first reserve game at sixteen, the last reserve game of the season at Blackburn, but after that I didn't seem to get a sniff.

Sadly, Wilf didn't last that long and Sir Matt came back in to stabilise the club and keep the team up. The following summer we had a new manager, Frank O'Farrell. It was unfortunate for Wilf when he was dealing with big characters like Alex Stepney, David Sadler and Pat Crerand. One minute he's their mate, the next he's the manager. It was a difficult job for anybody, following Sir Matt, and they obviously thought promoting from within was doing it the right way. Other clubs had done it and it had been successful but this particular time the board didn't have enough patience with him. I'd have liked to have seen Wilf get more time, and I think a lot of the young lads at that time would have, but unfortunately it didn't happen.

I had a nose operation in spring 1971 when Sir Matt returned. Then, in the early stages of O'Farrell's first season, I had my appendix out which kept me out for over two months, so I was a long way from the first team set-up. I never really knew Frank; I never really saw him while he was at Old Trafford as he didn't seem to be interested in the kids. We spent more time with his assistant Malcolm Musgrave. We'd have practice matches against the first team and that would be our chance to impress him. Other than that he'd just take notice of what the reserve team manager said, because we never saw him or came into contact. It was easier to find Shergar than it was to find O'Farrell!

I was waiting for my appendix operation when Sammy got his chance, scoring on his debut in the Manchester derby in front of 63,000 at Maine Road in November 1971. I was delighted for him - he was a fantastic lad who always kept his feet on the ground. Inevitably for a skilful player from Northern Ireland, he was labelled the next George Best. When you saw him you knew he wasn't anything of the sort. For a start he wasn't even that type of player, but what you did know was that he was going to be one hell of a player in his own right, which is what Sammy ended up being for the club.

Of course Sammy went on to make it but there were plenty who didn't. Eric Young, who I'd met on that England schools week, was someone I thought "Good God this lad can play". A few months after that, we played against Durham who Eric was playing for and he destroyed us. We lost 3-2 and I thought I'd had a good game but he was just head and shoulders above anybody on the pitch. I learned then that he was signing for United and thought to myself that they'd got themselves a player. Kevin Lewis was a good lad but had a little bit of a disciplinary problem. He once kicked a referee up the backside after being sent off! He was a good lad and wore his heart on his sleeve. Tommy O'Neill, from St. Helens, went onto play about fifty games for the first team at right back even though he was a midfielder. He was a very good rugby player, too. Then there was Tony Young, a local lad who came as a right winger who later played both full back positions. He eventually left because he wasn't getting enough games, which was a bit of a shame.

Tony Whelan was another Manchester lad who didn't make it at United as a player but went on to become a coach at the club. Ronnie Miller was the next Denis Law, everything he did was like Denis. He could have been a decent player but his head was so big he couldn't get it through the door, and that was a shame because he could play. He only lasted a couple of years before he went back to Scotland. Jimmy Fleming was from Belshill just like Sir Matt Busby, a lovely little left footed ginger haired lad but United was just a little bit too much for him and he ended up going back, but he was a lovely lad. Willie Carrick, the lad I was in digs with, was a good 'keeper who had the best left foot on any goalie I've ever seen. There was one game where we must have been that short of players in the B team that Willie and I played together in midfield against Chester. We won 4-2 – we both scored two! He could probably have made a good left winger, but he was a typical goalkeeper, mad as a hatter to put it politely! Paul Jones was a year younger than me, a centre half from Stockport, a nice cultured player who played in the Anglo Italian Cup for the first team. There just seemed to be something lacking with him, I couldn't quite put my finger on it, but he was another who left.

O'Farrell's departure caused further instability. The players used to go for a drink after games at a hotel in Chorlton and whenever they got together they obviously weren't talking about what they were going to eat! There were one or two who were still friendly with Sir Matt and would go and play golf with him. I don't think that helped Wilf or Frank, not that anything went on, just that it didn't help. By this time I had turned professional and was paying for my digs out of £20 a week - £4.50 digs and paying for my own travel home, so even though I was better off I didn't notice it much! But compared to my mates back in Barnsley, who were on about £6, I knew I was doing well.

We left Mrs Barratt's in early 1972, Willie was still living there and was still the blue eyed boy, and Smokey the cat was still getting better fed, it was on fillet steak while we were having burgers. One of the funniest things I've ever seen happened when Willie got himself a girlfriend who lived in Blackley. He was going to see her a lot and Mrs Barratt didn't like him having a girlfriend, saying "Oh Willie she's from Blackley, what you doing with a girl from Blackley?" One day they had a row, and he hit Smokey the cat with a copy of the Daily Mirror! Me and Sammy nearly fell on the floor laughing while they were having this argument and then he hit the cat - but that was it, out! He had to go. Not long after that, I moved in at Maureen's, with her mum, dad and brother, and Sammy moved in with Cynthia's parents.

In the summer of 1972 we went back to the Blue Star tournament in Geneva. We were playing at about quarter past eight in the morning, and I broke my leg at half past. I got carried off - not on a stretcher, just literally carried off! They put me down on the bench, and when half time came, they carried me into the dressing room and put me on the bench in the middle there. There was a lad called Kenny Ayres, he came up and thought I'd got cramp so pulled my toes back - when he heard me scream, he stopped doing it! They decided to take me to hospital in the back of a Morris 1100, with a deflated ball underneath my knee. Arnie was with me and Gordon Clayton came with us, they gave me an X-ray, told me I'd broke my leg and put some plaster on it. Then I had to wait to get the car back - no ambulance or anything – I was just left. "What's going on here?" I wondered.

They just stuck me in bed with no crutches! I couldn't travel back with the rest of the lads as they were going via Paris, so I had to wait to go back 24 hours later on a direct flight from Geneva to Manchester. They booked 6 seats for me on the plane, and got an ambulance to take me to the airport. When I got to Manchester there was an ambulance waiting for me to take me straight to Salford General. There was a doctor there, Doctor Bartlett, who cracked the plaster off and confirmed it was a break and went through everything that was wrong with it. He then asked if I had a sore foot. I said, "Well, yeah I have." He said "You've got a chipped bone." It was my metatarsal! For the previous six weeks I'd played with a sponge covering the sore part of my foot so I could put my boot on and play. I could run alright but if I kicked, God, it hurt! The sponge lessened the pain so I could carry on playing, but I never realised the extent of the problem until then.

As soon as I had my plaster off I told the club I was going on holiday to Lloret de Mar, and they told me to do plenty of swimming. When I got back, it was straight back into training at Old Trafford where Laurie Brown was with John Fitzpatrick and Jimmy Rimmer who had both had knee operations. At that time they had a little St. John's Ambulance room that had a little pulley which I would use to try and build my thigh muscles up. The other part of my rehabilitation was to walk up and down the Stretford End Paddock to build my muscles up. There were no proper weights to build them up, and I couldn't run on it, but it was just incredible. From breaking my leg in May, to going on holiday and then coming back, it was still another four and half months until I got fit. How I did, I still don't know, given the facilities that we had.

Laurie was the only physio we had, so he was treating so many players that you might have 5 or 6 injured and it was so difficult enough with just one. We still didn't have the gym at that point - it was some time until we had the multi-gym where we could run around to keep ourselves fit, so instead we used to go running up Wythenshawe Park with Joe Lancaster. I used to go walking around, heel and toe, to build my muscle up, all the time thinking "What am I doing here?" With proper training and rehabilitation I would probably have been back within three months, maybe not pre-season, but I wouldn't have been far off. Instead it was getting into October when I got back playing and by that time I had started having problems with my knee because of all the pressure I'd been putting on it, and the fact that my muscle wasn't strong enough.

I'd always had some kind of injury, even going back to when I was younger. I'd have problems with my thigh and I would be told "It's because you're growing". I'd go in and have treatment from Ted Dalton who'd be talking to somebody else while giving me a bit of ultrasound, a little bit of a massage, and then I'd ask what I needed to do next, and he'd tell me to go and run it off. How do you run a strain off! I once had a bad back and we didn't have a physio, so Jack Crompton used to do it. He'd put the heat lamp on it and give it a little rub, say "Go and have a run, see what it's like", but it still wasn't right. I had a bad back for about a month and they got another physio in – he was also called Laurie – and the first thing he did was tell me to lie on my back. He got hold of my knee, pushed it hard over the other one, and it was like a machine gun going off in my back! I'd had adhesions in my back, and he said in a few days I'd be alright. I was, but I'd been messed about for a month beforehand with no proper treatment.

When I think of the facilities and the treatment that is available today, we were treated very poorly. There's no disrespect intended to Laurie Brown or Doc McHugh, as they were the only two there. They could be treating seven or eight people. We did our own X-Rays, which was about the only thing we had that was better than other clubs. After games, when players would put ice on injuries and ailments, they'd have to take their chance as Jimmy Murphy and Doc McHugh used to put it in their whisky! When Sir Matt managed they'd have a bottle of whisky in the room before a game and they'd have a nip before they went out. Pissed in charge of a mitre ball! I think they put whisky in the treatment room, too. I learned the hard way with my injury in Switzerland – the organisation was poor, the aftercare was horrendous. Maybe in those days it was the best they could afford but this was hardly world class care at one of the biggest clubs in football.

I suppose my fortunes turned around the day Tommy Docherty arrived at the club. I was playing for the A team against Rochdale reserves on the day he signed. It was great to have Tommy at United. The first time I met him after his arrival was at the Cliff, he was coming out of the entrance and I was going in. He recognised me straight away from when he wanted to sign me at Rotherham. He was renowned for giving younger players a chance. Some managers get on better with younger players than they do with older ones, and if you were to take a brief look at Tommy's record, the older players tended not to like him while all the younger ones did. After a few years of instability around the club and concerns about my fitness, I was looking forward to finally getting a crack at the first team.

Bill Foulkes told me the new boss was keen to get a few of the kids in the first team. Meanwhile I continued to have problems with my knee and went to see a specialist, a man called Alan Glass. He had a reputation for butchering a few knees as John Fitzpatrick and Denis Law can testify. Alan told me I needed a cartilage operation but that he was away for a fortnight – so I thought "Great, another two weeks doing nothing".

I told Bill, who said, "Right, come on. I'm going to get you fit." He took me to Tommy Hamilton's gym near Longford Park in Stretford. He had made his own gym, which looked just like the ones you'd see today. This was unusual in the early 70's and Bill used to go there to keep in shape. He had a sauna there too, all in his cellar! Bill took me a long for a few weeks to build myself up and I felt a lot better. Alan Glass came back from holiday and I got a phone call from his secretary telling me I was due in St. Joseph's hospital the next day. I rang Bill and told him but he told me not to bother and cancelled it. I kept on training and within weeks I was in the reserves, and Bill got me playing until the end of the season.

At the end of the season I was picked to go on the trip to Switzerland again, which was my sixth year on the trot, and I didn't realise that it was make or break for me. Twelve months on from breaking my leg, I was back in Geneva. We only needed a draw in the last group game and they played me at centre half telling me to get hold of the ball and keep it. It's probably the only game I played in where I had the ball for what seemed like 60% of the game! We drew that match and got to the final to play Barcelona where I was told to play in midfield, and mark the number 10 who was their best player by a mile. If I stopped this player, I was told, we'd win the game. I stopped him playing, with one or two fouls. I got booked, and nowadays I'd have been sent off for a diabolical tackle that was almost GBH! I did my job but then we lost on penalties.

I knew the following pre-season would be crucial. After the tournament, Paul Jones was released while I was kept on – as both of us played in the same position, I knew the Doc had faith in me, now it was my turn to repay it.

3. RELEGATION

I F YOU SPEAK TO Sammy McIlroy, Jimmy Nicholl, Arthur Albiston, David McCreery, Stevie Coppell or Gordon Hill, then they would all say how much they love Tommy Doc and speak highly of him. He liked a laugh but he wanted to win, and he upheld the tradition of Manchester United, particularly after relegation – those were exciting times and he produced one of the most exciting teams of the decade.

The 1973/74 pre-season was an important one to me. We were playing a lot of games where the first team would play the reserves and I was thinking to myself, "I'm running these games", everything was going really well. I don't know if it still happens but we would always tend to beat the first team, more often than not, maybe because all of the younger lads had something to prove. Maybe it's because the first teamers took their eye off the ball thinking "what the hell are we doing playing in these kind of games?" That's what I would think later when I moved through the ranks to play them on the senior side – I used to hate it. You'd have the young lads running round trying to kick you and put a marker down – fair enough, as that's what I used to do.

Pre-season went alright; I was called up to travel with the first team for a friendly in Scotland against Ross County, and from there we played in Murcia in Spain for a few games. I wasn't originally selected but I thought I'd started in really good form so I wasn't too concerned; Bill was always encouraging me, I was playing regularly in midfield which was good as I'd been pushed around a lot but then one Friday lunchtime Tommy came up to me and said "Go on, get your passport, you're coming with us." We flew to London before flying to Inverness which made me laugh as we couldn't get a direct flight from Manchester, and the very next day I made my first team debut against Ross County.

I played as a number eleven, and I was surprised by that, I didn't expect to play at all. There were players there who I would have expected to be in front of me - particularly Ian Storey-Moore who I would have expected to wear the shirt or Sammy. I was in midfield and did OK. I felt quite pleased with myself. After that game we flew to Spain to play two games. It was hot and very difficult. I didn't play any part in the first game but in the second against Murcia I came on and got fifteen minutes. Tommy Cavanagh told me afterwards that it was always the plan to give me that time; they just wanted me to tag along after travelling to Scotland instead of sending me back to Manchester. They also gave me a little bit of time so as not to put so much pressure on me. Maybe it was to do with the heat - training in it was really stifling. It was good to have a proper pre-season though, having had injuries in previous years, I made sure I was ready for it. Nobody likes doing them but it was something we had to do so I made the best of it.

Back in Manchester, after starting to get involved in the first team set-up, I was beginning to wonder what would happen when we got to the season proper. I started back in the reserves and continued to play well and we had a midweek game at home against Huddersfield with The Doc in attendance. I probably had my worst game, I was thinking "Bloody hell, the first time the boss is here!" I was very disappointed. Yet on the Friday the boss came to me and told me to get my stuff as I would be travelling to Portman Road, Ipswich for the First Division fixture. I thought I'd be thirteenth man as there was only one substitute allowed, so I presumed I would be there to help with the skip as the kit man didn't travel to away games. Normally the thirteenth man would get there early with Tommy Cav and Laurie Brown to set everything up but I didn't realise that Jim Holton was having a fitness test. He had that at dinner time while we were being given our food and given the choice, I said I would have fillet steak, something I could never normally afford. I had just started to eat it when the boss came in and announced the team. I was half eating when I thought, "Did he mention my name then?" All the lads started offering their congratulations but that was it I couldn't eat the steak anymore - I just felt sick!

I rang Maureen to tell her I was playing and it was then that I realised I was playing centre half. It's not as if I wasn't used to playing there but I'd played in midfield for a while by then. I also realised that Martin Buchan was playing left back, while I was alongside David Sadler in the middle. It was great to play alongside David - he had bags of experience and that helped against their forwards David Johnson and Trevor Whymark.

We lost 2-1 but I felt I'd had a good game; it was much faster than I was used to and my feet hurt. The first team had better boots than the reserves. Dressing room rumour had it that if your boots started going in the reserves and you were told you weren't getting another pair, that meant you weren't getting a new contract! So when the powers that be told you that you were allowed some new boots, you got excited. To get a pair of boots was like being given a gold bar, it was such a relief when you signed a new contract - you'd get a couple of pairs of new boots – what luxury!

Anyway, Tommy said well done afterwards but didn't go overboard as obviously we'd lost the game. In the changing room Martin was annoyed that he'd played left back and had an argument with the boss. It was a surprise to everyone that he had been played in that position but he might have ended up there even if Jim had been passed fit, so I didn't feel awkward. I was just delighted to have played.

After that we played against Leicester at Old Trafford and I was substitute but didn't get on, we lost 1-2 in any case. Then we played West Ham, again at home, and I wasn't even in the twelve (we won 3-1) and then the week after we played Leeds away and I was called back in, this time to play in midfield. I was asked to mark Billy Bremner in midfield while Willie Morgan was on Eddie Gray, George Graham was on Peter Lorimer and Brian Kidd was on Johnny Giles, going for man for man. I'd known Billy and Johnny as well as most of the others for a few years because of my brother's connection, so I wasn't overawed.

There was a break in play and I hadn't given Billy a kick of the ball - Johnny hadn't had one either, I think they were a bit frustrated, and they took it out on me, telling me that they were going to break my legs! Billy used to pat me on the head when I was little but he couldn't do that anymore, and

I think both he and Johnny were a bit unhappy with the way we were playing. I just looked at them thinking I couldn't believe they'd just said that to me but that was the kind of intimidation Leeds were renowned for in those days – a team that was very much in your face and one of the first sides I can remember who would get stuck into the referee. They would contest every decision thinking it was against them and maybe there was a bit of truth in that. Their nickname after all was Dirty Leeds!

They had one or two lads who could dish it out. Everyone looked at Norman Hunter and thought he would bite your legs, but to me, he was not as bad as Billy and Johnny in that respect. The game wasn't even particularly bad tempered but the rivalry was fierce – probably starting from when Leeds had beaten United in an FA Cup semi final in 1970 which went to two replays before it was decided, and in fairness they were probably the best team in the country at the time. However we went there and got a 0-0 draw, which is what we set out to achieve. It was surprising to play for a Manchester United side that played so negatively, as we didn't really seem to have the kind of team players that could play that way. Yet rather than it being indicative of a general tactical plan from the Doc, I just think he took it game by game and thought, "If we get a draw out of this it's a good result" which given our league position was fair enough.

In the following game we played Liverpool at Old Trafford and I marked Ian Callaghan. He just ran all over the place so I had to run with him! Liverpool didn't get the best out of him but United in return didn't get the best out of me either and we finished up with another 0-0 in that game. From then on I played every game until the end of the season for the first team, plus the friendlies! We played a lot of friendlies that season, the club would be offered games and they would take the money but in the 1973/74 season there were also testimonials. I was fortunate that I really made an impression right away.

If ever there was a player to bring excitement back to the club it was George Best. George had quit a few times but had returned to training and played his first game back for the club in a home game against Birmingham City on October 20th. We went to Mottram Hall as we normally would the night before a home game and I found out when I got there that George was my room mate. We used to go and play snooker but George was in bed and when I got back to the room I asked him if he wanted breakfast in the morning. He said, "I've ordered it.". I said, "Well what about the newspapers", he replied he'd already sorted that too. That was the old pro, organised enough to make sure tea and toast would be coming up in the morning. So we had breakfast in bed – not together, I hasten to add!

We went on a golfing trip to Majorca soon after George's return and we stayed at the Son Vida hotel. We arrived after dinner had been served so all the lads were hungry; George organised for a taxi to pick us up and take us to the Plaza Camila. When we got there we went to a restaurant across the road where we had soup and veal, and a few San Miguels. We gave George about a hundred pesetas each which at that time was probably around fifty pence; that served as a tip, and we were never sure if George had paid for it or if it was given to us on the house! After that, we went across to a bar run by a friend of George's named Felix. This bar was our meeting point out there; during the day we'd relax and play golf, while George was on the beach pulling birds! We rarely saw him on that trip; to be fair, it was probably the last thing he needed. It was arguably the least fit he'd ever been at Old Trafford and he could have done with staying behind and having a mini pre-season to catch up. Though everyone was delighted he had come back, it was obvious that he wasn't fit. Looking back at old footage you can notice the difference between the George of 1973 and the man at his peak, and it was always a real shame to me that I never got to play with that George Best – what a player!

Yet this was still George Best - he could still beat people even if he couldn't get away from them anymore whereas in years gone by if he went past someone they wouldn't see him again. The goal he scored against Chelsea in the League Cup where he danced round them all - that was George Best and he just couldn't do that anymore. He scored a couple of goals after returning but he wasn't the same. His last game for United was January 1st 1974 against QPR away where we lost 3-0. The week after we played Plymouth Argyle in the FA Cup he was dropped, which surprised us all. It was disappointing for everyone as we wanted him to stay but we wanted a fit George. He was a good trainer but the only problem was his lifestyle; Tommy decided not to play him and he decided to finish with the club. It was a time we needed all hands on deck, entering a part of the season where we really needed to get going.

Sadly, due to his condition, it's difficult for me to say George was the best player I ever played with. He was still a bloody good player, but when I saw George in training before I got into the first team, he was incredible to watch, he could nutmeg someone with their legs shut! He would come in his fancy cars, always looking smart and you'd have read what he'd got up to at the weekend and think "Cor, I want some of that!" I think George suffered from trying to live up to the reputation of being the "fifth Beatle". He was a great, great lad who would never ignore you. I would have loved to have played with him longer and I wish he would have been fitter because our season may have turned out differently. Not only could George win games on his own but he could bring the best out of those around him. Perhaps him not being as fit had a negative impact on other players but not me; I loved every minute playing with him. Later in my career I would go on to play against Pele, Johann Cruyff and Zico but I played with George – and out of them all, if they were all fit, George was the best.

We only won two games during George's brief return but it was while he was back that I scored my first goal for the club. Against Chelsea at Old Trafford we were 2-0 down when I got the ball and laid it into Tony Young who drilled it in from the edge of the box. Soon after he returned the favour, laying it off to me inside the box and I just turned and hit it past Peter Bonetti in front of the Stretford End. I didn't know what to do to celebrate! In the dressing room afterwards Tommy Cavanagh said to me, "Go and buy a big cabinet because you'll need it to fit all your caps in." What a boost!

Relegation

That goal secured a draw but it was a difficult spell, nonetheless. In George's first game back we won 1-0 against Birmingham City but that was decided by an Alex Stepney penalty. Alex was a good striker of the ball and always had confidence in his ability to play; I remember he once scored a goal in a five-a-side game and ran right round the pitch celebrating, saying it was his thousandth goal! It didn't surprise me that he took them but it surprised me that the manager let him. Nonetheless, a goalkeeper taking penalties summed up the fact that we just couldn't seem to score goals that year. We lacked a top class finisher. The general play was good but we just couldn't score, underlined by the fact that there were 19 games in which we didn't register. Fifteen of those finished goalless or were decided by a single goal in favour of the opposition - we weren't getting hammered, but we couldn't score. Just before Christmas we played at Anfield and it was the first time Arnie Sidebottom and I played in the first team together. I was delighted for Arnie - he'd made his debut before me due to my bad luck with injuries - but it was great to play alongside him in the biggest game in English football.

We'd also suffered early exits from both cup competitions. We played Glasgow Rangers in a friendly that had been arranged on a weekend when the Cup games were being played and I was played up front - I think I only got picked because of Lou Macari's history having played for Celtic. Tommy didn't want to play him and I had played up front for the A team in the past. I scored early on when Willie Morgan pulled one back and I later hit the post and headed one wide. I was having a field day! I was also fouled in the build up for our other goal, a free kick by Alex Forsyth, but we finished up losing. One of the things that sticks in the memory about that game is that the Glasgow fans took over the Trafford Park Hotel! The week after that we played City away and again, I was centre forward. Lou Macari and Mick Doyle were sent off by Mr Clive "Watch me, not the game" Thomas. Thomas always wanted to be the star of the game and I found him to be a very poor referee, I didn't like him at all – we never seemed to win when he was in charge. The derby finished 0-0.

Then came the crunch game of the run-in when we played Birmingham City at St Andrews – I was picked at centre-forward, perhaps on the back of my performance against Rangers. For me to be playing there for Manchester United when they were fighting relegation summed it up – I tried my best but I wasn't a forward, I just did the best I could. That day we lost 1-0 to a Joe Gallagher goal. Joe was a centre half and went up for a corner, we were clearing it out and he was at the edge of the box. He just stuck his foot out to block it and it flew in the top corner. It was then that most of us thought "This just isn't our season". That result took Birmingham away from us, and put us under a lot of pressure.

Yet around Easter time we started to pick up results. We played Chelsea away and I started at centre forward and then Steve James got his teeth kicked out when he was trying to head the ball away so I had to move back to centre half after just half an hour. Everything ended well as we won 3-1, with Willie Morgan having already put us 1-0 up. Daly and McIlroy scored in the second half before Bill Garner hit a late consolation. The game marked a slight upturn in fortunes as we had now scored eleven goals in 5 games, helped by the signing of Jim McCalliog who made a big difference scoring four in three. He was a very clever player who I'd first met when he played for Leeds in the early sixties. He was actually working as part of the ground staff, as in those days you couldn't be an apprentice if you were from Ireland or Scotland so they would be on the ground staff to have a job "outside". At Old Trafford I believe players in a similar situation would work on the ship canal!

After beating Everton 3-0 on Easter Monday things were looking up, we had taken 9 points out of 10 and we were beginning to play attractive football and score goals but then we drew at the Dell and lost at Goodison Park, meaning when we played City at Old Trafford, our destiny wasn't in our own hands. We had to get a result and Birmingham City had to lose their fixture.

Before the end of the game, before Denis had even scored, we knew Birmingham were winning and we were going to be relegated. Denis's goal didn't matter. From that lucky goal we'd let in at Birmingham we could see the writing on the wall and it was that game that did the damage. We still had to go to Stoke City in the last game of the season – if we had gone there needing a result, I'm sure we would have. As it was the game was a dead rubber but it was also the first time I was named captain of the team. With our James captain of the Stoke side, it was a nice gesture from Tommy to make me skipper and still a great honour despite the fact we had already gone down. The players thought it was just because James was captain, but it was actually because the referee was

Keith Stiles from Barnsley. He asked Tommy if he could get a picture with both of us and so Tommy said he'd make me captain for the day!

Despite relegation we had played good football. You don't get an average of forty two thousand people turning up to watch you if you're rubbish; for the City game we got over fifty five thousand and at times we played in front of more than sixty thousand at Old Trafford that season. We were still the best supported club in the country – as United have been pretty much every season since the war. Everybody wants to play in front of big crowds, it must be soul destroying playing in front of empty terraces. To play in front of big crowds was exhilarating. It never made me nervous, it made me excited. Even when things were going badly, we were just keen to put it right, and that went through from the manager to the twelfth man.

Personally I'd had a good season. I remember Tommy coming to me at one point in the run in and saying "I'd like to give you a rest but I can't, you're too important to us!" I didn't want a rest anyway – and I lost count of the number of times I played carrying an injury or wasn't fully fit. In those days though you just had to get on with it anyway. These days you can be out for three weeks with a twisted sock! The twisted sock injury is so called because of the number of players who go down and suddenly when the ball is kicked out, instead of a physio coming on, they jump up and twist their socks!

At the end of the season there was no opportunity for me to get a rest as I was selected for England Under 23's for a game in Turkey. I was substitute and the game was abandoned at half time because of floods – I've never seen anything like it in my life. After that we played in Yugoslavia and I played in a 1-1 draw – I played the next game too, this time as a second half substitute in a 2-2 draw in France. It was a great tour which I really enjoyed. I roomed with a lad called Kevin Beattie who was the best young centre half I'd ever seen. In training he was an absolute colossus. People speak of Duncan Edwards and say he was some player; to be better than Kevin Beattie, he must have been one hell of a player because Kevin was the best player I played with outside of Old Trafford. The first I heard of the call up was a message from the manager telling me there was a letter at Old Trafford waiting for me. Later I got a cap for the tour and because I played two of the games I got Yugoslavia and France embroidered on it. It was delivered to me in a Jiffy bag which made me laugh – no pomp and ceremony with the FA!

That summer Maureen and I got married. I had met her at Brown's nightclub and moved into her parents. The relationship between Maureen and myself changed as we were seeing each other every day, spending all of our spare time together. After a while it seemed the logical thing to get married, but I didn't get down on one knee or do anything fancy; I just asked and she said yes. We had moved into a house I'd bought for £7,500. Some friends helped us decorate and we had an engagement party in Rochdale at a restaurant that was difficult to get into. It wasn't a long engagement; and we were married in the June at All Saints Church in Stretford. We went to Jersey on honeymoon where we met John McDowell, West Ham's right back who had just been on the England tour with me, who had got married the week

after. It was a great end to what had been an encouraging
first season in the first team. I didn't need much motivation
to return and hit the ground running the next season to get
Manchester United back into the First Division.

4. PROMOTION

LOOKING BACK, IT'S A MIRACLE Tommy Doc wasn't sacked following relegation. The supporters at United start grumbling nowadays over the slightest thing but relegation, well I dread to think what the reaction would be. I would hope that the board of the day realised that Tommy was building a side that could use that misfortune as a springboard to success. And so it proved.

We all knew Tommy had to bring someone else in, preferably another striker, knowing that if we could convert more chances we would go up – no problem. However being relegated we always knew some players would leave and that was the case with Brian Kidd who joined Arsenal. It must have been really disappointing for Brian because it was only six years before that, on his 19th birthday, that he was scoring in the European Cup final. But sometimes people need new challenges and Brian was probably one of those. All the players he'd originally played with had gone, there was nobody left from that side, so he must have found it difficult but it was a good move for him in the end as he went on to have a good career, particularly with Arsenal and Manchester City before he went on to be a coach at United (and later City) after his retirement.

Yet we signed the perfect replacement for Kiddo in the shape of Stuart Pearson, who made an immediate impact scoring two goals against the Belgian side Ostend on his first game in a pre-season tour. Pancho was a tremendous signing, a great player who would go on to play for England. He was not only a good finisher but a great target man; you could knock the ball up to him and he would hold it up and fetch people in. When you have people there like Sammy, Lou Macari and Gerry Daly, they could make the runs off him and they knew they wouldn't be disappointed by the ball they'd receive in return.

Despite slipping down a division, United were still making the headlines in the media even if a lot of it was down to the vast crowds we could still attract. We got the biggest crowd of the season against Sunderland (60,000) and still averaged over 48,000 at home. From the outset we expected to come straight back up. There wasn't a lot wrong with the team, it just needed one or two tweaks. The Doc had insisted that our general play was good enough and we were only lacking the goals; it didn't surprise me that we would end up taking the division by storm. The way we set off in pre-season was a marker – sometimes the way you play in those games sets it off and we hit the ground running. I think the way we started actually surprised a lot of teams. The arrival of Pearson had given us a great boost; it helped Sammy enormously as he was playing up front at the time, but it wasn't his game to hold it up; now with Pancho as a foil, Sammy would float around and get the ball in positions where defenders wouldn't want him to have it, as he was such a clever footballer. We'd also only recently bought a new left back, Stewart Houston, as we'd been struggling in that position, so Martin could move back into central defence alongside Steve James or Jim Holton.

Alex Forsyth was already there so we had a pretty solid back four. Jim McCalliog was doing a great job in midfield, Willie Morgan was playing fine on the wing. I was in midfield with Jim and Gerry Daly, we were probably only lacking a left sided player.

Though we had the self belief in our ability it was important to hit the ground running to justify ourselves; fortunately we did, and people began to notice we meant business. One or two teams visiting Old Trafford didn't fancy it, and it can be an intimidating place. In the Second Division teams might have been used to playing in front of 15,000 but suddenly there'd be forty or fifty thousand fanatics screaming at them at Old Trafford. This was the era of Doc's Red Army – in that crucible you either perform or freeze - most teams froze. We'd started the season in dominating fashion; notching 7 wins and 2 draws from the first nine games, scoring plenty of goals and funnily enough being awarded lots of penalties. Gerry Daly had assumed spot-kick duties. Alex had only missed one the previous season and I think that was it. It's a hell of a run back when you miss one and you're the goalkeeper! Gerry took a fantastic penalty, I think he only ever missed one which is a great record. The first game we dropped points in was a 2-2 home draw with Nottingham Forest in which I scored and came off injured – Sammy scored a great goal to earn us a draw but also might have won a penalty. Tommy suggested afterwards that referees might have second thoughts about giving penalties at Old Trafford but in those days you almost had to get shot or suffer GBH to earn one! In almost every game these days you see a penalty that should be given but it isn't, I just think it's swings and roundabouts. I always stick to the adage of things evening themselves out over a season.

After a good start I was disappointed to get injured and risk missing my first league match in over a year. On the Friday before playing at West Brom I went down to London with Laurie Brown as I was still having problems with my knees - it'd been lingering ever since I broke my leg. My left knee had flared up again and they wanted me to go and see what the renowned orthopaedic surgeon Sir Henry Osmond-Clarke would say about it. I didn't train on Friday, instead I went down to London, then met back up with the team on Saturday when we drove to West Brom and Tommy just said to me "I'm just putting you on the bench today". At the time I didn't realise that I hadn't missed a game for about a year so I wasn't too disappointed, and it was probably the right decision. We had a game against Millwall on the Monday and Tommy told me I'd be playing in that instead.

Though I had kept my place in the team I never got complacent about it; that was one thing that was drummed into you at United. Get complacent and you're down the road and very quickly at that. As well as the knee complaint I'd also suffered a problem adjusting to wearing new contact lenses. I'd had a problem with my eyes since I was twelve when I first wore glasses. I always seemed to get by and I didn't want to wear them. When I took my driving test I thought there was only one thing I was going to fail on, not being able to see the number plate. Instead I passed because of the contact lenses!

I'd got my new contact lenses in pre-season from a place in Denton called Kelvin Lenses, and they measured me for soft lenses. They didn't have any so they gave me some hard ones to try while I was away in pre-season. I lost two; one in one game, one in another, they would just ping out. Once I got the soft ones it took a while to got used to them. I was so used to not seeing clearly; I'd be able to identify players because of how they'd run. As long as I didn't wear glasses around the time I was going to play again, I'd be okay. So I wouldn't wear glasses, instead I'd get by, but I wasn't seeing the full picture. Having the new lenses was like having a black and white television and then seeing colour! I wanted to see a better picture and all of a sudden I could.

However after two pre-seasons of barely any trouble, it was a worry that I'd started to pick up knocks at the start of the new season, but then you'd never play a game at one hundred percent fit. There'd be niggles and a feeling that something was wrong but when you saw the physio and he asked if you were okay, you'd always say "Yeah". I'd carried the knee for a few games, but I'm sure others did too.

Against West Brom I came on as a substitute and less than ten minutes later I got concussed; somebody whacked me with an elbow which, had it happened today, would probably have seen him banned for three games because it was diabolical. I didn't expect it, just bump! And I was out. I got carried off, then put back on, then taken off, then put back on – like a football version of the hokey-cokey, it was all a bit surreal and another example of the type of care pros were used to back then. Afterwards we just got straight on the coach and headed down to London for the Millwall game on the Monday. There were no thoughts of getting me checked out or sent to hospital. The Doc probably had a quick look, but we didn't actually have a real doctor travelling with us, so it was a case of "Are you ok, are you seeing double?" Me answering I was alright again and off we went. I was ok, but obviously taking a whack like that wasn't pleasant.

Our good league form translated into the League Cup as well, as we went on a good run; in my view, cups are a bonus, especially when you're in the Second Division. That season, it ended up being an all Second Division final between Aston Villa and Norwich. The Canaries beat us over two legs in the semi-final, but earlier in the competition we knocked out Manchester City. It was our first meeting with them since the infamous game at the end of the previous season so it was good to exact some revenge. Gerry Daly scored a penalty after a debated handball from Jeff Clarke, not that we were too bothered that they were upset. It also didn't matter that people kept saying City sent us down; they didn't send us down, we went down over forty two games, not one. We were just delighted to beat our local rivals and give the supporters something to shout about.

That tie against City in October saw the debut of Arthur Albiston, one of a number of young lads coming through under the guidance of Frank Blunstone. It wasn't a youth policy in comparison to the academies that you see today with kids being taught from the age of eight or nine, these were lads being brought in at 15 and 16. Where I do think Frank was very good was getting players who were playing in the reserves to make that step up and be able to settle in the first team. I've always said what makes a good trainer is when you enjoy what they do and that was something in Frank's favour; players couldn't wait to get in of a morning because it was enjoyable. After all, you only played forty-two games a season but you train almost every day. It's a long time to keep players happy and entertained and that's what makes a good coach.

The youth setup had already undergone significant changes since I'd come through as an apprentice; they'd come in at ten, half past, train until around twelve, have a shower and maybe have a cup of tea and then go home. You didn't know what happened with them, what they were doing in the afternoons, which was different to when I was an apprentice when I had to go back to Old Trafford and do the cleaning. By then there were the proper changing rooms at the club and they'd also brought Billy Watts in to do the cleaning and the mopping up, so all the lads had to do was make sure the boots were ok. Billy was such a United fan he would have done anything for any of the players.

Arthur was a tremendous player and you could always tell that he and Dave McCreery were going to be good players; 'they'll always be in a job' is how I described them. Of course, Arthur went on to play many, many games and David went on to have a great career at Newcastle too. David's debut came a week after Arthur's, in a game down at Portsmouth. It was probably the worst game I ever played in. Portsmouth just played man for man on everybody, making it a complete non-entity of a game. A big centre half, Eoin Hand (who would go on to manage the Republic of Ireland), marked me. The manager at Fratton Park was Ian St. John, and Eoin said, "My boss must fancy you because I've got to run around with you all game." The highlight was David McCreery coming on as substitute for Willie Morgan. Willie went ballistic as he didn't like being brought off but I'm certain that anyone else would have been delighted to come off because it was such a poor game to play in. Willie was very angry at Tommy, saying "That's it, we're done, I'll not speak to him again, that's us finished", he went really over the top with his remarks. After the game we went and had a meal at the Playboy club at Southsea, I was sat opposite him and he just wouldn't let it go all night.

Despite the good form there was still some dissent around. It's been documented since that Willie and Alex Stepney claimed that earlier in the season they were told by Tommy Doc to pretend they had a problem with Tommy Cavanagh but I couldn't remember anything of that. I never had a problem with Tommy Cav. I had my run-ins with him, I'm sure most of the players did, but he was a winner and wanted to win. Maybe he upset the old guard but that was Tommy - if you were in the trenches he'd be there with you. The Doc certainly never intimated to me anything along the lines suggested by others. The game after the Portsmouth horror was a trip to Blackpool; a complete reversal as we played absolutely fantastically. Jim McCalliog crowned it off with a fantastic chip over the keeper in a 3-0 win. We played like Champions that day - there are a few games you play in which you afterwards stick in your mind and you think, "By God we really did play well", and that was one of them. Every player came off knowing they'd done well, it was just a great display of movement off the ball. We had some quick players in that side and then someone like McCalliog who could put his foot on the ball and dictate the pace of the game; Jim was on song, and when he was, he was a fabulous player.

Tommy said that he expected us to have a blip; he'd even

said it in the media, and you always do expect to have a run of fixtures that don't go so well. That was the case around the turn of the year. We went to Oldham and it was like a war – they scored a goal that was never given and I think they still have a picture of it at Boundary Park! Nevertheless it was a tough game and they fully deserved to beat us. Though we had expected to have a difficult run, the thing for us was how quickly we could get out of it and how we would come out of it. We were fortunate in that we'd had such a good run beforehand we weren't dropping down the league so we weren't really at panic stations.

In the midst of that run in January, as Willie and Tommy Doc's relationship continued to crumble, Morgan had the captaincy taken off him and he was replaced by Martin Buchan. I thought it was the right decision; Willie was being disruptive, his anger towards the Doc was plain to see and it wasn't pleasant. Martin was a natural leader and a steadying influence, he would fight the corner for the players and went on to become a fantastic captain. If there was ever any problem with the players he'd go to the management and sort it out, on the field if we had to make decisions he would do it. Martin was a natural – the perfect captain for us.

On February 1st we played Bristol City at Old Trafford. After that scare earlier in the season I finally missed my first league game for almost a year and a half through injury, as Bristol completed the double over us. I wasn't too concerned about getting my place back – especially after a home defeat. In those days you just played your best team and after a win it'd be a struggle to get back in. Nevertheless my return didn't help matters as we went down 0-1 at Oxford. We beat Hull at home before facing promotion rivals Aston Villa away – it was one of those days where we just didn't perform, they were the better side and won 2-0.

It was enough to provoke Tommy into making a change, signing Stevie Coppell. We'd not really heard of him before until it came in the papers about this lad who was still at university and the next thing we'd signed him for £60,000. He trained a few days a week and then went to college. His debut was in the next game against Cardiff. He came on and did really well, and then it was like "Aye, aye, who's this?" You could see players in training and think they're great players and you'd see them on a Saturday and wonder where they'd gone. Stevie wasn't one of those, he took what he did in training out on to the pitch. He was an intelligent lad, and he was always going to be a good player.

The form recovered with no losses and four wins out of six to put us in position to secure promotion at Southampton's Dell ground. Lou Macari scored the goal to send us up. It was a great feeling as that's what we'd aimed for all year, and with the long journey back we allowed ourselves a few beers. A home win against Fulham followed before a 2-2 draw at Notts County. I scored in that game but it will be remembered for a pitch invasion which got criticism from the Doc afterwards. The Red Army had been attracting a fair bit of attention over the course of the season and at times it did get a bit embarrassing but it had become something of a tradition that whenever a goal was scored the fans would get on the pitch. This time the Doc took exception, no doubt after being given a prod from someone 'upstairs'.

That draw put us in a position to win the league if we

beat Blackpool at home. The last game was like a party atmosphere; once we got the first goal, the second went in soon after and everyone started enjoying it. It was great to go up as Champions but not as important as just going up in the first place; it didn't really matter finishing first, second or third as you all got the same prize. The cup's just there to say you were first; you see teams go up in the playoffs these days and get a trophy. What do the team in second get?

We broke a lot of attendance records that year, I think it was good for the division. We always took a lot of followers and they gave a great boost to the clubs in the division. Whereas these days they would be restricted on safety grounds. I'm a believer that there should still be standing at games; there should be singing areas where there's standing. The Old Trafford atmosphere is criticised these days but that could go some way to improving it, I can remember when the Stretford End used to be standing and it was incredible. The European Cup semi-final against AC Milan in 1969 was unbelievable, I've never heard anything like it. Like the Kop at Liverpool, the Stretford End was swaying and very vocal, whenever anybody got into difficulty they were lifted out, passed over the heads to the ambulance men.

The supporters were just as good for us when we were in the second division. The away support in particular was unbelievable, the noise they made was incredible. When we were apprentices and young pro's, we'd go to games – I went to Sheffield United in April 1972 where Jon Connaughton made his debut and I stood with the travelling fans, singing with them. We went to Burnley and stood with the fans there too, it was fantastic. It's the kind of support that helps get that extra five or ten percent out of the players. When you're up against it and the crowd are behind you, it makes a difference. When the crowd goes quiet, the game goes quiet. In my view these days Old Trafford might be a difficult place to play even for the United players as it can get a bit too quiet – you don't always get away supporters like Athletic Bilbao brought in the 2011/12 season.

Promotion was welcome but what was expected of the club was to be challenging for the real honours at the top of the game; even ninth and tenth in the top division was not good enough for a club like United. With the team that we had, even though we had done so well, we still thought we would have to buy to strengthen, so we were expecting something to happen. In reality, there wasn't a lot of transfer activity and the same group more or less stayed together. We didn't have a long break that summer; the Doc knew that we'd need the spirit for a tough season back in the First Division.

5. BACK WHERE WE BELONG

A LMOST AS SOON AS the season ended we went on tour. I thought we were going to have a nice break and get ourselves ready for the next season, but we finished up playing a couple of games in early May in Germany against FC Basel where we lost 3-1 and against Lausanne in Switzerland who we beat 5-0 – I scored the fourth. After that we had a couple of weeks off but we still had to train, before going on a thirty-two day marathon "World Tour". It was weird because the challenge for the first season back in the top flight was going to be great but maybe the Doc thought keeping everyone together would be beneficial.

One player who didn't travel was Willie Morgan, who was transferred to Burnley while we were away. Willie was the master of his own downfall really. You don't know what goes on behind closed doors but when I looked at it I thought the relationship between him and the Doc had completely broken down. They went from being mates – good mates – to enemies in the space of a few weeks. Willie had a lot of friends at the club who Tommy referred to as the "Junior Board". Tommy took a bit of stick after Willie left from them but I think Willie had a lot to do with it; he didn't try to rectify what had gone wrong, he just made up his mind and that was it. He was a very good player who did well at United but he decided he wanted to leave and the manager let him but he didn't let it lie, he had to have the last word. I thought the Doc was good for him, and I think if Willie looks back and is honest with himself he will have seen that.

Willie didn't like the George Best tag even though he was a very good player; Sammy Mac was one who had to live with it as well but he never let it get on top of him. He just wanted to play and train; he loved the game and was great to play with. Neither were going to be the "new George" – Willie was a very good player doing what he did, he was a good winger who could beat people and cross the ball but he just couldn't dribble like George Best – who could? Ultimately I agreed with the decision. After the initial fall out way back when we played Portsmouth the previous autumn, Willie still played games for United. The Doc wasn't daft, he picked him because he was a good player, I think it was probably only when Stevie Coppell came in that Tommy thought he could afford to let Willie go. For team spirit I think it was the right decision.

It's not as if the fun and games ended there, though. In Switzerland Martin Buchan temporarily resigned the captaincy and I was thrown in to be skipper as I was vice-captain at that point. I went up to him and just said, "Come on, we want you to be captain", we all wanted him to sort out whatever his disagreement was with the manager. There was nobody more relieved among the players than myself when he changed his mind. He'd had some run-ins with the Doc, even going back to my debut at Ipswich but Martin stood his ground as a person and as a player; he was very good as a captain as if we weren't happy with anything at all he would be the one to go to see the manager and have it out with him.

A lot of the times he won, too!

Back to the World Tour... We played in Tehran, had two games in Jakarta and another in Hong Kong before travelling to Australia. In Sydney there was a bit of an argument. Me, Sammy and Stevie Coppell played a game of head tennis – it was only a bit of fun. We got paid for it and we didn't think we needed to tell anybody. One or two of the senior players weren't happy, led by Alex Stepney. They took us to a room and said that we had to split the money we'd earned and put into the players' pool. I thought it was a bit rich, I was on about £80 a week, Sammy around the same, Stevie around £60, all on peanuts compared to the more senior players who were on a lot more money than us and they wanted us to split the $200. They threatened us with throwing us out of the players' pool, so I just threw the money on the floor and said, "There you are, stick it up your arse!" and walked out. The next thing I knew we'd got about $40 each back. For them to take such a small amount seemed a little pathetic to me. It made things tense for a few days because after the game in Sydney against New South Wales we travelled up to Queensland but by the time we played in Auckland just under a week later everything was alright.

There seemed to be a few grievances floating around and Tommy Doc called everyone in to a meeting to get everything ironed out just before we went to Queensland. I can't remember much of the meeting but it was the older players who had more things to get off their chest; the younger players just sat and said nothing, as should be expected – we were only just breaking through and couldn't really be saying anything. Players in their thirties with less to lose could say what they wanted – Alex says this was when he was told by Tommy he wouldn't play for United again. Aside for one game in pre-season against a Hong Kong select team he didn't play again and it seemed that the boss favoured Paddy Roche, more of which later.

It's only after our careers ended and time passed that I realised that Alex had some real differences with Tommy. It has surprised me, as I didn't know at the time – maybe the head tennis thing irked him but I stepped forward and talked about that at the time... to be fair, I shouldn't have played in the tournament anyway as I had picked up an injury. I just thought it was nothing to do with anybody else.

The tour, and representing United abroad, was certainly a new experience. In that first game in Tehran, a place where you can't imagine many teams going to play these days, we drew 1-1. I lasted about an hour but I twisted my ankle and tore the ligaments in it, it was a real mess. I missed the next four games, the two in Jakarta, where we drew with PSSI Tantama and lost 3-2 against Ajax, and then the win in Hong Kong against Hong Kong Rangers and the first game in Australia where we won against Western Australia. I was asked to play in the next game, the Sydney game against New South Wales. I wasn't fit and I lasted half an hour, then I was asked to play in our next game against Queensland and I lasted five minutes! I didn't play in Auckland but then we went to stay in LA overnight before flying back to England.

The first thing I did back there was go to the treatment room as Sammy and I were going on holiday to Benalmadena a few days later, I had to pass a fitness test before they let me go! It was a nice trip to see all these exotic places but there was only really Hong Kong we got to see a little bit more of because we were there for about six days whereas the others we'd fly in, play the game and fly out. It wasn't glamorous, it was difficult, but at least we got a little spell where we could go and have a look around in Hong Kong. Wherever you went in the world there would always be United supporters there looking for autographs, though it was hardly like it is now. There were fantastic crowds in Jakarta - over 60,000 turned up to watch us play PSSI and against Ajax it was well over 100,000. It was incredible to think that in Jakarta that many people would turn up to see a Dutch team and an English team play but I think it was just a sign of the times that we drew such large crowds and other than Jakarta the grounds tended to be small. We got 20,000 at Sydney and that was at the Cricket ground! Going from those to then playing in front of 3,000 in Denmark was a big change.

Coming back after that tour we knew we had to start fast again and I think once again we surprised teams. We hadn't gone out of fitness from the season before as we'd kept ourselves ticking over with these games, we only had a couple of weeks off before we went back into a Danish pre-season tour playing a Halskov XI, Hvidore and Holstebro before playing Red Star at Old Trafford.

With Stevie coming in there seemed to be a lot more pace in the side; quick players like Lou, Sammy, Pancho and Gerry Daly who could all move. It used to be said that we didn't play offside - we did, we just pushed out quick and try to counter. The rules in those days were totally different, you could play that way tactically. It caught everybody out and we were in everybody's faces all of the time. We might not have had the players who would intimidate but we worked hard for each other which was a great thing by pressing the opposition. It was a relatively new tactic back then.

For me, having such quick and clever players alongside me was a dream. My theory was, if they make a good run, don't disappoint them, give them the ball, otherwise they'd stop making them! We had Lou and Sammy who couldn't tackle but they could pinch the ball and they were great at it - as was Stevie. My own preparation was good; all I had to do was walk around with a gammy leg while the others were playing games. I'd still done swimming, and played a bit of tennis so none of us had got a chance to really get unfit. We still had to do a bit of training but I was as fresh as anybody; in the Red Star Belgrade game, Jim got a kicking, and suddenly I was stuck at the back. I wasn't prepared, they were fantastic and ran us ragged. In no time they went two nil up, we dragged it back to 2-1, then 2-2, then 3-2 to Red Star, then three all, before they went back in front and we scored near the end to equalise again. It must have been a fantastic game to watch but it was very difficult to play in. After that I was glad to finish but was wondering whether I was going to play in central defence or in midfield. As it proved it was the former and I slotted straight in at centre half. I had played in both positions but still, to play centre half permanently when I'd only ever filled in there was a test. I was the one who was always moved around in the team; if there was a problem, I was the one to move into the position where there was an emergency.

The first two games of the 1975/76 season were both in the Midlands - we won our first at Wolves 2-0 with a brace from Macari and then an identical scoreline with a double by McIlroy won the next game at Birmingham. The game at St. Andrews was further evidence of my versatility. Birmingham had a corner in the first couple of minutes and their big centre forward, Bob Hatton, came and clattered Alex in goal. He just got up and got on with the game, we got to half time goalless and he said he was a bit sore; you could tell he wasn't right. He came back out for the second half and threw the ball out to Alex Forsyth and shouted – his jaw just locked, clicked out and he went down. Laurie ran on, straight away saying they'd have to take him off. They took his shirt off him and gave it to me; I was given his gloves, green gloves with no grip whatsoever, and that was it, I had to get in goal. Jimmy Nicholl came on as his replacement but in my place, and my first save was from a backpass from him! It was the best thing that could have happened really because not long after, Howard Kendall hit a shot from a similar distance and I dived and saved it. I had to make another save from him and made a bit of a meal out of another one that I tipped around the post but I felt I did fine. It was raining too, which helped a bit. The only problem I had was kicking the ball out of my hands – I could drop kick, but found it hard to volley – so I'd be pushing the back four up so I could roll it on the floor and I could pass it better. I claim I'm the first keeper to ever do that!

I had some experience of playing in goal and in those days, with one substitute, you couldn't really name a substitute goalkeeper as it was wasting the extra player. For me it was just a natural thing, it was something that I enjoyed doing in training. I had done a fair bit of training with Jimmy Rimmer and so it didn't bother me going in. I was just hoping the Saturday after I wasn't going to be picked there again! It wasn't so much the clean sheet bonus – I'm not sure if they even had them in those days, so I certainly didn't challenge Alex for it – but it was all about the win. The win bonus anyway was sometimes more than what we were earning – though I'd just had a rise to £130. The United supporters were singing "Greenhoff for England" and I was playing right in front of them – what an experience that was all the more pleasant because we won!

We beat Sheffield United and then drew with Coventry at Old Trafford, where Alan Green capitalised on my mis-hit back pass. I did make some mistakes as I wasn't the archetypal centre back like, for example, Jim Holton. I was put there to set attacks off and attack as well as I could. At times I found it difficult, at times I found it alright – I didn't really let the errant backpass get me down, as everyone makes mistakes. In the early days of playing with Martin the relationship wasn't the most fluid; Martin probably didn't want me playing alongside him and I didn't truly want to be at the back but that was where I was picked. While you're winning games everything is fine but when you don't, usually it's the one who people think shouldn't be there that shoulders the blame. I think once or twice Martin did blame me early on but I don't think I made many individual mistakes; some stick in my mind, but the slip at home to Coventry wasn't really one of them. For the last game of August, we travelled to Stoke City and won 1-0, where Tommy Doc once again made me captain as our kid was captaining Stoke. Keith Stiles wasn't referee this time, so it made it a nice touch.

After a home win against Spurs we had five wins and a draw from our opening six games – we were top of the table. It was a fantastic way to return to the top flight, although we all realised that maintaining our form would prove a more serious challenge. At United you had to think that anyway... according to the press we were now favourites to win the league, which in turn stirred the fans up but that's what it's all about anyway – United are the media's dream. We always thought we had a chance because we were winning games. Playing for Manchester United meant that we weren't bound by the convention of a newly promoted side having to struggle in the higher division – and there was a recent record anyway of teams having come up and done well in the top flight and we didn't see any reason why we couldn't follow suit. We were a young, enthusiastic side who worked hard for one another and our only real problem was squad depth.

We kept around the top of the table with three wins, two draws and two defeats from the next seven league games which also saw us get two 2-1 wins in the League Cup at home to Brentford and at Villa Park. Then we lost 2-1 at Upton Park and as a result of that game, Alex Stepney was suddenly dropped. After the pre-season bombshell from Tommy Doc, he'd kept his place in goal as the stand-in, Paddy Roche, had suffered a bereavement and when he returned Alex was playing so well there was no cause to drop him. He bit the bullet for the loss at West Ham and I was surprised that he was dropped – I always enjoyed playing alongside Alex, he was a good communicator, he was always talking which is what you wanted from a goalkeeper. If I made a run and I wanted the ball to set things off, it'd be there, he was very good at getting on with the game - once he had the ball he'd always be looking where to put it, he'd be aware of players' positions and he'd start a lot of our attacks. People didn't realise how quick he was at doing it.

Maybe it stemmed from pre-season and Doc thinking he had to get Paddy into the side; yet it was a big shout when he made the call. Paddy's first game was against Norwich - we won 1-0. For the keeper, as long as you keep a clean sheet and don't drop any balls you can think you did alright. Paddy had great agility and was very athletic, he had good hands but the worry to me was always with his lack of weight and presence. People today are worried about David De Gea in goal for Manchester United but Paddy was a lot lighter than him! For a keeper in the First Division in those days weighing in at around eleven stone it just wasn't enough; they had to withstand a bit of a battering as they didn't get the kind of protection that is offered 'keepers today.

Next up was a far sterner test against Liverpool at Anfield and barely a quarter of an hour had gone before we were in trouble - the ball was knocked in the box, a run of the mill ball that I could have headed away comfortably but then I heard this great big shout "My ball Brian!" so I left it for Paddy and the next thing I knew he came flying over the top of me and Heighway picked up the pieces and scored. Perhaps Paddy had a problem with his temperament as after that he was a nervous wreck, but I'm sure it was a ball that Alex would have left me to deal with - it was a cross I'd routinely deal with.

Good goalkeepers are your eyes, seeing an even bigger picture than you, so they can see what's going on and spot trouble on a wider scale. You would expect them to be telling you what you to do. That's what Peter Shilton and Ray Clemence would do. Paddy was trying to impress but it was the wrong decision to come out because maybe he was trying too hard; it was just unfortunate that it was at the Kop End as well to compound matters for him and the nerves got the better of him. To be fair to him he did recover somewhat – we never had a problem with him agility wise, if someone was having a shot at him you'd expect him to save it, but it was those other parts to Paddy's game that worried me. Not that I had a problem playing alongside him. I didn't pick the team and I would never contest the selection of a player. You might be able to do that in a pub side but not at Manchester United! It's the manager's decision and as a consequence he has to bear the brunt of the criticism too especially as he now had the 'experts' on his back asking him to bring Alex back when in all fairness he shouldn't have dropped him in the first place. After that 3-1 defeat at Anfield we dropped from top to fifth, as one point separated the top five. This was going to be a tight title race – could it be that the Doc's decision cost us the league?

Before Alex was recalled, Paddy had to undergo further turmoil. Next up was a League Cup game at Manchester City in which, to be fair, everybody had a bit of a nightmare. It didn't seem too bad but every time they went through they seemed to score, it was just one of those games. We had to dust ourselves down and recover; we beat Aston Villa in the league at Old Trafford and Paddy kept a clean sheet, but the week after we had a trip to Highbury. Unfortunately Paddy didn't get another chance after this game.

When you've got a goalkeeper behind you who you've got confidence in, you do things naturally but when you have someone behind you who you aren't totally sure of, you try and protect them a bit more and then as defenders you start to get into positions you shouldn't really get into. Maybe it was partly the defenders' fault with us getting into trouble; every time we made a mistake, we got punished. Everyone has little runs where things don't go right. This was Paddy's great big chance and he didn't take it. Perhaps he was unfortunate that the games he had to impress included games away at Liverpool, Manchester City and Arsenal but he got five games on the trot to impress and he failed.

We'd probably got too close to the keeper too. Whereas Alex would have pushed us out – Paddy, not being a vocal keeper, or perhaps through lack of confidence, didn't do that. He might shout but Alex would tell us with the authority that comes with being a top keeper and that's probably why Tommy brought him back in, which immediately restored the status quo at the back. We'd still concede goals but you had to look at the bigger picture to see why and that was in the way we played. We didn't play with holding midfield players, we just had players who wanted to attack, so suddenly if you've got defenders like Alex Forsyth, Stewart Houston and myself who all liked to bomb on and start and join in the attacks, you'd sometimes only have one defender left! It becomes a difficult situation when you're then asking a team like that to change the way they naturally play to protect a goalkeeper. We didn't have to do that with Alex so we shouldn't have had to do that with Paddy, but still, maybe he was a little unfortunate with the run of games he was handed.

Perhaps the decision itself was also an unsettling one, particularly going into a run of fixtures like that. Alex was a calming influence but he made mistakes too, just like I had earlier in the season, just like everybody does in the game. The thing is that Alex could put them behind him and contribute to trying to win the game, thanks in no small part to his communication skills. Tommy must have learned a lesson in keeping the team stable as, after the following game against Newcastle, a 1-0 win with a clean sheet for Stepney, we had an unchanged side for over a dozen games in which we went unbeaten. There's nothing better than a settled team - over forty two games it might be a big ask to pick the same team for all of them but we worked very hard and very well, complementing each other and we could only play one way - having a settled side made all the difference.

One player who had arrived and made his debut just before the team was settled was Gordon Hill. When he played for Millwall, Eamonn Dunphy had written a diary of the season that had a picture of Gordon on the front with a tennis racket on it that said "Gullible" on it! That was Hilly, who always wanted to be funny but was gullible. One of the first games he played for United was at Middlesbrough. Lou sent him to a TV interview and he ended up doing a radio one because the TV one didn't exist! Nothing seemed to bother him, he was always trying to be funny - fifty percent of the time he was, fifty percent he wasn't! He thought he was Norman Wisdom. But he was a good addition to the team as he scored goals and looking at that front line - Hilly, Stevie Coppell, Sammy, Pancho and Lou, there was some serious pace in that side.

Greenhoff!

In January 1976 Arnie Sidebottom left; he hadn't played for the team since the loss at Aston Villa the previous season and cricket was taking over for him so in the end it didn't come as a great surprise. He moved to Huddersfield and it was a bit of a surprise that he kept on playing football! It was still slightly sad to see him go after spending such a long time with him, he was a good lad who I liked very much – he was best man at my wedding, we'd go out socially too. He went on to have a good career playing for Yorkshire. Sadly he only got to play for England once and couldn't finish the game as he split his big toe open but when he got that cap I think it was a bit late, he should have had one earlier. He finished up being a bowler and I always knew him as a batsman!

That run of fourteen unbeaten matches included nine wins, three of which where in the FA Cup against Oxford and Peterborough at Old Trafford and then at Leicester in the fifth round. The unbeaten run was ended by Aston Villa but we drew our following game against Derby and then won 4-0 against West Ham before drawing the sixth round tie with Wolverhampton to take it to a replay.

The replay at Molineux proved to be a classic still talked about today. We went two-nil down to bullet headers from Steve Kindon and John Richards. As if we weren't under enough pressure, Lou Macari had to come off and Jimmy Nic replaced me in defence and the Doc moved me into midfield. Even at 2-0 we never thought we were beaten; it only takes one goal to get back in the game and that's what happened when Pancho scored to halve the deficit. From then on we were pressing and were all over them, finally getting the equaliser with a quarter of an hour left, when I scored. From then on there was only going to be one winner and that's how it turned out, when Sammy scored in extra time. If he hadn't put it away, I was right behind him and would have scored myself. It was a great win. Having played in midfield so often it was no difficulty to move up there against Wolves and I was pleased to make a difference.

It was good to make that contribution but I never had any restrictions on me even when I was in defence. I was always encouraged to join in with the play. Though it was a risk, if I was bringing the ball forward then more often than not it meant we could get an extra midfield player unmarked and that's what I tried to do, and it worked a lot of times. My strength as a defender was always contributing to our attack – every centre forward would be six foot plenty and I was five foot ten and a half. I found it difficult in the air but the understanding between Martin and myself was just that he expected me to miss every one, and he was always prepared to pick up any balls lost. I was the same with him too and we were both like that with Alex. If a shot came in, we always reacted as if we expected or thought he was going to drop it, so you'd be back and quick to react, covering to second guess the worst case scenario.

The communication with Martin and myself had certainly improved since those early days. He came up to me not long after and said, "I didn't think you were a centre half, but I do now." He shook my hand and there was never a problem. I always had the utmost respect for Martin, he gave me a bit of a bollocking at times but again that's part of the game as a captain – I might have had my say once or twice but I certainly respected him as a captain. Having spent so much time moving around and playing in so many different positions I was beginning to feel like "Brian Greenhoff, centre half for Manchester United." I thought as long as Tommy would be at United, that's where I would remain. He was happy with how things were going, how we were playing and the fans were happy too. I felt a bit bad for Jim Holton as he had endured horrendous luck; he was a big honest lad, a lovely lad – people wouldn't believe that he would put his foot in on a football pitch. He wasn't imposing in the air but he was a fantastic header of the ball. With a bit of luck with injury he might have had a lot longer of a career but from one man's misfortune comes another's chance...

I'd done well but it really felt like a team effort; and we were a team. We didn't have standout individuals, nobody who people would say "this one makes them tick", we were a fantastic team and worked so hard at it. We defended and attacked as one. I think that's why the fans really fondly speak about that side, because of our character, it was such a fantastic team to play in and watch.

Following the cup tie against Wolves we won three and drew one of our league games in March to keep us in with a chance of doing the League and Cup double as we entered April. Not that we were greedy, we would have been delighted with one of them! The cup semi final was at Hillsborough against Derby County and everyone called it the Final, as the other semi final was contested between Crystal Palace and Southampton, two lower division teams. The game was tough, fast and furious, but we just had too much for Derby. I helped set the first goal up with a drilled ball from the back towards Gordon Hill, who swapped passes with Gerry

Daly and then whacked it in. He scored again to make it two but I almost got a goal when I was clean through in the last minute but I put it wide. Frank McGhee, who was chief sports writer for the *Daily Mirror*, wrote of the chance in the final paragraph of his write up, "I don't know what he was doing there, but I liked it", which I thought was nice. That was how we played that season; it wasn't as if we didn't have our hands full, either. Derby played with another six foot plus centre forward, Roger Davies. It wasn't easy for Martin either as he was five foot eleven, in fact the best header in our team was Stewart Houston. He would be the one picking up the best header from the opposition at corners and free kicks, Martin and I would pick up the next best, Pancho would come back and help out too. We weren't a tall side, though, so we had to make sure our challenges were good and we didn't let people have free headers. And in fairness, Martin and I didn't have many direct headers scored against us. It was something we practised.

After the semi final we picked up a few injuries, and as much as I'd like to think we didn't take our eye off the ball in the league with a Cup Final approaching, maybe there was a bit of that. We'd been measured up for suits, everyone paying attention to the final and talking about it, everything sort of hectic. We certainly didn't mean to have our attention diverted but it didn't help as we suffered three defeats (to Ipswich, Stoke and Leicester) in five league games to knock us out of contention for the title.

For us it was a brand new experience to be competing in Cup Finals but for Southampton and, although they were in the Second Division, they had players with plenty of experience. Jim McCalliog had just signed for them and Peter Osgood played in the Cup Final ten years before for Chelsea. Perhaps where we had enjoyed the benefit of playing with a settled team, this was a game too far. Taking into account the pre-season tour, we'd had a long old time of it and there were one or two tired legs. That's not to make an excuse; I still felt that on our day we had enough to go and beat them. We were expected to win; the only people who probably thought Southampton were going to win were from Southampton and unfortunately they were right. We just didn't perform as we know we could have done, something seemed to be lacking.

We could have had a couple of goals in the first fifteen minutes, and everyone has said that if we had got a goal or two we would have probably run away with it and I agree but in the end we just got caught out. One or two players didn't perform, our semi-final hero Gordon Hill was substituted, he just couldn't get into the game and it got gradually more difficult to get going. We didn't make their keeper do enough, and even if we'd still been playing now, we probably wouldn't have scored.

They say your first Cup Final passes you by and that day, for a lot of the lads, that's what it did. There's little in the game aside from their goal that sticks out – the goal which decided the destiny of the trophy was offside and it should have been given offside, the linesman made a mistake, but then again the referee was Clive Thomas! The best referees are always the ones you don't see, where you ask afterwards who the ref was, but Clive made it all about him. At the time we weren't happy and perhaps we were a little bitter but it happened and there was nothing we could do about it. It was a game that as soon as it finished I wanted to forget about. I didn't want to remember anything of it.

As soon as the whistle went I just slumped to the floor and I don't even think I shook any of their players' hands, I was just so upset, I didn't want to go up and get a loser's medal and I couldn't watch them pick the Cup either because I wanted it to be us. I wanted to go to the fans but we'd been told we weren't allowed to, win or lose, because they weren't at the tunnel end, so as soon as we'd got our medals we had to get off the pitch. There had been a meeting before the match with the FA and Ted Croker and that's what he said; we weren't even allowed to do a lap of honour, which was a bit disappointing for the fans who had followed us all year. We'd entertained them all year and the one game they'd come down to celebrate with us, we couldn't do it.

We had a do after the game at the Russell Hotel in London, which was surprisingly good as everyone drowned their sorrows. When we got back to our room, I tossed the losers' medal to Maureen and said, "There you are, you can have that, I'm having the winners' next year!" It may have been a bit of bravado in my case, a little bit of wishful thinking but I was determined – as were the rest of the lads – to get there again. It was the second time I'd been to Wembley, the first as a ball boy in that League Cup Final in 1968 and I wanted more of it, not realising I'd be back within two weeks.

The week before the Cup Final I'd received my first call up to the senior England squad for the Home Championship tournament that started the week after, which meant I missed the final league game which was a two-nil win at home to

Manchester City. They'd won the League Cup that year but we weren't viewing the FA Cup as a chance to gloat over them; it wasn't like what Carlos Tevez did disgracing himself, and what Samir Nasri did disrespecting his old club. In later years we were pally with plenty of their players; Sammy and I would knock about with Dennis Tueart and Dave Watson. They might have played for a different club, they were our rivals but they're only rivals when you play them. You don't hate them and you don't want to kill them all the time... there are a lot of players who play for the clubs who haven't come from Manchester or haven't come through the ranks so they don't know what it means to play in a proper derby game with seven or eight from both sides having come through the youth team. That's when it really meant something to the players, nowadays it probably means more to the fans that it does the players. All we wanted to do was do the best for our football club, and if theirs couldn't win, then that was their fault.

Coming back from the Cup Final, we were on the coach at ten o'clock on the Sunday morning driving up to Stoke and the lads decided to start on the beer. By the time we got there we'd had a few, then it was straight in the bar - me, Alex and Lou (even though he doesn't drink) decided to stay there. We ordered a plate of sandwiches and just carried on drinking. By the time we got to Bowdon, I think we'd had enough. I wasn't in the best of shape when we got back on the bus - I knocked my glasses off and broke a lens. Someone came running up to give them back but I was drowning my sorrows and looking back maybe this was why I didn't play against City! There was little Tommy could do or say to cheer us up before we went to the Town Hall in Manchester to tell everyone we'd win it next year. Amazingly, there were a quarter of a million United fans there to greet us and we'd lost! City didn't get that many for winning the league.

There was much to look back on and be proud of in 1975/76. We'd finished third and reached a Cup Final, which made it successful, it was just disappointing to have finished empty handed. Then again, we were now in contention for the highest honours; it must be much more difficult for those sides who enter competitions knowing that they don't have a chance at the outset.

There was plenty to look forward to the following season too; we wanted to improve as a team and build upon what we'd done, we wanted to start well again. I trusted in my team-mates - I trusted Martin, Alex Stepney, Lou Macari, Sammy, Pearson, Stevie. I knew when it came to it nobody would let us down and nobody would hide. It doesn't matter which of the top clubs you play for, you sometimes find top players who hide but there's no hiding place at Old Trafford, as anyone will tell you. You were always in the spotlight from people in the press who were very quick to criticise. The difference with the press in those days was that there were good lads who you could have a drink with and tell them anything, which you don't get these days. In return, they'd be honest with you. We'd be in the spotlight next season even more - we'd qualified for Europe which was the first time the club had played in the competition since that AC Milan tie I saw at Old Trafford in 1969, so we had that to look forward.

On a personal note, having broken into the England side, there were World Cup qualifiers to look forward to so it was going to be a busy season. But, having put right the wrong of relegation by being promoted and doing so well, we had another wrong to right the following season.

6. GLORY

FINDING OUT you'd been selected for the senior England squad was by letter back then. Tommy pulled me to one side and said, "You've been picked for the England squad. Your letter's at Old Trafford." The document detailed the complete itinerary for the game against Wales on Saturday, 8th May 1976 at Ninian Park, what I needed to take and what was expected of me.

That call up for the senior squad in May 1976 was a bit of a surprise. The previous game for the under 23's had been a home game at Old Trafford against Hungary. We won 3-1 and I was captain. I had a very good game and I knew it'd put me in the picture after a good season; the England manager was Don Revie who had been in charge of Leeds United for thirteen years from 1961-1974, and of course I'd made many trips to go and see the club when our James was there. I always had a feeling that he would pick me, perhaps because he had let my brother go at Leeds, so I just thought that if I did well enough he'd give me a chance.

The manager of the under 23's was Les Cocker who had been Don's assistant at Elland Road. I'd known Les for a long time as he had given me my first proper pair of new boots. In the Hungary game there were four of us from United picked to play; myself, Stevie Coppell, Gordon Hill and Stuart Pearson. There were around thirty thousand in attendance which was a good crowd for the under 23's in those days. It was a cracking game where we were trying to overturn a 3-0 first leg deficit, and we nearly did it, getting to 3-1 and having chance after chance but we just couldn't get a fourth.

The situation resembled when Tommy had arrived at Old Trafford and I was hoping that my familiarity with the manager might give me a chance – you knew you would get one, it was just a matter of taking the opportunity when it came. Don had come to watch me quite often, not least because at that time we were the team to watch. Me being a centre half that was able to break forward might have been something that he wanted in the team as, like Tommy, he never put any restrictions on me to say "You're just a defender, stay back". If that's what he wanted me to do he could and should have picked somebody else, but I was perfect to get on the ball and start attacks going.

It was weird as I played alongside the Liverpool player Phil Thompson, and I'd always played on the right side as a centre back, but Phil liked to play there so I had to play on the left. I found it a little bit awkward to begin with because when you've never done it you have to gather your bearings but I felt okay. It was similar to when Nemanja Vidic was injured and Rio Ferdinand switched to the left hand side of centre defence while Jonny Evans played in his old position in the 2011/12 season. It was just a little bit weird early on. A positive for me was that when balls were being crossed in from the left hand side, and I was covering, I would be hooking away with my better foot which was handy. The game went okay, I felt I played alright and we won. It was nice to keep a clean sheet in a 1-0 victory where Peter Taylor scored.

The best kind of feedback I could possibly get from Don is that he selected me to play in the next game and that was all I could ask. England was that sort of thing; like a club, teams didn't rotate much, particularly when they were winning. You picked your best side and that was it. There certainly were no wholesale changes like you see today. I think in those days you really earned your caps, there weren't many one cap wonders around. The only one I can remember is Alex Stepney who was so very unfortunate as he played in a period where all the other goalkeepers were fantastic. In any other period Alex would have had a lot more caps.

That second cap came against Northern Ireland at Wembley and Sammy Mac and David McCreery turned out for the opposition which was a bit weird. Despite that, the best they were going to get out of me was swapping my shirt. It was fine and we just got on with it. When you're turning out for your country and you're coming up against your team-mates, I'm sorry but if it's him or me, it's got to be me, and that's the way it had to be. That's how it was with Sammy, who I was best mates with, who got my shirt and that's all from the game! We won 4-0.

United were on another post-season tour, this time to North America, but I missed this as I travelled with England to the States for the US Bicentenary tournament. I'd missed the third home international game in Scotland after damaging the medial ligaments in my knee - and I wasn't going to travel but Tommy Doc convinced me at the last minute. I travelled with them to Los Angeles where they played Brazil and I sat on the bench not even as a substitute and then onto

New York against Italy at Yankee Stadium where again I sat as a spectator. The Brazil game was lost in the last minute and against Italy we recovered from two goals down to win with a couple of Mick Channon goals.

Then it was on to Philadelphia where we played 'Team America'. I played and we won 3-1. 'Team America' weren't in FIFA so the game isn't recognised officially; players from the NASL represented them; the likes of Pele, Bobby Moore who had captained England with such great distinction and Italian forward Giorgio Chinaglia, who started out his career at Swansea and finished up being president of Lazio! 'Soccer' as it was called in the States, was coming of age and these great players were attracting a lot of interest. Sure enough, within twenty years the Yanks had hosted a World Cup – that's progress for you! Although perhaps money had something to do with it!

Nevertheless it was a good game but just another England game, feeling a little like preparation for the next game. After the match Pele was quoted as saying, "England are more impressive as a team than they are individually" which was seemingly meant as an insult! After that tournament we played Finland in a World Cup qualifier and Don played Paul Madeley instead of me, purely to perform a man-marking job on a centre forward, a role to which he was far better suited.

We didn't go on holiday that summer - it was the famous long hot summer of 1976 and Maureen was heavily pregnant. My first son, Paul, was born on the ninth of July, in Park Hospital which is now Trafford General, the same hospital as where his mother was born. It was a very proud moment. I did my part; everything I needed to do as a husband and father. I changed his nappy, winded, bathed and put him to bed. When it came to football though that was it; I had to make sure I was fully prepared and rested, as that was my job. If I had to sleep in the spare room, that's what I did.

United's pre-season tour was in Scandinavia which was a bit of a relief, not just because of welcoming a new born. We'd needed a good rest as maybe the long season and not having any proper time off the year before had caught up with us and started to show in those final games of the 1975/76 season. This time around I got a five week rest, and with it being the hot summer, even though we didn't go on holiday, it was great. It wasn't so great for the wife when she was eight months pregnant! But I felt like I'd had a good long rest that year.

The disappointment of Southampton had been eliminated from my mind – you have to forget these things very quickly. Once they're gone, they're gone, you have to look forward and see what's around the next corner. At United once again we were seeing if they were going to sign anybody. Stuart Pearson had arrived, Stevie and Gordon had joined, and we were wondering if anybody else would come in. Yet nothing happened immediately. Not that I would attribute either the lack of new players or a hangover from the Cup Final as reasons we started the league season so indifferently.

We won just one of our first five league games, losing one and drawing the other three. It was just one of those things; the previous two seasons we'd started really well but this time around we just didn't; we were thinking and wondering what we were doing wrong as there didn't seem a lot wrong. Sometimes it's just a little tweak here and there to put things right, yet the team more or less picked itself and there were no changes in there either, perhaps rightfully so, as we'd come so close the previous season. With Cup games aplenty at the start of the season we just had to take it one game at a time; not just League Cup games, but Europe and the World Cup qualifiers for those playing for their countries, which was most of the first team now. There was no real opportunity to prioritise anything given the fact that you could be playing a League game, then a League Cup game and then a World Cup qualifier all in the same week. With the successful season just gone there was expectation but then there is always expectation at Manchester United. When you're running out in front of anywhere between forty five to sixty thousand, the expectation is there and you know what you're required to do. Team talks would be less detailed at home, because you were just expected to go out and entertain at Old Trafford.

The reward for finishing third in the league was to play in the UEFA Cup, and our first opponents in the competition were three times European champions Ajax. The first leg wasn't played in their home stadium but in the Olympic Stadium. At United every game is a big game but this was the first time they'd played in Europe since the controversial 1969 defeat to AC Milan. The difference between European and domestic football was very quickly clear. It was the first time you could see at first hand that they were much better at keeping possession, having a lot more of the ball than we enjoyed and we had to work a lot harder than they did to get the ball back.

We gave it back far too easily – one thing I learned from

the experience was the importance of keeping the ball because they were so good at it. It was a good game even though we lost 1-0 to a Rudi Krol goal, we had a few chances and did well. After that we fancied our chances at home and we knew what was expected. We knew that we had to be good on the counter as they were so good at holding the ball and moving it so quickly. We rode our luck a few times but then Gordon Hill hit a fierce shot that was parried, and Lou Macari nipped in to make it 1-0 and level it on aggregate. The second half began and Tommy took Gerry Daly off for Arthur Albiston, and I wondered what he'd done that for, until he told Stewart Houston to move into centre half and told me to get into midfield. It was never explained to me exactly why but I presume it was because Tommy thought I'd be stronger on the ball than Gerry had been, who was a little bit lightweight even though he could run all day.

It worked. Tommy wasn't made to look a fool. Sometimes a manager can make a bold decision and it doesn't work but this time it did, as I was able to make the winning goal for Sammy, squaring it in the area in front of the Stretford End. The atmosphere was fantastic, creating a reminder of those days I'd watched European nights on the terraces at Old Trafford. I didn't finish the game thinking "Oh, I've played really well there". It was the reaction from the Doc as we were leaving the pitch that did it - he was waiting for me with his arms out, which somebody took a picture of and it ended up being a famous image. Afterwards, all the press were waiting for me and I thought, "Did I play that well?" Sometimes you go through games and you don't realise how well you've done until afterwards. Maybe the adrenaline and the atmosphere influenced how I felt; remembering back to the game with AC Milan in 1969 with the hairs going on the back of my neck, and now playing in that kind of atmosphere, maybe it got that bit more out of me. It really sunk in afterwards but perhaps that was down to the fuss people were making; I just thought it was a job well done!

We were having a bit of a run in the League Cup, too, having defeated Tranmere 5-0 in the second round, we were drawn against Sunderland. It was a game that went to two replays; it didn't get settled on the night in those days, if you couldn't get a winner, you played again and so on until somebody won. We played at home first and drew 2-2, went away and got another 2-2 draw. I scored at Roker Park and it was a little bit of a fluke, I crossed it in for Stuart Pearson but he couldn't reach it and neither could Sunderland goalkeeper Jim Montgomery who was flat-footed and the ball went into the opposite corner. In the second replay, I scored the winner to finally settle the tie, Stevie played the ball in, I hit it towards goal with my right foot and it hit Sammy in the face. The ball broke and came back to me so I hit it with my left and it went into the back of the net. It had a bit of luck but it was a bit funny; Sunderland were just one of those teams I seemed to score against, as were Wolves. A month or so later we played Sunderland yet again, this time in the league, and I scored again in a three-all draw at Old Trafford.

That Sunderland result earned us a fourth round tie with their local rivals Newcastle at Old Trafford. We were at Mottram Hall before the tie and Maureen was in hospital awaiting an operation to have her gallbladder out. We had something to eat and went for a sleep as usual but I couldn't settle so I told the Doc I wanted to go and see my wife. He said 'no problem' so I found Norman Davies and we went back to his house and his wife made me tea and toast, then I drove to St. Joseph's hospital to make sure Maureen was okay. She'd come out of the operation but she didn't know I was there, I just had to go make sure she was ok. I drove to the game, played and we won 7-2, then afterwards I went back home as I wasn't allowed back to the hospital. That's my main memory of such a high scoring game - well, that and Jimmy Nicholl scoring!

Sandwiching the Newcastle game were two games in Europe against Juventus. That was a tough tie as they were a naughty team. They had a lot of lads in that side who could kick, they really weren't a nice team to play against. They had Claudio Gentile - who was anything but gentle - Antonello Cuccureddu, Marco Tardelli, Francesco Morini, and then the biggest animal of them all - Romeo Benetti. They had a big flat-nosed centre forward called Roberto Boninsegna who kept telling me what he was going to do to me, "murder in Turin, murder in Turin", that's all he kept saying to me. They were unbelievably tough, but we beat them 1-0 at Old Trafford and probably just about deserved to win.

When we went over to Italy it was a completely different kettle of fish. They treated us with disdain; they were a good side who could play as much as they could dish it out and even though at times I thought we played well, they were just toying with us and we got a proper European lesson, losing 3-0 and getting eliminated from the competition. In the days when you could get a relatively easy ride, to get Ajax and then Juventus was a hell of a baptism. Juventus went on to win the tournament – their first European trophy. They were so organised whereas we certainly weren't. We had a way of playing and we had specific jobs but we were not on the same level as the Italians, they really were organised. It was the first time I'd played against an Italian side and they were so hard to break down, and had so many great players.

I played against some of them in a World Cup qualifier a couple of weeks later. I was away when Kath, the club telephonist, called me at the England hotel and said the boss wanted to speak to me. The Doc asked how I was doing. "Go on then, what have I done wrong?" I asked. "Somebody wants to speak to you", he said and then he put our James on the phone. I was gobsmacked, absolutely gobsmacked. I never thought I'd get a chance to play with our James professionally. He was getting on then at the age of thirty and was well set at Stoke where he was loved. He had no need to leave there but then one of the stands blew down in the wind, the roof went off, and the club needed to have it repaired.

One of the directors at Stoke went to their manager Tony Waddington and said, "You need to sell somebody. Is there anyone who you could sell quickly" and he answered by saying, "I could sell Jimmy quickly, but he goes where I want him to." The story goes that he rang up Tommy Doc to tell him that James was available for £100,000. I played the game in Italy and then flew back, the next morning James drove up to our house where we were living in Davyhulme and I took him to The Cliff. The Saturday after we played at Leicester, which was Jimmy's debut. Martin didn't play, so I was captain, too. It was brilliant. It pleased my mum and my sister so much, dad would have been really proud too, it was so good for the family, a very pleasant surprise. It proved a good signing. We needed a striker and we'd got someone with a proven track record, someone who'd done well in the top league for years who we were sure would score a few goals. The fee was a bargain too, even in those days – it was only a couple of years after that that players started costing over £1 million which seemed daft even though now it's nothing.

Elimination from the UEFA Cup had an effect on our league form which also translated into the League Cup too. We didn't win in eight games in the league and were eliminated by Everton in the Cup. Football is a confidence game and when you start suffering defeats, it gets to you. Still, looking at the team I couldn't imagine the Doc making many changes. We just had to stick with what we had, fight through it and hope things would change. We worked on things in training to see if it would make a difference and we'd keep working until we found the right formula. With elimination from two Cups and the form in the league ruling us out of a serious title challenge, focus and attention turned to the FA Cup. That was something that I wanted badly, ever since the previous year since I'd said I didn't want the losing medal. There was unfinished business; I wanted to go back to Wembley. I'd been there with England and won but more so, I wanted to go back as a Manchester United player and win. Not that we were ever going to concentrate solely on one competition and neglect the league; you can't do that at a club like United, it was important to pick up form anyway to build up momentum, as it's momentum that ultimately helps you win things. We had to get back to winning ways in the league to help us in the Cup as well.

Our third round victory against Walsall at Old Trafford, a 1-0 win thanks to a goal from Gordon Hill, started a run of 15 games where we went unbeaten. James had taken a short while to settle in – and sometimes great players do – look at Juan Sebastian Veron, the Argentine playmaker who signed in 2001. He was a fantastic signing, but at United he didn't do it enough. He had spells where you thought he was unbelievable then there were games where he'd just go missing. You have to give these players time to settle in, sometimes it doesn't matter how good a player you are, and it was like that with James. He had a new working partnership with Stuart up front and that was going to take time, and the midfield players had to get used to the way he played, the little ways he would lay off balls that were knocked into him, and once they tapped into his way of thinking, it was then we knew things were going to happen and that we were going to get better.

Lou Macari's goal in the FA Cup fourth round was enough to defeat QPR and set us up for a replay of the previous year's final, a trip to holders Southampton. The week before we went to the Dell, James hit a hat-trick against Newcastle in a 3-1 win. Going back to Southampton after losing to them was massive. They'd added Alan Ball to their side so they had even more experience, and we knew it was going to be a tough game. We drew 2-2 with goals from Hill and Macari and we really should have won the game, but we got them back to Old Trafford and to play at home was a bonus. In the replay, Ball scored a penalty to put them one up but then we dominated the game. They were playing a different

Manchester United team than the one they'd played the previous year and there was no way that we would let up. As it proved in the end, when we ran out worthy 2-1 winners, with James getting both goals.

That earned us a sixth round tie at home to Aston Villa. On the Thursday before the game, I was supposed to be guest of honour for an event in Altrincham. I had to pull out and Tommy Docherty told them it was because I had flu, but I had actually got an abductor injury and I was required to rest up so I could be available for the game. I got to the game and I really wasn't fit, I shouldn't have played, but as was typical with Tommy, he could talk me into doing anything and I agreed to give it a go. I think I lasted about fourteen minutes, I just couldn't play as it was pulling all the time and I was worried that it was going to rip. I was brought off for David McCreery, and it was disappointing as we were 1-0 down. The lads pulled it round and Lou got the winner after Stewart Houston had equalised. It was a great relief to me as I really did think I'd let the lads down by playing but as I say, the Doc could have talked me into running through a brick wall for him. David coming on meant we had a disjointed team and I was just relieved when we got through. A lot of people were saying that our name was on the trophy but we weren't thinking that way, we just wanted to get to another final.

The semi-final draw had us in the pot with Everton, Liverpool and Leeds United, and I think everyone wanted Leeds. We'd won our last four games against them, and we got what we wanted. We were also drawn to play them at Hillsborough which had been good to us the year before against Derby. We always thought that if we could hit them hard the first fifteen minutes, we could go on and win, and that's exactly how it happened. Goals from Stevie and James put us two nil up. They pulled one back with an Allan Clarke penalty which shouldn't have been given. The ref should have sent off Joe Jordan for elbowing Jimmy Nicholl in the face, but he got away with what I saw as a naughty act.

After the Villa game, the league form had dropped off once more. We won just four and lost six of our last fourteen league games, and we finished in sixth position, ten points behind Liverpool who won the league. I've often been asked what was lacking from the side that stopped us really challenging for the league as we'd come so close the year before but I've always reply that I never thought the side we had was set up to win a league. When you watched that Liverpool side – they were a lot more solid than us, we just didn't have the same type of players, so we played to our strengths which was attack. If you took that away then you took our strength away. You can't ask people like our midfield four, Lou Macari, Sammy McIlroy, Gordon Hill and Stevie Coppell to defend. They were just better going forward. None of them could tackle but they could pinch balls, the majority of the time they did it well.

Liverpool were our opponents in the FA Cup Final. They were league champions and were in the European Cup Final, so they were chasing a treble. For our own preparation we changed what we did from the year before. In 1976 we stayed in Sopwell House just north of London and this time we stayed in Selsdon Park in Croydon, where Southampton stopped the year before. It was a long way to the ground and we had a police escort all the way to make sure we got there in plenty of time. I sat with our kid on the bus and he was nervous as hell, saying to me "I hope we win, I hope we win". I was telling him to relax, to go and enjoy it.

When we got to Wembley, we had a little walk around and a couple of interviews, saw the crowd and gave them a wave, tried to see if the family were there and then gave them a wave. Then we went to prepare and they named the teams. There was a big shock as Ian Callaghan wasn't playing. They decided to play David Johnson and Kevin Keegan up front, but we thought they might push Steve Heighway forward or Jimmy Case as that's what they had been doing. So it was a bit of a shock, but a pleasant one. It didn't necessarily give us more confidence but I couldn't understand why Liverpool had made the decision. A lot of the pundits were saying that if we didn't score in the first fifteen minutes then Liverpool would win. I think Don Revie went on record saying on the BBC that it was "men against boys" meaning we were the boys. He later apologised to the United lads who joined up with England for saying that.

In those days Liverpool weren't the fierce rivals they are today. City were our "rivals", Liverpool were just a team we looked at and wanted to have their success, because they were the team who were winning. I was quite friendly with a few of the Liverpool lads, which was normal in those days. Phil Thompson was one I got on with who actually missed the Cup Final, Phil Neal, Ray Clemence, Ray Kennedy and Terry McDermott, we knew them with England – Emlyn Hughes was someone I got on really well with too. They were good lads and you wanted to have the success they were having, but it was more from a determination aspect than jealousy. I was envious if anything, but I'd rather they won than City!

It was a tough game – it was a hot day on the big Wembley pitch, but I think Martin and I played as well as we ever had played together at the back. Jimmy Nicholl did fantastically against Steve Heighway, Arthur Albiston coming in for Stewart Houston (who had unfortunately broken his leg two weeks before against Bristol City) was brilliant. The back four was probably as solid as I can ever remember them being in a game, and Alex was his normal self, talking, shouting and encouraging, telling you what's happening. Lou and Sammy ran a thousand miles, or at least it seemed that way to me, they just never stopped running. Stevie was up and down the right wing, Hilly was doing his bit. Gordon was probably the only one who would have been disappointed with his performance. Stuart and our kid up front were working hard, trying to keep hold of the ball as they were against two tough centre halves – Tommy Smith was hard to play against, as was Emlyn Hughes, two defenders who wouldn't give you anything. It was a very difficult game, we just kept plugging away, then it got to half time, and we did the same in the second half, going for that chance. Then suddenly the chance came and Pancho whacked it in and we thought, "Oh, that's it!" You just couldn't relax against Liverpool though, and within two minutes, they'd levelled and that's what they were like. I think if there's one thing United learned from them in years to follow was the resilience, to never give in.

It's always said that teams are never more vulnerable than when they've just scored, and it was proved twice in that game.

The next thing, we get the winning goal! Jimmy Nicholl on the right looped the ball into the box. Lou, who for a little lad was always fabulous in the air, flicked it on. Our kid was challenging with Tommy Smith, when Lou came in and hit it, I think James was trying to move out of the way but it hit him on the arm and looped past Ray Clemence. When you look at it afterwards you think maybe our name was on the Cup when stuff like that happens!

We defended really well after that, Alex didn't really have a shot to save. The hardest thing he had to deal with was a backpass from me when I headed it back. A lot of people have said to me that I was lucky with that, but I tell them I wasn't - Alex shouted for it, and I just headed it back to him! I didn't think anything of it in spite of the crowd reaction, until people mentioned it after. Watching it back now, you can see that as I was running away I turned round and applauded Alex for the shout. After being asked about it I did confirm with Alex, "Did you shout for that? You did, didn't you?" and he said he did. It was an instinctive thing we were used to doing and had done it before so the surroundings and settings barely mattered; it was a free-kick from Phil Neal and it was a funny ball in, I could either head it over the cross bar or do what I did, and it just seemed natural to head it back to Alex. It wasn't a thunderbolt or anything, it was a cushioned ball back to him. It's only a bad header if it goes in the net!

During the game I felt absolutely fine; I just didn't seem to care, I think whereas the year before there was an expectancy on us to go out and win, we weren't expected to in 1977. Liverpool were just going to go and do the treble, but we stopped that and it was a great, great feeling. It was a strange sensation; I was going up and heading balls throughout the game – David Johnson, like myself, wasn't a big lad. I'd been playing against 6 foot plus centre forwards all season and then suddenly there was David who was about 5'11 and Kevin Keegan who was around 5'7, so I felt confident in the air. I probably won more headed challenges that day than I did all season, I think at one point I actually controlled one as a pass to Martin! It was just one of those days where all the confidence came out and everything I did, apart from maybe one occasion where I stood on the ball in the first half, I was composed. I felt good, so good that at one point I cleared a corner kick with a header and it nearly went to the half way line!

A few years later I went around with the video of the game to our kid's house to watch it, and he said, "Oh no, I'm not watching that. You want to watch it because you had a great game. I was crap!" I insisted he wasn't and we watched it, and he said "Hey I wasn't that bad was I?" Sometimes you come off the pitch thinking how badly you've played. On that day, he might have thought he'd had a bad game but I knew I'd had a good one. In saying that though, I was more positive than him going into the game. He actually did fine but maybe it was his perception going in and out of the game that influenced his opinion of how he'd done.

The 1976 Cup Final had gone in a blur because I was so upset about it. This one, I wanted to savour. After the game we jumped on the coach and went back to the Royal Gardens Hotel, we met the wives and had a glass of champagne, before getting on the bus to be taken to the Royal Lancaster Hotel where we were having the reception. There were all sorts of people there. I can remember saying to the wife, "Hey there's Jimmy Hill, let's go and have a chat with him," and she said, "I'm not talking to him! I can't stand what he says on the television!". We ended up going to talk to him for about half an hour, and she said "Ee, what a nice man he is!" He was such a nice man and sometimes the people you see on the television aren't a reflection of who they really are.

After that we had a nice meal and went out; me and Mick Docherty with the wives and Steve Coppell with his girlfriend. We went to a Greek place where we'd arranged to meet a Alex, a Greek-Cypriot friend of mine. He wasn't there when we arrived and we found out that a big friend of his he'd come down with, Tommy Thorpe, had died in the hotel the night before. Alex was understandably upset afterwards. We still managed to have a good night, we ended up throwing plates on the floor, Stevie and Mick were dancing in the middle of the plates being thrown, it was a pleasant couple of hours there before we went back to the Royal Gardens to finish off celebrating. When we got there, both my mother and Maureen's mother who'd travelled down as our guests, were still there drinking champagne at about three o'clock in the morning!

At that time I was still buzzing, and at 7am we were walking in the park; me, Tommy Doc, Lou, Gordon, Clayton and Jack Trickett, the boxing promoter. I finally got to bed not long after and at half past nine there was a knock on the door from Martin Tyler who had come to pick us up to take us to the studios to appear on London Weekend Television. We went and did the programme which was going to be recorded, then jumped in a car that took us to the train station. This time, I didn't drink. Everyone else was on it but I wasn't. I wouldn't even have anything to eat, I just thought, "Right, I'm going to take this all in".

We were due to get on the coach at Wilmslow and from there to the town hall in Albert Square is a long way. We had to go down the M56, all the way onto the M63, onto the A56, past Old Trafford and down through Deansgate to the Town Hall. We went in there and had a bit of a reception, some pictures with the Cup. The crowd were unbelievable. We then went back to Old Trafford, and my niece was on the coach with us – my sister's little girl, Kay – she loved it. We got back there and got in our cars to go home, I went back to where I was living in Davyhulme on Whalley Avenue, and they'd decorated the street for me which was great. All they wanted was to see the FA Cup winners' medal, and I didn't need much persuading!

To cap off a great season I was named Supporters' Player of the Year, which was a fantastic privilege. We used to get the magazine every month and they'd tell you the positions. It was done by all of the supporters clubs in the country who would send the votes in and I was top for nearly all of the year. Stuart Pearson was probably the closest to me and I finished up winning. It was massive – when the fans think you've been the best player all year, it really is a massive thing and it was a great honour. I still have the award to this day. 1976–77, with my England caps, my son being born, my brother joining United, winning the Cup and then being given the supporters award really was the standout season in my career.

My first season had gone well, my second year a little bit indifferent but still a good season. The first year back in the

First Division was a good year but this was the one that really stands out – every player has one where they look back on as their standout best, that's unless you're called Lionel Messi or Cristiano Ronaldo! It was always going to be hard to top that year.

At United though it was all about the next challenge. I was so pleased for Tommy to have won the cup after all we'd been through, and his own personal attempts to win at Wembley too. Tommy had only ever been good for me – he never told me any lies, he was only ever honest which was all I wanted from a manager. If there was something I was doing wrong, I wanted to be told, and it never bothered me as long as it was good, honest criticism. Knowing that we could beat Liverpool gave us the motivation to try and really push on in the league. I think we all knew the squad needed strengthening in order to be able to accomplish that – it wasn't the strongest but then again it was difficult to have a strong squad in order to keep everybody happy.

When we signed our kid, we had to let Gerry Daly leave. Nobody wanted to play in the reserves every week and it wasn't like you could take a squad of twenty five and rotate it back then. Nonetheless, I don't think it's any secret that our squad needed strengthening to get to that next level, nor do I think it was a secret that Tommy was trying to get a new goalkeeper. He'd tried to sign Peter Shilton but his wages proved to be a problem; United had always been notoriously poor payers. Mine had never been a problem for me over the years – Tommy had said to me back when I signed a contract to go onto £35 a week and that if I did well, it would go up every year. It did, he was as good as his word. If we stood a

Greenhoff!

chance of winning the league, it was going to be in the year after we won the FA Cup. We just needed one or two names in there; and if anyone was the manager to lead us to the title, it was going to be Tommy...

7. THE DOC AND DAVE

I WAS ON HOLIDAY in Malta in July 1977 with our kid. There was a girl who knew Tommy very well (her name escapes me) who worked at the Piccadilly pub in Manchester who broke the news to us that he had been sacked from his position as manager of Manchester United. She gave us a number to call. We rang Tommy from the hotel to find out what was happening; James and I were both so disappointed, though I took it harder because of the long history I'd had with him. By all accounts it was a long drawn out saga with a "will he, won't he" storyline but by the time we got to speak to him he'd already gone. We hadn't known anything was going on, it just came completely out of the blue.

It was an even bigger shock to discover he'd been having an affair with Mary Brown, the wife of our physio Laurie. Nobody knew about it - at a club the size of Manchester United you would imagine that somebody would have had a good idea of what was going on. Tommy himself was covering for certain people committing similar acts. Personally, I was more surprised than anything else. These things do happen, even in today's game, it's just that it had never really taken place in the public eye before. It was something that Tommy would have to live with. Both the Doc and Tommy Cav used to say that "players are ships in the night" and the same rang true for managers at United in the seventies. We'd had such a swift turnaround after Sir Matt retired, with Wilf and Frank given relatively short spells. I think when boards get used to sacking managers it comes so easily. To put it in context – United have only had seven managers since the war and I played under four of them!

I believe there were underlying issues. That there were one or two people outside of the board who obviously didn't like Tommy and they were friends with Sir Matt. Maybe there was a bit of pressure put on from outside but once the news broke it was always going to be difficult for both Tommy and Laurie to remain in their positions and work together. If it was down to me, I would have said to keep hold of Tommy and let go of Laurie because he wasn't the best physio in the world.

No matter how disappointed I was and no matter how much I didn't want to see Tommy go, it wasn't my decision; it was obviously very difficult for me as he had been so good for me. As I mentioned earlier, I would have run through a brick wall for him. The number of times I would play when I wasn't fit or when I was carrying an injury – not that I was the only one – was down to my loyalty to Tommy, he could get players playing when perhaps they shouldn't have. My loyalty to Tommy was simply down to the fact that my relationship with him had lasted such a long time and we'd been through so much together professionally.

On a personal level, he had always stepped in to do the right thing for me also. While Maureen was pregnant and she wasn't doing so well with it, I went to Tommy to ask if I could take her away for a few days. Typically, he said it wasn't a problem. I didn't know how long I was going to go away for – we were on the way back from a weekend away game against Coventry in the February and I was meeting Maureen and her mother at Knutsford as we got off the motorway. As I got off the coach, Norman Davies gave me a kit bag with boots and a ball in and Tommy said, "See you Thursday". If he'd have said Tuesday or Wednesday it wouldn't have bothered me, as I just thought Maureen needed a couple of days break from it all, yet to give me that long spoke volumes about him.

The break did Maureen the world of good – and I'd be lying if I said it didn't do me some good, too! That summed up the Doc. To me he was nothing but helpful, no problem was too little, he would never tell me to go away, he would always try and sort it. When I was buying a house he put me on to a good estate agent and insurance broker, and helped sort it so I could get my mortgage. Even when I was buying my first house, and I needed a little bit more money, I went to see Tommy and ask if I could borrow some money from the club and he sorted that out for me too. Managers don't always have to help with solely football related matters and I knew that no matter what my problem, I could go to Tommy and he would sort it out for me.

It's been said that you could love or hate the Doc. I only realised in recent years the depth and extent of Alex Stepney's issues with Tommy. Despite their feisty relationship I never thought it was that bad; if anything, I thought that Lou Macari had more run-ins with him. Nothing runs smoothly with managers anyway, no matter who it is. It's been said that those who were on the good side of Tommy demonstrate a stubborn refusal to see bad with him; but that doesn't really bother me. He was nothing but good for me, and at the end of the day you make your own relationship with your manager. Mine was fine and if others couldn't have a great one with him, then that was their problem. Make no mistake, there were plenty who did have problems with him, not least Laurie. One of the pair had to leave the club, and it was Tommy. I was gutted, it was very upsetting.

When Tommy came to the club he did what Wilf had tried to do, and that was to make the squad younger. The 1968 side that had won the European Cup was getting on a bit and though Wilf – and I'm sure Frank, too, to an extent – tried to bring through the younger players, the bottom line is that they didn't manage to do it successfully. And so when Tommy came, they all had to go. Bobby Charlton, Tony Dunne, Denis Law had all left, Paddy Crerand and Bill Foulkes were finishing, and there was a lot for Tommy to replace. At Rotherham and at Chelsea Tommy was noted for using younger players. That can give those young players a lift and I had a relationship with him that extended back to when he was at Rotherham. I don't think I let him down and he certainly never let me down. He also never let Manchester United down.

Whoever was going to follow Sir Matt knew it would be all but impossible, as Wilf found out. And when Frank arrived from Leicester City he didn't seem to cope with the size of the club. To manage Manchester United, it's not only a big club, it's different from other clubs. It's got such a high profile and the media attention is far greater. I thought Wilf had done a good job but Frank hadn't taken it forward at all. Most managers start well and then you learn much about them from their reaction to adversity. Unfortunately, Frank didn't deal with that too well. When the Doc came in, although he kept the team up he could tell there was going to be a big problem, which we realised with relegation.

Yet the board must have seen something in him not to sack him after that, he was still upbeat about his chances of returning the club to it's former glories, and I think the board that eventually sacked him was exactly the same as the one who backed him in 1974. He was what the club needed after Sir Matt but he was a totally different character; he was always laughing and joking, taking the mickey, and he had a perfect sidekick in Tommy Cav, making training so much fun. We'd have to be there at quarter past ten to start at half past but I'd be there at half past nine, I couldn't wait as I was so excited. They were such good times, I would say ninety nine times out of a hundred I came off with a smile on my face.

It's flattering that people hold the Manchester United team of that period in such high regard and that it occasionally gets compared to the exciting teams that Sir Matt and then, much later, Sir Alex Ferguson assembled. I'm very proud if people think that, and I would have to agree that we were the most exciting team of the mid-seventies. We played at a hundred miles an hour, a philosophy that others had described as a high offside trap but we always simply called, "attack the ball". It was a prototype of the pressing game that Barcelona and Spain perfected recently. Our strength was going forward. It wasn't easy having defenders under six foot against strikers well over, so we used to turn it around and try and play in their half instead, which is something we did very well. I suppose we were ahead of our time in many respects. In others we were a throw back to a more innocent era, we seemed happier winning 3-2 than 1-0.

Soon after taking that message in Malta, James and I started talking about who would be the next manager. The names who were mentioned in the media included Brian Clough, Laurie McMenemy and Dave Sexton. We didn't have that much time to speculate or really decide on who we wanted it to be; not that it would have mattered anyway, as it's always a decision that the club takes. As a player you just sign the contract and you have to deal with whoever the manager is.

When Dave Sexton did get it, I think all of the players thought it was a good choice, as he had a reputation for his sides playing good football, and he was known as a hands on manager, even more so than Tommy. Tommy had been hands on but Dave was apparently part of a new breed, and he had already succeeded the Doc in managerial roles before and done a good job. To follow him again seemed natural; not least because when we'd finished third, he was manager of Queens Park Rangers, who finished second. It remained to be seen if he could do that at United but as players we were curious to see his own ideas; which players, if any, he wanted to bring in, so the first months were all about proving to him that he didn't need anybody else.

We knew that for a title challenge we would probably need one or two players as we didn't have the strongest of squads. We certainly didn't have great depth - if Martin or myself were injured, Stewart Houston would come into centre half from left back, and for an example of versatility from within the players we did have, you didn't have to look any further than myself, of course. I was one of the fortunate people who could do a job in most positions, so I imagine to a manager someone like me would have been perfect.

We kicked off the season taking on Liverpool at Wembley in the traditional opener to the English season, the Charity Shield. Kenny Dalglish was making his Liverpool debut, replacing Kevin Keegan, but it was a bit of a non-entity of a game which finished in a drab goalless draw with us sharing the trophy. That game rounded off a strange pre-season for me during which I had travelled to South America with England and also had my wisdom teeth out before returning to training.

Everyone was curious to find out Sexton's plans for the future and one of the first things that struck us was how defensive the new man was. Then it became apparent that changes were happening on the training pitch too. We rarely finished with a five a side, it would usually be some routine where the clipboard came out. He would mark things down, scoring things and tell you what you'd done - I always felt under pressure, which for me isn't what training should be about. There's a time to work hard, and as professional footballers we knew that, but there was time to have fun as well. I've always believed players should walk off after training smiling, and unfortunately that wasn't the case.

Dave's monitoring may well have been intended to motivate but it certainly didn't do that for me; writing every little thing down into sections. We'd play eight against seven with the intent on keeping the ball and he'd be marking who made most interceptions, who did this, that and the other, and it felt like we were back at school, or at least it felt like that to me. He brought in a method of training called "Third man running", a routine where you'd touch the ball once every two minutes, which was something I thought we did naturally anyway, we certainly didn't need to be taught it! We did some exercises under the Doc and Tommy Cav but those would mostly be things like shadow football, where we would set out in our formation but against no opposition. Those were the kind of things that were helpful to us, things that we could take on to the pitch, but there seemed to be little of that with Sexton.

We'd always finish with the eight against seven and we'd all be knackered and couldn't wait to get off! At least with the five a sides, we'd have a bit of a laugh, something like Alex scoring his thousandth goal and running around the pitch, and you'd walk off having a laugh and joke. Dave tried to be funny but he just wasn't. I'm sure Tommy Cav told Dave the kind of players we were and what we responded to but Dave was his own man, and eventually it got to the point where instead, Tommy Cav became a different man from the one that we'd known under Tommy. Even though I'd had my own share of run-ins with Cav, I still liked him, but I could see the change in him. And for me, personally, after Dave had been there for only three or four months I started to get the impression that he didn't like me.

We started the season fairly well and those results translated onto the training pitch; there's always a good mood when you're winning, and we started with two wins and a draw from our three league games in August. Wins create confidence and get players wanting to come in and train, and we were still trying to impress the manager. He'd obviously not come in with any pre-conceived ideas of changing it right away. Our chance to really impress him came in the European Cup Winners' Cup. We were drawn to play Saint Etienne of France with the first leg away. At the time, there was a bread strike in England, and the home fans were throwing bread at the United fans would you believe. In return, the United fans threw heavier bread back! We could see it going on as the game continued.

We played very well and got a 1-1 draw but unfortunately due to the crowd trouble United were thrown out of the tournament. We were re-instated after an appeal but we had to play the 'home' leg at Plymouth Argyle. Our choice was to either play there, or Aberdeen, as we had to play a certain number of miles away from Old Trafford. Home Park was a lovely pitch and we won 2-0 with goals from Stevie and Pancho in front of over 30,000. One thing I can always remember is that we had to borrow Plymouth's coach to get to the game and it was far better than our own. When you think about it, Plymouth need a good coach because of all the travelling they did for away games, they obviously needed something comfortable. There were only something like seventeen seats but then we only needed space for twelve players, a manager, coach, physio, and maybe a director or two who might travel with you.

It was weird playing a European home game away from Old Trafford but the speed with which UEFA acted to get the game played at a new venue was almost as weird! If only things were resolved as efficiently nowadays. Still, it was better to have played at Plymouth than to be kicked out of the competition altogether. Again, crowd trouble was still rife just as it had been back in the season where we were promoted, even if it did always seem to be away from home rather than at Old Trafford, where we never seemed to have a problem. At one time the club had a meeting with supporters at Old Trafford to discuss the trouble yet I'm certain it was genuine fans who attended the meeting, not the ones who caused the trouble. Of course you wouldn't get people coming saying, "It was me who ripped that roof up". It was a difficult time, and it was difficult reading about the trouble as well, but it got better. I don't think I've ever seen any trouble at Old Trafford.

The win over Saint Etienne sent us through to play Porto. The first leg was away again, and I travelled even though I had picked up a knee problem and knew I wouldn't be playing. Our kid was taken ill before the game and then Pancho didn't play either. With a few players out, Porto were up for it and came out of the blocks, defeating us 4-0 with a hat-trick scored by Duda - a headline writers dream - and another from Antonio Oliviera, who would go on to coach at the club. In the return fixture it was always going to be a difficult game. It's not often you see a team reverse a 4-0 first leg deficit, and it was even harder not being able to play in the game. They were a good side and even though the lads did well to win 5-2, Porto always looked dangerous on the break as United pushed forward so much.

It was a great game to watch, though. The atmosphere was fantastic - it was getting so that European games had an even better atmosphere than the FA Cup games. Having reached two Finals on the trot the atmosphere was always electric at Old Trafford for Cup ties. The little 10 seconds before the referee blew the whistle for kick off did something to you, it gave you a real buzz. It's a shame that the players don't get the same thrill for the cup these days; the League Cup or the FA Cup, because I think the clubs are demeaning them by not playing their best sides. Then again, clubs have such massive squads whereas in the Seventies we had to play our best side. Nonetheless, we all wanted to get to Wembley, the goal was to win all three trophies. The FA Cup was second to the league but only just; the whole day of the final would be massive in terms of coverage. Cameras would be at your hotel at eight o'clock in the morning and it lasted all day. ESPN covered the 2012 FA Cup Final between Chelsea and Liverpool in such a fashion, for the first time probably since the Seventies, and that was really good to see.

Following our exit from the Cup Winners' Cup, it was obvious that things weren't right. Under the Doc he'd always tell us to go out and enjoy it, whereas Dave would be telling the players to do certain things or think about this, think about that. It wasn't the same. Sometimes you want the lads ripping the door down to go out and play, particularly when things aren't going well, but Dave didn't have that, he just had players going out to do a job. We had started to pick up a few injuries and we'd lost seven games in the league by the end of November. Martin and I both had spells out of the team through injury. December didn't get any better.

The worst it got was just before Christmas when we were hammered 4-0 at home by Nottingham Forest. I remember it for being the worst performance I ever had at Old Trafford. Martin and I had just come back from injury and I just could not put a foot right and we got run ragged. Forest were a very good side and we were very low on confidence; it was a mix of things destined to go badly for us. The defeat against Forest must have been when Dave decided he wanted to change things and start bringing players in. He wanted to change the direction of the team, which was the start of a difficult time for me.

In an FA Cup tie against Carlisle, I was sent off for two bookable offences and was suspended for the replay. These days I might have been sent off for both incidents - the first one might well have been violent conduct! Sammy gave the ball away at the edge of the box and I was left with no choice but to bring the player down. For the second one, our kid gave a free kick away, they took a quick one and it was going over my head so I caught it and was booked. We won the replay 4-2 the following midweek. The next game was against Ipswich Town at Portman Road on 14th January 1978, and with my suspension over, I was available for selection again and was expecting to be in the team. Not only was I not picked, I wasn't even told I was dropped. Sexton just named the team and I wasn't in it. If it had been Tommy, he would have taken me aside and told me, just like he did when I went down to see Sir Osmond-Clarke. I was fuming about it afterwards so approached Dave on the Monday to ask him why he hadn't told me I wasn't playing.

"I didn't tell you because I thought it would upset you," he explained.

"Upset me?" I replied flabbergasted, "Well, what do you think I am now? If you don't want to play me, just tell me!" Those words still stick in my craw; I realise now that it was a completely stupid thing to say. This relationship wasn't going to get better, as Dave had done one thing to me that Tommy had never done, and that was be dishonest with me, or probably more accurately, he had not been entirely honest with me. It didn't sit well with me, particularly as he was a slightly nervy character at the best of times and when he knew he'd done something wrong he didn't handle it very well. The manager should have you on the back foot but it was the other way around.

My first game back in the side after that was against Chelsea on 11th February. Martin wasn't fit to play and with me as vice-captain I picked up the ball to go out. Dave took the ball off me and said, "Stevie's the captain today" and gave the ball to him. He said it in front of everybody! To publicly take the vice captaincy away from me was punishing me for no good reason yet again but the thing that really got me was the fact he didn't tell me. It was the second knife in the back from him in just a few weeks. He didn't like confrontation; that much was obvious. His way of doing things was to just commit the act and not argue about it; if he had called me in and had a row with me, I'd have thought better of him. If he had told me that I wasn't guaranteed my place so he wanted to give the captaincy to somebody who was, such as Stevie, that would have been better. I didn't have a problem with Stevie doing it, my problem was with Dave not being honest with me again.

When Dave came in to the job a lot of people thought he could be the man to take us to the next level but so far that was far from the case; despite an impressive win against Liverpool in the league in October, we'd lost a further four games since the start of December and, by the time of the

Chelsea game, had been eliminated from the FA Cup in a 3–2 loss at West Brom, a game I didn't play in as I had flu. To be knocked out as holders when it was the only trophy we could realistically win was very disappointing, but as they say, anything can happen in the FA Cup.

It was essentially the same bunch of players that less than a year previous had finished sixth and triumphed at Wembley against the European Champions. My theory is that it was down to the training and the profound difference now was that players simply didn't enjoy it, and I think if the players now look back at some of the things they did, they'd think "God that was boring!" It most definitely didn't excite me and I didn't enjoy it. I went from being there at half past nine to start at half ten, to getting there at quarter past ten with just a few minutes to get ready. Training, as a huge part of a player's life and career, has to be something for them to look forward to and with Dave Sexton I didn't.

I felt sorry for Tommy Cav, a man with his own ways that revolved around training with a football. You couldn't necessarily say that Dave's way was training without a football, because it was, it just wasn't the same and it wasn't as good or enjoyable. Once players don't enjoy the training, you start to have problems. I can only speak for myself; it started to affect how I felt on the field. You want players to go into training happy and I wasn't a happy bunny. I'd like to think that it didn't have an impact on how I played but I'm sure sometimes in one or two games it showed.

Collectively it didn't feel as natural or easy flowing; Tommy was able to motivate us quite easily, as a team we'd try and defend and attack together, but with Dave Sexton it was a bit different. He'd be instructing the full backs to pull wide, telling certain players to do this or do that, but these would be natural things we'd be doing with Tommy. The things that came naturally, Dave Sexton seemed to make too much of an issue over. He didn't like me bursting forward too much, but that was my game. The very purpose of me playing at the back in the first place was so I could start attacks from deep. When I got hold of the ball, I could get forward more efficiently and attacks would gain momentum from deep. If the centre forward doesn't chase, the first person to pick you up would be a midfield player, which in turn would release one of our own. I never overdid it and always had it on my conscience to defend but I had so much confidence in the fella behind me, Martin, and he would have been the one to tell me if I was overdoing it anyway.

Years later I re-watched a game on television, the home game against Aston Villa in the Second Division, and we were 1-0 down. Brian Moore was commentating. I got the ball and went well into their half with the ball before passing it, and Brian said, "Brian Greenhoff's going to have to do more of that." He'd said that because he'd seen us play and knew how we chased games; sometimes little tweaks just don't suit the team, such as giving a player too much or, in the case of what Dave wanted to do with me, too little freedom.

The two players he brought in to try and rectify the poor form were Joe Jordan and Gordon McQueen, both from Leeds United in just a matter of weeks. Joe, a centre forward, Gordon, a centre half, both stood over six feet tall and indicated the direction Dave wanted to take the team. It was clear he wasn't going to play me at the back with Gordon when he had Martin there and it was obvious I was going to be left out. Again, the signing of Gordon and the effect it had on my position in the team was something Dave decided not to talk to me about. So it was up to me to force my way back in and find myself a new position in the side. It was probably just as well that I didn't have that conversation with Dave, as I'd have asked him where he intended to play me, and he wouldn't have been able to answer, because he wouldn't have known himself.

From then on I'd play right back and midfield, wherever he needed me, but I'd felt the writing was on the wall ever since I'd been dropped for the Ipswich game. Towards the end of the season Martin picked up more injuries which meant I was unexpectedly recalled into central defence to play alongside Gordon. Gordon liked to play on the right hand side, which meant I switched to the left where Martin would normally play. I was more comfortable on the right but I wasn't that bothered as I knew every ball coming in the air, Gordon would want to head it, he wasn't going to leave it to me. The partnership that I had with Gordon was alright, we didn't do too badly, due to his strength in the air – it was reminiscent of my days playing alongside Bill Fairhurst in the youth team, it was very rare I would have to go and head it, I'd just pick the bits up. I was quite happy with how I did and when Martin came back in, I was moved to right back, so I'd done enough to stay in the side. In reality that was enough – I always knew Martin would come back in his normal position so that didn't upset me. You don't have one of the best defenders in the league to sit on the bench, and it wasn't as if he would come on and change the game if we

That's me aged 5 sat on our back steps, wearing the Park Road School kit, my first football kit.

In Blackpool - Mum, me, Dad, my brother in law Bill holding my niece Ann. My sister Joan must have been taking the picture.

My first visit to Wembley was as a ballboy at the 1968 League Cup Final. I saw James help Leeds beat Arsenal 1-0.

Can you spot? Bobby Lomas, Eric Young, Kevin Lewis and myself who signed for United and also Steve Daley who signed for Wolves and later played for City - Northern Schoolboy week.

line-up - B-R: Ronnie Miller, Jim Hall, Ian Donald, Willie Carrick, John McNally, Tony Whelan, Eric Young, Kevin Lewis. F-R: Damien Ferguson, Ian McMurdo, Laurie Millerchip, Bill Fairhurst, Tommy O'Neill, Tony Young, Myself.

MUFC 1968-69 - My first official club picture as a professional.

BRIAN GREENHOFF, Manchester United's brilliant young midfield star, met his match on Saturday—pretty Maureen Stanley . . . and it was a real soccer showpiece. Brian and Maureen were married at All Saints' Church, Stratford, and there to take a supporting role were (left) best man and United colleague Arnold Sidebottom plus Brian's big brother, Jimmy, of Stoke City fame.

TOP LEFT: *A press report from my wedding day with Maureen.*

TOP RIGHT: *I arrive in Spain on crutches for a holiday after breaking my leg in the Geneva tournament in 1972. The after care for these types of injuries wasn't up to much back then!*

HEARTBREAK *I am inconsolable as I am led off the Wembley pitch by the Doc following defeat to Southampton in 1976. We vowed to make amends the following year…*

PEEK-A-BOO! I am behind Sir Matt and Tommy at the remarkable homecoming in 1976. 300,000 reds turned out despite our defeat, although I was a little worse for wear!

MY ENGLAND DEBUT: One consolation during May 1976 was a call-up for England. Here I am keeping an eye on Wales' Alan Curtis during the Home Championship. I would later line-up alongside Alan for Leeds.

AT LAST! The relief and joy is evident as we celebrate following our 2-1 win against Liverpool.

THE CELEBRATIONS CONTINUED:
(right) Here we are doing our Benny Hill impressions after winning the FA Cup.
(below) Naturally the press wanted a picture of James and I with our mother - over James' shoulder, Maureen's mum can be seen in the background!

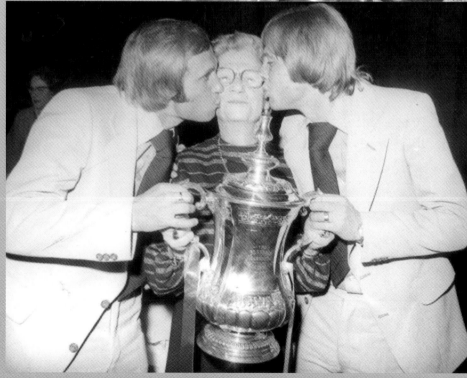

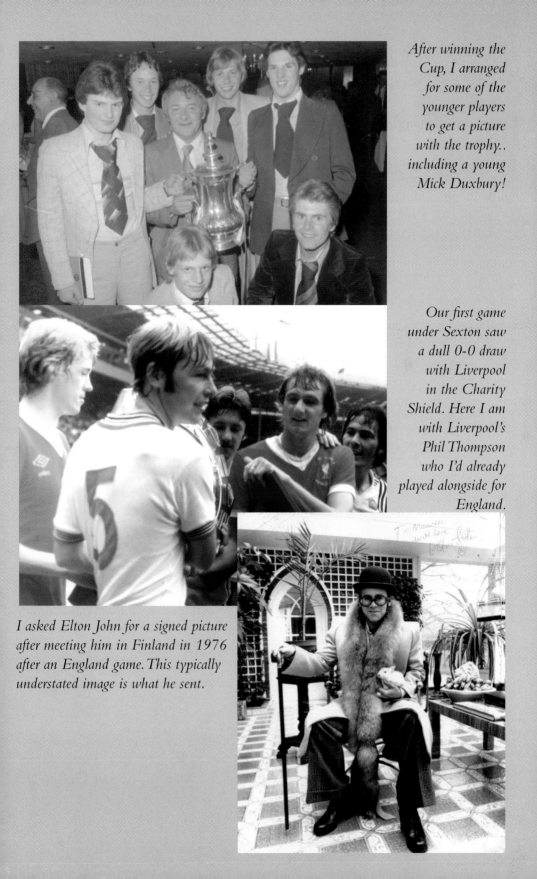

After winning the Cup, I arranged for some of the younger players to get a picture with the trophy.. including a young Mick Duxbury!

Our first game under Sexton saw a dull 0-0 draw with Liverpool in the Charity Shield. Here I am with Liverpool's Phil Thompson who I'd already played alongside for England.

I asked Elton John for a signed picture after meeting him in Finland in 1976 after an England game. This typically understated image is what he sent.

I celebrate my only goal for Leeds, a thirty yarder past Nottingham Forest's Peter Shilton

(Right) With Mike Kenning and Raymond Hack signing for Wits. Playing in South Africa was an experience!

My sons with their partners in Barcelona - from left to right, Lou, Brian, Joanne, Pete, Paul and Fara. I couldn't ask for more wonderful sons.

were chasing, so I just had to play well enough to keep my own place.

Another player who left was Gordon Hill. Hilly was never a Dave Sexton type player. He could be a bit of a liability, but he could win you games, so on one hand he'd frustrate you but on the other you'd be chasing him around the ground because he'd scored a fantastic goal. He made for a contrast to Stevie on the other side, who was always up and down, working for the team. Steve Coppell might not have scored as many goals or been as exciting as Gordon but he was a great team player. Gordon moved to Derby County to be re-united with Tommy Doc but even though I had my own problems, I wasn't tempted to have the same reunion. I didn't want to leave Manchester United, and as I'd been there for nearly ten years, I would have found a move very difficult to contemplate.

1977-78 had been an indifferent season that, even though it ended with a positive run of four wins from the final five games, saw the players realising how much we had underperformed. At the end of the day, though, the buck stops with the manager. He picked the team and how we played, and if we couldn't play successfully under those methods, then he's either got the wrong players or the wrong system. It was becoming more obvious he was going to get his own players to play the way he wanted to, rather than the other way around.

At the age of 25, and having had an extended and settled defined role in the first team of Manchester United, I wanted to keep that, not just be moved to become a bit part player where I would be played anywhere or moved to be the stand in when someone else was injured – sometimes versatility can be your worst enemy. When managers have their own ideas, such as Dave Sexton not wanting a 5'10 centre half, you have to accept those things and fortunately enough, despite having my preferred role taken away, my ability to perform in different roles got me in at right back. I did well and struck up a good partnership with Stevie; but to be honest, if you don't have a good partnership with Stevie then you can't have one with anybody as he was so easy to play behind. He'd come back and help you and you'd just be a supporting act to him going forward. I was happy to play anywhere apart from left midfield; it just didn't suit my natural balance to play there. It was more or less the same at left back too; Denis Irwin would go on to be a fine right footed left back for Manchester United, but it never suited me. The very first game I played for Barnsley Boys had been on the left wing, and every time after it must have brought memories of that back! I'd more or less accepted that wherever my future was at the club it wouldn't be at centre half unless somebody got injured; and even then I wasn't sure as Stewart Houston could have moved in, as Arthur Albiston was emerging meaning we had two good left backs!

With the team undergoing transition and Hilly having departed, I played the final game of the season in midfield and scored in a 2-1 defeat at Molineux. We finished tenth in Division One, winning and losing 16 games and scoring 67 goals while conceding 63. Post-season we knew changes would continue to occur and one of those was the departure of Alex Stepney. Gary Bailey was emerging and Paddy Roche had played much of the 1977/78 season. Alex's experience might well have been handy to keep (and he went on to pass all his wonderful experience on as a coach at Manchester City) but it was around this time that Harry Gregg, the hero of the Munich disaster in 1958 and legendary United keeper of that era, had joined the club as goalkeeping coach.

It was a good move by Sexton yet, although he made the right noises in the press and although he had brought Harry back, after ten months in charge at Old Trafford and especially after succeeding Tommy Docherty, it would have to be said that Dave Sexton wasn't exactly at one with the philosophy of Manchester United as a football club. The Doc may have been a bit gung-ho but I think most punters would agree that Sexton's side were not the best on the eye to watch. He had good players, but if you were to ask if he got the best out of them or as much out of them as Tommy did, I would have to say no.

Whereas pre-season tours in the modern era seem to be more about earning money than getting the players fit for the new campaign, it was common for us to go on the more commercial tours immediately after the season's end. In 1978 we went to America and our first game was against Tampa Bay Rowdies with cheerleaders called the "Wowdies"! We did okay in the game, going one-nil up, but in the second half Alex Stepney got a whack which earned him broken ribs. It took about quarter of an hour to get him off the pitch, and the temperature was around ninety degrees. We just melted and with about twenty minutes to go they sent Rodney Marsh on as a sub, and he looked like a world beater. They equalised and in the last minute, Paddy Roche and Ashley Grimes collided and the ball dropped to Davie Robb who tapped in for the winner. Two days later we played in Tulsa against the Roughnecks, who Billy Foulkes was managing. They played on Astro carpet which was absolutely terrible but we won and I scored two goals, identical half volleys which was strange. A few minutes from the end I hit the same shot again but the keeper saved it and said, "I wasn't going to let you do that again!"

Following that game we flew to New York to stay overnight, even though we weren't playing a game. We stayed in the hotel where they filmed "Saturday Night Fever" and the day after we flew to Bermuda for six days. It was fun, and we all hired little bikes or mopeds. I met an old friend from Barnsley - I thought, where can you go in the world where there isn't someone from Barnsley? I didn't know they had pits in Bermuda! We stayed in a five star hotel called the Hamilton Princess and only had one bit of trouble where Ashley Grimes and another lad "borrowed" two bikes from outside of a nightclub for a joyride. I think they had to go to court and they got fined, but that was probably the highlight of the tour! Due to being in the England squad, I wasn't getting to many of the post-season tours, and I missed one to Hawaii which was a shame. They don't do the post-season tours anymore - our pre-season tours were generally in Norway, Germany or Spain. Perhaps part of the reason was the fact that we were going to have about nine weeks off, so they wanted to make sure they were doing something with us after the season was over. These days the players have about a month off, but I loved to have at least six weeks.

The Doc and Dave

Heading into the 78/79 season, I wasn't given any indication about my own future in the team, or Dave's plans for me, only that Gordon and Martin were first choice centre halves and I would have to find another way in. Though he had dislodged me from my position, I always got on fine with Gordon and had a good relationship with him. You're not going to spend £500,000 on a centre back and stick him on the bench; he was bought for a specific job, and Gordon was a Scottish international, a good player and just what Dave Sexton wanted. The problem was with Dave's tactics and the way they had brought about that change. I was playing centre half and was used to playing a certain way; Dave went and changed that, and when it turned out to be not as successful, instead of changing it back, he went and brought somebody else in. It was his decision and I had to respect it the manager; when he makes an honest decision and he doesn't get it right, he has to move on and make the next decision because that's his job. I didn't agree with it, I thought he was wrong and that there were other areas that could have been strengthened more.

The start of the season was steady though we were getting a fair few draws; of our first thirteen games we won five and drew six, including a win at Molineux where I scored again. On 11th November we played at Birmingham where Martin and myself were back at centre half as we got murdered 5-1. Don Givens destroyed us – we used to lose very few goals with headers but on this day Don could have jumped over a roof, he was that good. Afterwards Sexton admitted he had made a mistake, that he should have put Stewart Houston back in there to play centre half. It was one of the only times that Dave admitted to making a mistake but even then it looked like the blame was being put onto the players. We didn't play that badly, it's just that Don was unplayable that day.

That was the end of myself and Martin at centre half, though again I believe it was down to a bad managerial call rather than our inability to play together when we had proven that we could. Martin missed the next few games and I partnered McQueen but on Martin's return, I was put back to right back. Sexton still hadn't replaced Gordon Hill after his April transfer, but did soon after the Birmingham game when he brought in Mickey Thomas, who made his debut in the 1-0 win at Chelsea at the end of November. Mickey's work ethic was very similar to Stevie's which is something that Dave wanted and it wasn't a surprising transfer as that's the way he wanted to go with the team.

No disrespect to Gordon, Joe or Mickey, but they weren't the exciting players we had become used to with Tommy Doc. With Gordon Hill and myself there were players who took chances and risks in the positions we were in and that helped create the identity of Tommy's side; you have to be a brave man to do what Tommy did because the way we played at times could be described as suicidal. It wasn't as though we were disorganised; Martin would make sure, on the pitch, that we were countering the opposition's strengths even if we were going gung-ho. He would be the one who might spot a problem somewhere and tell one of the players what to do.

Now the party was well and truly over as Dave calmed everything down and tried to make us harder to beat while retaining flair but with the side we had, we couldn't have both. Perhaps under Tommy we were more reactive and under Dave maybe it's fair to say we were more organised or more prepared prior to the games. But doing that took the creative license away from the players. Admittedly, Dave would go on to finish second in the league in 1979/80 but I would say that side were more efficient than they were entertaining.

Seven defeats in the league before the turn of the year meant that once more the FA Cup was the only trophy left to play for. We hadn't qualified for Europe and we'd been knocked out of the League Cup at home to Watford. Once we got past Chelsea in the third round and then knocked out Fulham after a replay we started to really believe we had a chance of getting to the final again. A win at Colchester United in the fifth round set us up for a tie with Tottenham. I was getting a good run at right back but then I missed the league game at Bristol City before the Tottenham game after suffering a problem with my calf. I didn't realise how bad it was. On the Friday I'd gone in to training and because it wasn't right, Tommy Cav gave it a massage and told me it felt funny as there was a little lump on it, and I said that's where it was sore. We travelled down to Bristol but it got worse and Tommy noticed I was limping on it, so he called Dave over and we decided I shouldn't play to save me for Tottenham in the Cup. I had treatment before the Cup tie and when we went down we stayed at Selsden Park to train down there for the week before the game. I didn't train all week until on the Thursday when I was asked to give it a go. I did and lasted about five minutes. So suddenly, from being fit and having a run in the team, I'd got this calf problem from nowhere and it was going to keep me out for a few weeks.

Any uncertainty around my position was not on my mind when it came to considering my career and where I was in life. We'd bought a house in Rochdale and were delighted with our lot, and in March 1979 we welcomed another boy into the family, baby Brian. The wife always said she wanted four lads, and we were halfway there. We were settled, I still had another two years on my contract, and everything was going okay aside from my relationship with the manager. I was always happiest when I was out on the pitch playing football, but I always had an underlying thing with Sexton where I was wary because he hadn't been honest with me in the past. Sadly, it was a feeling that would be proven right again.

I recovered from my injury and on my recall was played in midfield, where I played when we drew Liverpool in the FA Cup semi final. The game was played at Maine Road and the pitch was terrible and muddy and it just felt like one of those games that pass you by. I didn't feel as if I'd done much in the game, I didn't really get on the ball and I was still struggling with my calf but I got the goal and we looked like winning it 2-1 until Alan Hansen equalised with under ten minutes left. I should have come off as my calf was causing me pain. As it was, it ruled me out of the replay in which James scored a famous goal in a 1-0 victory to send us back to Wembley for the third time in four years. We weren't as well looked after as the players are these days but we earned a couple of thousand through the players' pool for getting to the final.

Following the semi-final and replay, once I was fit again I was used sparingly and in different positions. Coming up to the final, with Sammy and Lou fit, I wasn't sure if I'd get in midfield and Jimmy Nicholl had come in at right back. If I was to play, I always thought it would be at right back, but Jimmy was a good player and playing well. We played Wolves in the last game before the final at Old Trafford, and I started in midfield, but I came off early. I came off with what was officially termed as a groin injury but on reflection, it was just nerves. I'd got so worked up about wanting to play in the final but knowing that I wasn't, when I came off my stomach and lower half were in bits. It was the most weird sensation I've ever had, but in a day or two I was right as rain. I knew I was going to be in the squad for the final and I had a feeling I'd be in the twelve, but I just had a gut feeling that I was never going to play.

When the game went to 2-0 to Arsenal and United made their dramatic late comeback to equalise, Tommy Cav said to me, "Get your tracksuit bottoms off, you're going on".

Dave Sexton said "No, stop, we'll put him on in extra time", which was probably the worst decision he ever made. Having had the stuffing knocked out of them with United getting the equaliser, the perfect thing would have been to stop the game on such a red hot day, get a substitute on the pitch and get Arsenal thinking about the game for a bit longer. It didn't happen, and they went right down the end and scored. I wonder if Dave still regrets that decision.

In the end, it didn't matter that it could've been my last appearance for the club. The manager makes the decisions and has to live with them; he was wrong and Tommy Cav was right. The consequence of his action was that we didn't win the Cup. I was never aware at the time that that early substitution against Wolves would be the last time I would represent the club. I would have loved to have done it in front of a packed Old Trafford, wave to the crowd, a chance to say "Thank You" and have the crowd applauding me and say the same. It wasn't to be, and unfortunately the way it turned out is that my last appearance for the club on any level was for the reserve team.

We went on a family holiday to Fort Lauderdale in the summer of 1979. We had booked it through a fella called Peter Johnson who organised some of United's tours and we stayed at the Seagull Hotel. We arrived at five o'clock in the morning after a nine hour delay; we were sat on the plane, had been given something to eat, and Paul fell asleep. He woke up as we were getting off and asked if we were there, but we were having to get off as there was something wrong with the plane! When we eventually did land, we were picked up by the owner of the hotel who told us that a few players from Fort Lauderdale Strikers were staying there. He mentioned George Best but I was so tired I didn't think anything of it. When we woke up the next day some of the players were milling about; I recognised a few of them, though I didn't know them personally. I was recognised by Tony Park, a former Stockport player who came over and introduced himself. I said, "George is here isn't he?". He said, "Yes, but we can't get him up!"

George had missed their training session, but we met him later on and he was great; he took a few pictures with us and the kids, and I actually ended up training with them a couple of times to keep my fitness up. They played first against seconds; I was obviously in the seconds as I wasn't one of their players, but George was also on the same team as he was in their bad books for missing that training session. We beat them 3-0 and George was marvellous. I went with my friend Colin to watch the Strikers play against Tulsa, coincidentally enough. Tulsa, managed by the former Derby player Alan Hinton, took a two nil lead. With about seven or eight minutes to go, George was sent on as a substitute – they immediately pulled a goal back, and the legendary German striker Gerd Muller equalised to send the game into overtime. I said to Colin, "That's cracking, let's get another beer". There were the vendors walking round selling snacks and beer, so we called him over and got some in. They kicked off, and after about 11 seconds, Bestie whacked one in the top corner. "Oh, we've got a game on here Colin!", I said excitedly. But then everyone seemed to get up and leave; we didn't realise that they were playing golden goal! We had a great holiday, and we managed to fit in a trip to Disney World too.

Of course the destiny and future of the manager and football club wasn't my decision, but if it was up to me, after the end of the 1978/79 season I would have got rid of Dave Sexton after a ninth place finish which showed marginal progression from the previous year but a substantial regression from Tommy Doc's days. My relationship with Dave had hit rock bottom and there was no communication between us; once it was clear that he was going to remain in the position, it was only ever going to end with me leaving the club.

On the pre-season tour of the 1979/80 season we were in Germany and I'd heard that my son Paul was in hospital. I didn't handle it well and in the game I played poorly, got booked, and came off at half time in a bit of a mess. I apologised to Dave on the way back from the friendly - and after travelling back we were due to have an open day of training on the Sunday. I explained about Paul being in hospital, suggesting I could play in the reserves against Northwich Victoria on the Saturday, and skip the open day on Sunday so I could go and pick Paul up from hospital. Dave said, "But we've got an open day," seemingly missing the point, and I just re-iterated the point that my son was in hospital. I played at Northwich thinking I'd get the next day off and Jack Crompton, who was looking after the reserves, brought me off with about two minutes to go.

Dave asked why I'd been brought off and Jack said it was because he didn't want the crowd to get at me because I was a popular lad. He didn't like it, but I said, "Right boss, what's happening now?", and he said, "See you tomorrow" and just walked away. So my son came out of hospital and I couldn't even go and pick him up, I had to go and do this open day, which to have missed wouldn't have meant anything but to go and get my son would have obviously meant more to me. Dave knew that and he just didn't respond to it, which was yet another kick in the teeth. It was disappointing as earlier in the pre-season I'd approached Dave about the differences between us and after that I'd decided to give it until around the end of September and see how I felt. A few days later I was at home when I got a phone call from John Lyall, the

West Ham manager. He said that Dave Sexton had given him my number and that he was allowed to speak to me. I couldn't believe it, I had literally just had a word with him about stopping until the end of September. John asked if they could come and speak to me and I told him what I'd said to Dave, asking once again in disbelief whether it was Dave who had given him my number.

John drove up with Eddie Bailey in horrendous weather, we drove up to Rochdale and spoke for a few hours and then arranged for me to go down the next day. I went down with Maureen but drove to the Cliff first and went to see Dave in his office. I said, "Right, I'm going down to West Ham to speak to them" and he asked "why?"! I told him it was because he had given them my number, to which he replied, "Yeah I know but I thought you'd tell them that you didn't want to go." I said, "You what? You're joking me. Look, I'm going down to speak to them." I walked out and went down to hear John out again. He took us out for a drink and a meal, took me around the club and the training ground. West Ham were a good outfit. Stuart Pearson had moved there, recently. John dangled a contract in front of me which had more money than I was on at United, a rise from £350 to £450. I was very close to signing but held off, saying I just needed to speak to a few more people. One of the problems I had was when I was being shown around houses and thinking to myself, "Could I live down in London?". As a Northern lad it was difficult to get my head around it but when I look back, everything that John Lyall said he would do, he did. I feel that I made the wrong decision to turn down West Ham and go where I eventually did.

I went back to Old Trafford and Sexton told me that Leeds were interested and I ended up playing for the reserves against Blackburn. We won about 5-0, and after the game I was thinking about Leeds. I met Jimmy Adamson who was the manager and Dave Merrington, one of the coaches, at Birch services on the M62 to discuss a contract. They offered me £450 a week which was the same money as what West Ham were offering, but I had the added bonus of staying in the north. I still hadn't spoken to Dave Sexton but I got another phone call from John Lyall who then offered me £600 a week which almost had my head spinning at the thought of the jump. Tommy Docherty was at QPR and offered me a lot of money, £500 a week, as well as a handsome signing on fee but the idea of staying in the North was appealing to me and to be honest if I had decided to move to London then I would have chosen West Ham. Perhaps I should have done but I made a geographical decision rather than a footballing one.

Dave called me in to the office at about 4.30pm one afternoon a few days later and I had to head in rush hour to Old Trafford. "I don't want you to go," he said, which was possibly the worst thing he could have said to me. "But you've just given someone my number and somebody else permission to speak to me and now you're telling me to stay?" By this point if he had said he was glad I was going, I would have told him I was staying! Anything he said, I would have said the opposite. It just got to the point where the deceit and lies, the dishonesty I'd had from him was too much. I couldn't play for him anymore. I loved the club and I didn't want to leave, I'd been there for eleven years and I was bitterly disappointed to be ending my time there but it had become impossible for me to remain.

I signed for Leeds United solely because they were based in the North, and I wouldn't have to move house. I should have listened harder to John Lyall as everything he said, he did. He said he was going to buy a right back, and a right sided midfielder and did exactly that, and to be fair to them they went on to win the FA Cup the following season. At Leeds they were honest with me too, to be fair, telling me they had no money but they had plans, I just didn't realise how badly they were struggling. I believe that a part of my exit was orchestrated by Dave; he'd just brought Ray Wilkins in and must have thought we weren't compatible but if he'd done his research and saw the way we played together for England he'd have realised we had quite a good relationship. Yet to let someone ring me - and, in what was now typical fashion, not even telling me about it beforehand to let me know - was something that caused a total breakdown of the relationship. He'd obviously got no respect for me, and my respect for him had disappeared a while back. I found the constant dishonesty appalling and he'd done it so many times we had to part ways; I wish it'd had been him that left but it had to be me and I realised that if I wanted to go on playing professional football I had to move on elsewhere.

I went to Old Trafford to pick my boots up, and bumped into Martin Edwards on the way out. I said to him, "That man is not befitting of the title of manager of Manchester United" and those were my final words at the club. It was my decision to leave. I had two years on my contract left, I could have stayed and told him to sod off and stick me in the reserves for those two years but it was either leave, or put myself through purgatory for the next twelve months at least, so I made my decision. It wasn't nice and not what I wanted but I had a family to support and I was getting a rise, a percentage of the transfer fee, and an ex-gratia payment for service (which they didn't have to give me, but most certainly didn't come from Sexton, as I spoke to Les Olive about it) were important factors to take into consideration.

A couple of years later and I might have got a testimonial, but it wasn't to be. I don't hold a grudge against Dave for effectively forcing me to end my career at United, I just hold him in contempt for the way he handled me and my career. I know for sure Tommy wouldn't have handled me in such a fashion. I've met Dave only once since I left, and as I always am, even if I have misgivings, I was cordial with him. He didn't apologise, he probably thought he did nothing wrong, because that's the way he managed things. A lot of people probably wouldn't think he did anything wrong as, aside from the captaincy thing, nothing was ever said or done to my face so it's my word against his. Even stripping me of the vice captaincy in front of everyone seemed like the wrong thing, because of it being done in front of my team-mates.

Everything just built up and in the end it doesn't matter if you're manager of Manchester United or Rochdale, it shouldn't be done that way. I had wanted to stay at the club and was motivated by that, not by the possibility of more money. I'd proved that by staying in the north when I had big offers to move down south - my wages at United were never anything other than the yearly raise I'd been offered. Even the offer of £450 at Leeds was because Trevor Cherry, who I'd played with for England, rung me up and told me that he'd told Jimmy Adamson that I was on £450 at Old Trafford! The reason he'd done that is because he was on less money, but he had a clause in his contract where he would earn as much as the highest earner as he was captain. So when I was asked if that was what I was on, I just said yes – I wasn't going to argue. They said they couldn't pay me a signing on fee, but I responded that it was alright due to the payoff I was getting. John Lyall had said West Ham couldn't offer me a signing on fee either but that they wouldn't charge a fee when my contract was up. The Leeds move seemed a perfect scenario. I didn't have to move and the training ground was just 35 minutes away.

The fee Leeds United paid for me was £388,888. The reason I remember that is that I got 5% and another 5% went to the players' benevolent food, and the transfer fee was the highest received by Manchester United at that time. It was a big transfer fee but what with the 5% clause, it would have been nice for it to have been £1million! Not long after, Steve Daley transferred to Manchester City for £1.4m and he wasn't even an England international.

Having spent so much time at Leeds United when I was a young boy and with Jimmy playing there, it was strange to join the club as a player. Naturally, some of the people had left, but a fair few were still there – Bob English and Maurice Lindsay were just two names who I could remember from our kid being there. But with Jimmy Adamson, Dave Merrington and Syd Farrimond all with a Burnley connection, there was a new feel to it at the same time. I was welcomed and I didn't feel out of place at all. I was looking forward to the new challenge and next step in my career.

8. LEEDS

I F I'M BEING completely honest, the breakdown of the relationship with Dave Sexton had made me want to leave so much that Jimmy Adamson could have spun me any line and I would have joined Leeds. While I was always going to leave Manchester United, the only decision was going to be my destination – I didn't want to uproot the family. I didn't have to move house, and what with getting a £100 a week rise, that made my mind up. My last wage at United had been £350 and Leeds put me on £450, and the other additional payments made sure I was settled. So Adamson didn't have to say much; although from our chat, he didn't make it sound as if they were building for the future. I got the impression that at that particular time they were more interested in steadying the ship, also because they'd just sold their best player, Tony Currie. Yet I didn't have any regrets moving, and I immediately wanted to prove myself. Maybe everything Dave Sexton did was to try and get me out but it was my decision and I had to take responsibility for it.

The move happened so swiftly. I signed for Leeds on a Friday, all the forms were completed between the clubs on Saturday, and I went and started training on the Monday in preparation for a home game on the Wednesday in the League Cup against Arsenal. My debut was a 1-1 draw and the following game was also at home, also against Arsenal and also 1-1! We were up against Arsenal once more in the following game at Highbury in the second leg of the League Cup tie. I was thrown into midfield not really knowing anyone around me and I found it quite difficult. I know the saying is that great players can fit in any position but I'd been playing and fitting in at right back, centre half, midfield, basically being messed around at the end by Dave Sexton. With all these positional changes coming in a short space of time, I wanted to go to Leeds and get settled but going straight into midfield was difficult, especially the first two games.

In that third game against Arsenal, I felt I was doing really well in the first half even though we were getting beat, but then my knee flared up and kept me out for two weeks. The game finished 7-0 to Arsenal, which was the heaviest defeat I was ever involved in. To be fair, it was one of those games where everything they hit went in, we didn't seem to play that badly. At that early stage it looked to me as if Leeds were going to have the same problems that we had suffered at United when we went down - scoring goals. There were two big lads in the strike force, Ray Hankin and John Hawley but there were big doubts over whether they could get us twenty goals a season. They weren't going to hurt defenders by running in behind them, they were basically two target men and we needed somebody else to bring something different.

The players as a bunch had welcomed me alright; I just wanted to get the first win, have a really good performance and settle down, and for those first few weeks I did find it quite difficult, even though the club itself and the people welcoming were fine. Brian Flynn was still living in Burnley and he would travel into Leeds, so he would pick me up and take me into training. Sometimes I'd go and pick Paul Hart up, who lived in a funny place called Sowerby Bridge which is near Halifax. If we had games, Flynny would come and pick me up, leave his car at our house and Maureen would drive us to Leeds. The bus would drop us off somewhere and Maureen would pick us up after and Flynny would go home from ours – there were little quirks like that, and it was good as I always got on with the lads.

Flynny and Trevor were good friends and Byron Stevenson was a nice lad I got on really well with: there weren't any that I could turn around and say was a bad lad. It was the same as at most clubs. You'd have a go at each other in training sometimes and during matches but once you've finished with that, you'd get on with it. And there was some cracking quality in the side. Two top young keepers, John Lukic and David Harvey. Paul Hart at centre half, Trevor, Paul Madeley and Eddie Gray were there. Terry Connor came into the side that season and he was just what we needed, he was able to play off Ray or John. Terry did very well and that was due in no small part to the fact he wanted to learn. With some young lads they don't want to listen, but Terry did, and it never surprised me that he went on to coach.

I always found the atmosphere at Elland Road good; they always got behind the team and depending on who they played the atmosphere could be electric. I never found their support of the team anything but good, but there were some things that, being a former Manchester United player, didn't sit well with me. The expectations at Leeds were quite different. When you play for Manchester United away from home, every ground is full, every team wants to beat you but you were expected to win no matter where you were going.

Leeds had been hated under Don Revie but that feeling had more or less passed. Sometimes you'd go away and think for example, "Is this the Tottenham team I played against last year for United?". They didn't seem to be trying as hard yet it's not as if I could look at any player at Leeds and say they didn't give their all as they were all honest lads and with one or two they just loved playing football.

The club always had a great away support as well and when your support is good, you try and give everything to the cause, yet I noticed there just didn't seem to be the same fervour there playing for Leeds as there was for Manchester United. Leeds were at least playing in Europe. I was ineligible for the first two rounds after my transfer and didn't travel with the squad to either Malta to play Valetta or Romania where the team played Universitatea Craiova. Instead, I stayed at home and played in the reserves. When the first team went to Romania, my reserve game saw the debut of a 15 year old kid in goal by the name of David Seaman. We played against Preston and won 2-0, and I thought "God, he's got a chance".

My first return to Old Trafford was on December 8th, 1979. The warm reception wasn't anything less than I'd expected; everyone wanted to say hello and shake my hand, I had a chance to catch up with one or two of the players as well. After the pleasantries it was all about getting out there and getting them beat; we came away with a 1-1 draw where Connor scored for us. It was a point in the middle of a seven game unbeaten run before Christmas; but we won only six league games after the turn of the year and finished in eleventh position. Our final game of the season came against

United at Elland Road and my old team had a remote chance of winning the league. If they beat us and Liverpool lost at Anfield, they'd be champions.

I can remember how much we wanted to beat them. With the rivalry starting to get stronger following Dave Sexton poaching of McQueen and Jordan, a lot of Leeds fans weren't happy. We were really wound up for the game and we ran out easy 2-0 winners. United were playing in a slower, more methodical manner than I'd been used to; they had Ray Wilkins who liked to get hold of the ball rather than burst forward. We just got behind the ball quickly and that day we played really well. There was an incident in the game where I kicked our kid to stop him from scoring; it should have been a penalty but it wasn't given. The goal difference was so great before the game that it would barely have mattered if United had won - but with it being Dave Sexton in charge, I felt nothing. If it had been someone else there I might have felt something, but I didn't want him to win anything at United, and I certainly didn't want him to win the league at the club I had played for in when I was on the opposition. "You're not kicking me in the teeth again," I thought.

That eleventh placed finish for us didn't fool anybody; we needed players, notably another striker despite how well Terry had done. Ray Hankin was having injury and fitness problems. On his day when he was fit and lean he was a top player but he was going through a spell when he needed somebody to get hold of him and sort him out. Both him and John left with Derek Parlane coming in. We needed one or two changes - like at United when you knew the squad needed to be strengthened in order to challenge, at Leeds it was looking a similar way.

The training at Leeds had been different and something I had to get used to; as I've always said, I liked to train and come off smiling, at Leeds we always used to finish with a five a side and give a yellow jersey to the worst player. The winning team would vote who got the yellow jersey, and whoever got it had to wear it the following day throughout the session. In the three years I was at the club I only got the jersey a couple of times, and one of those was in the early days to introduce me to it. You'd try and do things to get out of getting the jersey, but in later times, we'd all keep trying to give it to Allan Clarke every week because nobody liked him!

Under Adamson, the training was always taken by Dave Merrington and Syd Farrimond and they were two nice fellas but the manager was never there. It was a crying shame, because when he did come out and join in everybody enjoyed it. It was interesting, fun, enjoyable and you could see why he had such a good reputation from his days at Burnley. At Leeds, he spent too much time in the office when he was needed on the training pitch and as the season went on, and we were just going along as nothing special, it needed something else.

In the end, he brought in Stan Ternent, but he hadn't been there long before Jimmy Adamson left the club in the autumn of 1980. Obviously, when a manager goes, the backroom staff usually follow. Dave and Syd left and so did Stan, but for the few weeks that we had him, the training was different and enjoyable. It was such a shame that they went; but off they went to be replaced by Allan Clarke as manager, who brought in a fella that I'd known for years since my days in Barnsley called Barry Murphy.

As is generally the case with a new manager, they came in laughing, joking, hoping to ignite a spark, wanting to change the tactics around a bit. It had an instant impact; we'd been reeling in the bottom half when Jimmy Adamson left after a really difficult start to the 1980/81 season and under Allan Clarke our form really picked up. Shortly after Allan's arrival I scored my first - and only - goal for Leeds. Nottingham Forest were European Champions; they came to Elland Road and we played well. The ball came to me about twenty five or thirty yards out - thinking about it, it could have been thirty five or forty yards, I'm not sure! - and I just whacked it and it flew in to the top corner. I knew Peter Shilton was weak there. The goal gave us a 1-0 win.

I was playing really well at full back; so well that Allan said to me that I should be picked again for England, which was nice and gave me confidence. Allan was like that but it was funny, as I'd never liked him as a player! Allan changed the system in the team to a 4-5-1 and it worked quite well. I was an attacking right back and it suited me; likewise Eddie Gray on the other side, a natural left sided midfield player who could also play centrally but was played at left back. In midfield we had Alex Sabella who was a talented player and Gary Hamson, a prospect who'd been at Sheffield United. Things seemed to be picking up; with such a good run of form in the second half of the season, we were thinking that if Allan could convince the directors to pick another couple of players up, we'd have a chance at pushing on. We'd got the foundation of a decent squad, it just needed a little bit more. We had a couple of young lads from the youth team such as Keith Parkinson who played a few games but you couldn't rely on them every week and we needed to flesh the squad out. The drop in expectations was quite a contrast. As players, you play in games all the time and you want to be competing. That was the way it was at United but at Leeds we never had a proper Cup run and there was never anything left to play for after February.

Yet we were still playing well – from the middle of January 1981 to the end of April we won nine out of fourteen games, including a victory at Old Trafford. Allan Clarke was still hated at United and he loved it, he thrived on anything like that. Sometimes in games like that he'd walk on to the pitch just to wind the crowd up. He did it at Liverpool once; he told me to go and have a fitness test. There was me, him and Barry Murphy, we went out on to the pitch about 75 minutes before the game and there were already quite a few in. I could hardly walk and I was wondering what I was doing there, I was struggling with my ankle strapped up. The physio, Geoff Ladley, had even asked what I was doing having a fitness test when there was no chance I could play – I said "I know that and you know that, let's just go out there and show him."

So I went out, they passed me the ball and made me run, I was limping around. He was only doing it to wind the crowd up as that was what he was like. He loved the confrontation of those atmospheres and if there was a good thing about Allan, it was that he would be there in front for you. He'd put his own neck on the line first, and the players responded with a good run that saw us finish ninth. Allan strengthened the squad when he bought Frank Gray, Peter Barnes and Kenny Burns to help us push on in the 1981/82 season.

The training had started to become fun under Allan; we were still ending the training with five a sides, we were still always trying to kick Allan, and he'd still put himself about – in the time I was there, two lads had to go and have stitches because of him. He was still competitive and one or two of the lads still wanted to kick him. I might have been one of them! But then he changed the training, and it became hard work. We'd go in some mornings and you wouldn't see a ball. In the afternoon we'd have a short session in the gym and on the track, we'd just have days where we wouldn't see the ball. We'd get weighed every Monday, which used to really confuse me. I couldn't understand the sense in it, I felt it should happen on a Friday, the day before a game. If a player isn't right before a game, or overweight, then by all means have a go at them but on a Monday when the lads have taken a little time to relax, perhaps had a couple of pints, a nice meal and a nice Sunday roast? Surely this was a time to relax and not worry about your weight.

With me being weight conscious as I had been throughout my career, it was terrible. I hardly ate as I didn't want my weight to go up, my goal was always to weigh in at 11 stone 11 pounds. When I went to see a dietician in later years he told me that I'd played a stone under the actual weight I should have played at but because there hadn't been anyone like that when I was playing, we had to manage it ourselves.

Once when I was at United, I went with Jimmy Rimmer to a place in Chorlton where he would have injections. I thought that I didn't want to go down that sort of avenue. I wanted to enjoy my football and enjoy my weekend, which started on a Saturday afternoon, and to me the introduction and timing of the weigh-in's at Leeds spoiled it. The lads would wear sauna suits to try and counter the new system – they'd train in sauna suits on a Monday, go straight into the sauna with it on, just try and sweat an extra pound or two off before they were weighed. It's sad when players have to do that; it culminated in a meeting after a weigh-in where four of us were called in to see Allan.

Me, Frankie, Peter and Kenny were there and we were all told to lose weight. Allan pointed at me and said, "Four pounds" before he went round the rest of the lads saying we all needed to lose four or five pounds. With Kenny Burns, he could have said a stone and a half! Kenny carried a lot in those days and I'm sure he knew that; but after that, we never heard anything of it! We never knew what weight we were from one week to the next there. At United, I was always in control of my weight. Sometimes I went a little bit over the top; at times, when I had got conscious about it, I made myself sick. I'd go down for the meal the night before a game and I'd have a meringue afterwards. I didn't – and still don't – particularly eat sweet things a lot, but I'd have a meringue as I knew it wouldn't sit well on me and it would make me sick, which is something I would do regularly to keep my weight down.

I suppose looking back I suffered from bulimia a little bit; if I didn't feel right, it was just something I did. Having said that, if I would weigh in at 11'8, I might go out and have a couple of bottles of Guinness! I didn't want to be too light – a few years back, just after I'd had my wisdom tooth out, Tommy Cavanagh had a word with me and told me to put some weight on as I'd weighed in at 11'8 at pre-season. The year after that I weighed 12'2 and they told me to lose weight, even though it was pre-season. I never thought that if people came back from pre-season overweight that it mattered very much; in fact, sometimes I thought it might be better if they came back overweight, as they would have to work that bit harder.

Paddy Roche used to come back from pre-season about two stone underweight! I asked him what he did to lose that much, and he said, "I just play golf and drink Guinness!" I questioned him in disbelief but he said the reason was that back in training he ate like a horse and the more he trained the more he ate. I didn't want to be nine and a half stone as Paddy was when he came back, I just wanted to be 11'11. I knew after I finished I would put weight on and that didn't bother me, it was just a matter of trying to control it while I was playing. The weigh-in's were a bad sign of where things were going and the training was getting that way too; training without the ball is something you might imagine doing in pre-season but during the season it was unheard of.

I didn't think our squad was good enough to stay up, and I wondered who we could get to score the goals. The first game of the 1981/82 season was at Swansea City. We were all ready for it, all wound up. I'd travelled with the team, had my little bag with the contact lenses and solutions in it, and I walked in the dressing room and hung my bag up by the number two shirt. Allan Clarke came in and named the twelve and I wasn't in it. I played all pre-season and just like that I was out. I took my bag and went and had a cup of tea somewhere with Bryan Flynn who also wasn't playing. I think all of the lads were surprised I wasn't playing - the team went on to lose 5-1, which I took no pleasure in, but it had set us off on a really bad start.

After ending the previous season doing so well with a certain system, he changed everything and paid the price. I'm not saying I'd have made a massive difference but I was part of the system that had been successful. Allan came to me during the week and apologised, saying he should have played me. The damage had been done, though, as he had created the same problem that Dave Sexton had. He didn't tell me, and all I wanted was that honesty. He could have pulled me to one side and told me his reasons. I would have disagreed, naturally, but he could then re-affirm his decision and that would have been it. At least then he would have had the guts to have told me, but he didn't, and straight away I was thinking, "Aye, aye, here we go again."

I could feel then that something wasn't right; not just with me, but with the club as well, as if it was really getting into a problem, even though we'd got three players in. Allan had enjoyed a honeymoon period and now he had to show what he had as a manager; it wasn't just about running, it was about producing on the field. He didn't show any change in his methods despite the poor form and I for one started getting fed up of the slog on a Monday morning and being told to run, run, run, run, run. It was awful. You'd played Saturday and try your best, had the Sunday off and then we started to dread going in on a Monday morning because the first thing they'd do is put you on the running track. Sometimes after a game at United, Tommy Cav and the Doc would let us have Sunday and Monday off, saying we should have 48 hours rest after a match. Even if we played on a Wednesday, we might have Thursday off and we'd go in on a Friday to be told "Do what you want" and we could have a little jog or a massage. It was all about preparing the players for Saturday, and if there were two games a week, it wasn't always seen necessary to have extra training.

A bad start to the season with just one win in the first eleven games was temporarily halted with five wins in nine league games, but after a 2-0 home win in the return against Swansea, things started to go downhill. My relationship with Allan Clarke had deteriorated and I wasn't enjoying my time at the club. I knew one of the directors, Jack Marjason was trying to get rid of me behind my back without paying me. I had three weeks off to have a nose operation. I ended up not having the operation as it was postponed to the end of the season; but Marjason was trying to get me sacked for having the time off, I later learned from Martin Wilkinson who said the club were trying to cut costs and save money. On my return, I hadn't been paid any wages, so I went to see Keith Archer, the club secretary, and told him I hadn't been paid. He said, "Well, it's because you haven't been here". I said that I had a contract. "You know where I've been", I told him, "I think you'd better sort it out". I got my money back – they had no right to take it off me in the first place. I'd even offered to get them a sick note and they declined.

Five players were put on the transfer list – Paul Hart, Trevor Cherry, Flynny, Peter Barnes and myself, as the club were clearly trying to get some money in. Leeds were starting to struggle, and after returning from my spell out, Allan wanted to put me straight back into the first team despite me not having played for three weeks. He reneged and named me as substitute but nonetheless I was encouraged that I was back in the fold. Soon after we attended a supporters dinner at Queens Hotel near the rail station in Leeds. I talked to one of the directors, Leslie Silver – we used to call him Hi-Ho – and told him I'd had a word with an agent named Brian Tiler who said he might be able to get me a club in the NASL called Seattle Sounders. After the pay incident and the concerns raised by Martin, I wasn't going to have my future dictated by anyone, instead I was going to raise the issue myself.

Mr Silver said that Leeds wanted £100,000 for me, to which I responded that I was out of contract at the end of the season and they'd have to give me away then anyway. I said if they wanted to save money, they could let me go to Seattle on a free transfer and save money on wages. It was a perfect scenario. He said he would think about it but ultimately they wouldn't let me go and stuck to wanting £100,000 for me. I knew they weren't going to get that kind of fee and told them so and I would just wait until the end of the season and get a free transfer.

By now my relationship with Allan had completely broken down. He was ignoring me completely in training, which was fine but even Barry Murphy would shake his head and ask me what was going on. Before the West Ham away game in the April, Martin came up to me and said, "Look, Allan's told me to pick the team for Saturday. Will you play?" I said I'd have a think about it, which I did, but I said "No. He doesn't want me in the side – if you pick it and name me, he won't like it. It's better for me and it's better for you if I don't play. I just want to play in the reserves now if that's okay." He said okay, and that's how I continued, waiting for the tap on the shoulder in training to let me know I'd been given a free transfer.

By that point Leeds had suffered a drastic decline; just a pitiful three goals in twelve games after that Swansea game, all by Frank Worthington who to be fair had done well. However, he needed service from the back, and if he had played with Eddie and myself at full back then he would have good service, in the end I don't think he was enjoying it. I felt sorry for him, coming to a club which was very obviously going the wrong way. It was a similar scenario to what I'd been involved in at United in 1973. There was some nice football but in the last third of the pitch there was nothing happening, no end result, and I could see the inevitable coming. At the end of the day if you don't score goals you don't win games – we had decent players up front but we needed an out and out goalscorer, something we just didn't have. The team picked up three wins from the last eleven games which included a brief Easter revival of seven points from fifteen available (under the new format of three points for a win, which had been introduced that season) but it was never going to be enough, and Leeds were sadly relegated.

Even if they had survived, my own time with the club was definitely going to end. I was looking for other things and had had an offer from a "Rebel Tour" to South Africa – something I'd known about for a while, but Dennis Roach, one of the agents involved, wanted everyone to keep quiet. The Seattle move had fallen through and Martin Wilkinson had told me I wasn't going to get offered a new contract, which suited me – if they'd had offered me a contract then it would have proved tricky for me to be able to move for free.

This was in the days before the Bosman ruling where clubs had more power - if a player was out of contract and a fee couldn't be agreed, then a tribunal would decide.

Thankfully that wasn't the case. I left the club - Leeds let Allan do the retained list after the season and then he got sacked. Martin and Barry both left the club too. Just like when I left United, I didn't have a problem with Leeds as a club, I was just happy to be away from the manager and though I didn't have any issue with the board either I was quite happy to be away from Jack Marjason. He could quite easily have come to me and told me the club wanted to get rid of me and we could have sorted something out, and I would have bitten their hand off, but to do it the way they did didn't sit well. All I'd done in the first place was be ill! It's that kind of situation which make you start losing respect for people and the manager was no help.

Since leaving Leeds, I have never returned to watch a game. I've been back to the club once - one of my neighbours was the manager of a wholesaler that was just around the corner. I wanted to go and have a look around there and I had a few hours to kill so I went to see Paul Hart who was looking after the kids there at the time. The first person I bumped into was John Lukic, who took me to see my old physio mate Geoff Ladley, before I saw Harty. It was just before Christmas and they were in Portakabins as they were doing the dressing rooms up. There were a load of Puma boots knocking about and I said I wanted to buy some; he gave me a pair which I ended up giving to my son Paul as an extra Christmas present. It was great, a brand new pair of Puma King that he didn't know he was getting. As I came out of the office, Harty was having a whiskey with the legendary John Charles, the gentle giant, a legend for Leeds and Juventus.

The first supporters dinner I went to was in the first season I was at the club; they were singing anti-United songs, most notably a song making fun of the Munich air disaster. That was the first and last time I attended one of their dinners. It's one thing singing songs; in fact I played there when United fans would sing, "All Yorkshiremen are twats"! If in return they wanted to sing the same about Lancastrians, then that's fine, but to sing about something like that... it's always been a bone of contention with me. It's something I despise. Any club I hear singing songs like that, I hate them, and I hate the fans that sing them, no matter who does it. They're a disgrace, and they should respect the history of other football clubs.

Regardless, just as I didn't have any regrets signing for Leeds in the first place, I look back on my time at Elland Road as an enjoyable one. We had some good laughs and some good performances, it was just the last six months which soured things and made it a shame. Allan Clarke made a big mistake changing the tactics and for us to have played so well at the end of the campaign prior to the one where we were relegated was a huge shame.

After turning down a move down south just three years previous I had begun to consider the possibility of moving further afield. America was a place where you could make a lot of money and playing there for just a couple of years was appealing; my wage was around £22,500 a year and the wages on offer were around £50,000. The prospect of going away for two years and coming back with my mortgage paid off sounded good – but with the Seattle moving never materialising, after leaving Leeds we realised we would have to sell the house we were living in as we couldn't afford it – we eventually managed to sell it a year later, moving from a big detached house to two beautiful cottages.

Martin Wilkinson had taken over at Peterborough, and he wanted me to go there to be his number two as a player coach. Neil Firm had gone there from Leeds, as had David Seaman. I thought that I mustn't have done too badly at the club for the assistant to want to take me with him, but I think he knew what had gone on there and appreciated the way I handled it. Some people might disagree, but I thought I handled the Leeds situation very well. I felt that I had been messed around a bit and that I was going nowhere in my career – I'd had six months where I hadn't been enjoying it at all, and I was concerned about looking after my family and worried about what was best for them. I had interest from Burnley and I'd even offered to go on less money as I was only bothered about my pension, but their offer was quite insulting and I decided not to go to Turf Moor.

We went on holiday to Greece and talk of the Rebel Tour began to pick up pace when we returned – the prospect of six months on good money sounded very decent. It wasn't long until I was back on a plane.

9. ENGLAND

YOU'RE PROBABLY wondering what happened to my international career. Truth is that by 1982 I'd given up on it but it's probably best I re-cap on the 17 appearances I made for the national team between 1976 and 1980. There were a few highs and several disappointments, not least the failure to reach the 1978 World Cup, but this was a tricky period for England when tactics, managers and players seemed always to be changing.

It's best I start back at the beginning, before I actually made it into the senior squad. The disappointment of being relegated in 1974 with Manchester United was softened a little by a call up to the under-23 squad for a three match tour of Turkey, Yugoslavia and France. As one of the substitutes for the Turkey game, I didn't get chance to play as the game in Ankara was abandoned at half time with the score at 0-0 due to a waterlogged pitch. It was an absolute monsoon, going back on the coach after we were going through two foot deep water. I'd never seen rain like it. In the following game we played against Yugoslavia and were defeated 1-0. I made my debut in a 1-1 draw. I came on again in the following game, another draw, this time in France. The highlight of the tour was rooming with Kevin Beattie, the Ipswich defender. I thought he was a good player when I saw him play for Ipswich, but training with him I realised just how good he

162

was.

I continued to play in the under-23's, even scoring a goal against Czechoslovakia in a 3-1 win at Selhurst Park in October 1974, but it must have been the second game against Hungary in March 1976 that had attracted the attention of senior manager Don Revie. The first game had finished 3-0 to Hungary - our kid and Alan Hudson had turned out for that game as over-age players, but Les Cocker decided to go with a younger team for the return. I was made captain and Stevie Coppell, Stuart Pearson and Gordon Hill all played at Old Trafford in front of 33,410. We won 3-1 in an absolutely fantastic game. I had played so well and thought, "If that doesn't do me any good, nothing will do me any good", especially after such a good season for United. The England senior team played the night after the under-23's and Peter Taylor, who was playing for Crystal Palace, had already been taken out of the second leg against Hungary to play in a friendly for the full side at Wales in Wrexham. He made his debut as a half time substitute and scored the winner.

With Les Cocker and Don Revie, I thought I'd get my chance if I kept playing well. Don had selected our James for the Wales game but in those days, clubs would sometimes play on the same day as the country, and it was a friendly rather than a competitive game so the club could decide whether or not you were allowed to play or had to stay with the team. Nine players made their debut for England at Wrexham; James didn't get called up again. It was disappointing, of course it was, but there were lots of good players who didn't get a call up for England. If it had been nowadays, he definitely would have got a cap, because to me now they give caps out like confetti and I can't see why it happens. Much of the time it's down to pressure from the press, who are pushing for players who haven't done anything or proven themselves enough to be selected. Howard Kendall was another one; he'd played at almost every level, and was even captain of the England Youth team. He'd come through the ranks and even played in a Cup Final when he was eighteen, but he never got his chance, and I think the fact that he and James never got a cap surprised a lot of people. The same could be said for a host of other talented players.

The call to say I'd been selected for the full England squad at the end of the 1975-76 season was a surprise, but to be called up and then selected straight away to play in the Home International Tournament was an even bigger shock. I thought I would be called up into the squad and have to wait for my chance to play, that I might just have been taken along for the experience. Panch had been selected too, and we both made our debuts in the tournament. We had a strong side for my debut at Ninian Park with a team that read – Clemence, Clement, Mills, Towers, Greenhoff, Thompson, Keegan, Francis, Pearson, Kennedy and Taylor. It was Peter Taylor who got the winning goal yet again just before the hour. I played in defence alongside Phil Thompson, but had to play left side centre half as Phil always played right side for Liverpool and because he'd already been capped, he got the choice. We'd never actually practiced together before the game – we'd trained, of course, and played five a-side but with the team being named the day before kick off we'd not had opportunity to train in the shape of the team. In saying that, it went well, we won the game and that's all that really matters! Looking back, that first international cap was probably the start of when people would say, "Jimmy, brother of Brian, England international". When I first read it, we both laughed about it, but it was nice to see. I'd had it since I was seven, wherever I went I was known as "Jimmy's brother". It was important to me to finally be recognised as a player in my own right; it was nice to have my brother play alongside me as he would go onto do shortly after with United, and it was also nice just to have him in the game. If I wanted, I could ring him up for advice, with James being nearly seven years older than me.

It had been a source of pride to represent Yorkshire playing football – as it was when I represented the county at cricket – but to do it for your country is your goal, it's the ultimate achievement and nothing gives you more pride. I'd like to think that is the case these days. In those days you were paid rather handsomely. I was on £135 a week at United around the time of my first cap. For just going away with England, you were given £100. It was a further £100 a game, so to go away for the Home International Tournament where there were three games in a week was mind-blowing. Don Revie went even further and changed it so if we drew we got £100, and if we won we got £300, meaning that we could earn around £1000 for just a week. It'd be seven or eight times my club wages and it must have been an even greater incentive for the lads, though with it being my first time with England I didn't need the monetary reward as incentive. Only on reflection do I think, "My god, we earned some money playing for England". Despite the money, and the obvious step up, after the first game I must confess I never really felt any pressure playing for the national side.

The following game was against Northern Ireland, and I was up against Sammy and little David. We won 4-0, played really well and I felt more comfortable, as if I was really accepted into the squad. When you play against the lads you play with for your country you don't really know them, but when you're away for a week as we were, suddenly you might develop friendships. I roomed with Peter Taylor and I really got on with him; we enjoyed it, and I think the more established lads enjoyed us coming in. Whenever new players came in, all the established players would always be welcoming. There was no club segregation, everyone would eat together for example. You might get a little bit of mickey taking about club performances but our mind was always collectively on the job for England. If you go and watch England in a pub you can tell who supports what team by the players they cheer or give stick to but it wasn't like that with the lads. I never felt any back-biting, we all wanted the same thing and we all wanted to win for England.

Unfortunately the next game for England wasn't a win. The Home Championship finished with a trip to Scotland. We stayed at the Marine Hotel in Troon, right on the golf course. We went training on the Thursday, but getting up on the Friday my left knee was throbbing. I went to see Fred Street, the England physio, and told him I was in pain. He examined me and told me I'd strained my medial ligaments. I was bandaged from thigh to foot and was told I'd miss ten days; I watched the game on Saturday 15th May which England lost 2-1 at Hampden, then I got friends to pick me up and drive me back to Manchester. The national team were going to America straight after the Home Internationals (which was lost by the defeat in Scotland) to play Brazil in Los Angeles, Italy in New York and Team America in Philadelphia in the US Bicentennial Tournament.

My injury was going to keep me out of the tour, which started with that Brazil game on the 23rd. I got a phone call from Tommy Doc on the 18th with the team due to fly out on the 19th; he told me to get down to the ground. When I got to Old Trafford he said, "What are you doing, sat on your arse? Look, you're going with England." I said, "Well what about my knee boss, I won't be fit", to which he replied, "You'll be fit when you get there. You'll miss the first game and you'll be right then." He rang Don Revie and they booked me on a plane to get me to Heathrow and I joined up with the squad and went with him. That was yet another example of Tommy looking after my career; there was nobody that would have got away with that but him! England could have turned around and refused but they didn't.

I trained for the first time after England lost that first game with Brazil (0-1) following a late goal from Roberto Dinamite! I trained lightly with a hope of being fit for the following game five days later against Italy. I was on the bench but wasn't fully fit, so I didn't get on – nevertheless England overturned a two goal deficit to win 3-2. Though the game with Team America was next up, we were also due to play Finland in a World Cup qualifier on 13th June, and I was hoping to ensure I was fit for that. I was selected for the Team America game, and thought I played well, but afterwards I was told by Don that he planned to play Paul Madeley against Finland. I thought it was fair enough and didn't have a problem. Paul was a great player who I'd known since his early Leeds days - England won the game 4-1 in Finland, which was important as in the qualifying group there was no play-off for second place, and we were in a group with Italy.

After that game, with it being the end of the season, we let our hair down a bit and we had to sing for our supper. Kevin Keegan and Mick Channon wrote a song about the journalists, and I can only remember one line from it - "When I grow up, I want to be a journalist, a journalist, always pissed, a journalist, I want to be like Frank McGhee, only drink when it's free!". Frank wrote for the Mirror, but it was all good fun. On another table was Elton John, and he was sat with the London lads who all sung, "Maybe it's because I'm a Londoner" - Elton nearly took the piano apart to play the song! We went in the nightclub afterwards, Elton came in with us and ended up going on the organ and playing a few of his hits, and all the lads stood behind him singing away. He flew back with us on the charter plane which was dropping us off in Manchester before going to Luton. I asked him if he could sort an autograph out for my wife and a friend, and his manager at the time John Reid sent us two beautiful photographs. It was a bit odd mixing with such a celebrity; he was the first one we'd really met. Afterwards, Don Revie said that he'd given Elton a framed picture we'd all taken together and signed. While we were in Finland, we'd run up such a bar bill that the FA questioned it and didn't want to pay it. Don went out for lunch with Elton afterwards and told him about it; Elton rang up and paid the bill! I've still got the signed picture of Elton to this day (see photo section); I wonder if he's still got ours!

Our next game with England was a friendly in September 1976, against the Republic of Ireland at Wembley. Revie tried a different system, playing five at the back with me as sweeper to try and get me on the ball a bit more. The thinking was that it might be an effective way to play Italy who we had coming up, but we didn't play the system very well. It didn't work against a very good and organised Ireland team under Johnny Giles, and we drew 1-1. In the system we played I didn't think the sweeper role was right for me, as all Ireland did was push the striker further forward. I couldn't do what I wanted to do - it was the first and last time that system was played so it proved Revie didn't get what he wanted out of it. The following game was another poor performance, a 2-1 win against Finland where we just couldn't get going. It was a poor game where everything we did just didn't work. You don't normally get awful nights at Wembley with England but that was one of them, it seemed like a continuation of that poor performance against Ireland. Maybe if we had played our normal system against Ireland the momentum would have helped us out, but we didn't and we just didn't play well.

Playing so poorly and only winning by one goal was probably what ultimately cost us qualification for the World Cup – Italy went and hit six past them later in the qualifiers.

Our own game in Italy came a month after that win against Finland. It was always going to be very difficult, but I thought we played alright. Yet they would always punish you for any little mistake you made as they had a good side; Antognoni scored the first goal from a free kick and Bettega got the second in a 2-0 win. I had the two best chances, but

Zoff made two good saves – it was said that I was one of the few players to come out of the game with credit. I'd recently faced some of the Italian team for United against Juventus and I knew they had one or two players who could dish it out. Benetti, Tardelli, Gentile, Cuccereddu, names that roll off your tongue. Fabio Capello played and I came up against him more than anyone in the game, with us playing three in midfield, but I didn't really notice him so much. The system again didn't work, but they were a good side, and losing against them wasn't a huge surprise. In February 1977, we welcomed Holland for a friendly at Wembley, but after 40 minutes with the score at 2–0 for the visitors, I came off with a suspected broken arm. I went in a tackle but whacked my arm, and it was quite painful for a few days – they didn't take any chances with it being a friendly, and I was brought off for Colin Todd. Jan Peters scored both their goals. The Dutch had a good side that would go on to reach the World Cup Final the following year.

I missed the next game, a qualifier against Luxembourg, but was back in the squad for the 1977 Home Internationals. The first game was in Northern Ireland which ended 2–1 thanks to a late goal from Dennis Tueart. We had to stop in Manchester and fly in on the morning of the game, having police and army escorts to the hotel and to the game afterwards. Straight afterwards we had to go to the airport and get back – for my first trip to Northern Ireland, it's not what I would have preferred but due to the troubles at the time we couldn't risk it. It was a bit eerie playing at Windsor Park, and it was a different kind of test to the team you played against at Wembley. The crowd were really behind them and the players were more up for it – on that day I think we were probably a bit fortunate to come away with a 2-1 win.

Up next was a 1-0 loss to Wales; I wasn't originally picked to play, but Peter Barnes picked up a bit of a knock so I was drafted in to play left side midfield at the last minute. It was a disappointing defeat and I was disappointed to play where I did; people say that footballers should be able to play anywhere, and I agree with that to a certain extent but you obviously get the best out of them where they're more comfortable and I would have been better playing in the centre. I was back in the more familiar position of centre half for the next game against Scotland but I was substituted through injury again; I aggravated an abductor injury I'd previously suffered playing against Aston Villa for United. I would occasionally get problems with it and it was uncomfortable; at half time I thought it was alright and said I would give it another go but then I went on a long run into the box and I could feel it start to pull, so I had to come off. Minutes after I came off, Kenny Dalglish scored and Scotland ended up winning the game – another Home International lost.

The Home Internationals were fiercely contested and I think the tournament is missed, particularly by the Scottish, Irish and Welsh. It was a surreal thing to play at Wembley and have what seemed like 99,000 Scottish fans there! The build up would last for months, with the Scottish lads asking to buy your tickets for the game. They'd all go down, be lying in gutters, and hanging in trees – they had nothing underneath their kilts, I can tell you! But they were incredible, the noise they made and the atmosphere was unbelievable. There was a lot of pride involved and you didn't want to lose any of those games, not least because you didn't want your team-mates at club level who might play for the rival countries to mention it! It was a big tournament, enjoyable and it would happen over a short period of time. The competition was tough and fierce; there have been attempts to bring it back and try and replicate what once was but I don't think it's been done right. If it was, I think it would be good, I used to enjoy playing and watching it and think it is sadly missed.

I was worried about missing an upcoming tour of South America where England were scheduled to play in Brazil, Argentina and Uruguay in hopeful preparation for the World Cup in Argentina in 1978. It ended up that I came off at the right time (against Scotland) – I knew that if I'd stayed on, I'd have no chance of going away. As it was, I made the squad and was fit enough to start the first game of the mini-tour against Brazil at the famous Estádio do Maracanã. It was the first time I'd ever played in a stadium where you had to come up from underneath to get to the pitch; the changing rooms were huge, and they had a "football area". I'd never seen anything like it, but even so, the pitch was a huge disappointment. The grass was weedy and awful, but it was at least a decent surface to play on. To be fair, I think we had the best chances through Kevin Keegan which he might have put in on another day. We thoroughly deserved the draw in front of 77,000. The stadium seemed half full, and it had been known to pack in almost 200,000, but it still felt like there were more than 77,000.

Brazil had some good players; the likes of Rivelino, Zico, and the number 6 who I swapped shirts with after the game, Cerezo. I helped set up a goal early in the next game against

Argentina - hitting a ball down the wing that was crossed in for Panch to slot in after only a couple of minutes. Daniel Bertoni equalised not long after. I came off at half time to be replaced by Ray Kennedy, I wasn't feeling at my best - maybe it was because of the long trip and the tour - and Don decided to give me a breather. Late on in the game, Trevor Cherry got sent off for what must have been nutting Bertoni's fist! He smacked him, knocking his teeth out, yet Trevor got sent off! Something we noticed playing in this part of the world – more so in Argentina and Uruguay - was that they weren't afraid to give you a kick, but they also weren't averse to cheating either. Bertoni was sent off for his part in the incident but he'd actually blatantly dived to win the free kick in the first place. Referees react, particularly in stadiums where the crowd seem close. There were 60,000 packed in and playing against England they were baying for our blood! We stopped in Buenos Aires for a few days, flying in and out of Uruguay for a non-entity of a game that finished 0-0 that really felt like an end of season game. It was a funny old trip that just seemed too far; it might have been in hopeful preparation for the World Cup, but waking up after a friendly to face a 20 hour journey home seemed a bit too much.

The game in Montevideo against Uruguay had been my 12th cap; the win over Team America the previous year wasn't officially recognised by FIFA. Soon after that trip, Don Revie left his post as England manager. He hadn't joined up with us on the trip until we got to Buenos Aires, and we didn't realise until afterwards that part of the reason was because he'd been in the United Arab Emirates to sort a contract out. I wasn't surprised that he left as he was under massive pressure after the loss against Scotland, and the crowd didn't really take to him at all. When he originally got the job I think most people wanted Brian Clough, but I found Don fine. I enjoyed his training and talks, even if some of the other players didn't. Before the Italy game he'd created a dossier, he'd taken the time to write down about every player we'd be up against, but one or two of the players didn't take to that. There was also a big card school at England which I couldn't believe – they used to play three card brag, and there'd be more in the pot after the first round than what I was earning in wages. It was a different culture, and a lot of managers didn't like it as it could cause problems.

Ultimately Don had to leave the country; the contract they were offering him was worth an absolute fortune. That summer the Doc left United, adding to my uncertain future at the time. With England, though, I never went expecting to play. With your club you get to a stage where you might expect to play unless you do something drastic to put yourself under pressure but I honestly never expected to always play for England. In South America I'd been given a new role just behind the midfield of Brian Talbot and Ray Wilkins and it suited both me and the team. It worked really well, and the three of us clicked. I had a good playing relationship with Ray, and alongside him and Brian, who was possibly the hardest midfielder I ever came up against, was a really enjoyable time. Not many teams go to South America to play against those teams and come away undefeated.

Ron Greenwood replaced Don, and unfortunately I missed his first game, a friendly against Switzerland. I travelled to Luxembourg in October 1977 but I didn't get on; I was happy to have at least been selected in the squad as sometimes when a new manager comes in, they just discard players. Ron was an absolute, total gentleman with me at all times, and as long as I kept fit I thought I would make Ron's squads. I missed the following game against Italy, which was the final qualifier. England won 2-0 but needed to score six. It was a major disappointment to not qualify; we had a lot of good players but we weren't a great side like the team that had won the World Cup just 12 years before. The expectancy was so high because the standards had been set by that achievement and also a good performance in the 1970 World Cup. It was up to those players afterwards to try and emulate that success but unfortunately we never quite met the expectations.

In February 1978 I was again part of the squad that went to play a friendly in West Germany, after not being named in the original squad. I was actually at the dog racing at Belle Vue when I got a call from Maureen's mother to tell me I was to join up with the squad the following morning. I didn't get on the pitch, and England lost 2-1 late on after taking the lead through Panch. In April we played Brazil who featured many of the players who we'd played against before; the squad was notable as we didn't have any Liverpool players. We played really well in a cracking game. Gil scored early on past Joe Corrigan and Kevin Keegan equalised in the second half. It was a competitive game, underlined by the fact that we didn't use any substitutes – friendlies these days are ruined by six or seven players coming on. Although this has improved recently.

At the end of the season we once again competed in the Home Championship. Sometimes it is nice to get away from your club and have a change of scenery and, after the difficult season I'd had in Dave Sexton's first year in charge at Old Trafford (even more so as the club were embarking on another post season tour to America), it was good to see different faces and do something different. Stevie was in the squad and I roomed with him; we used to knock around with Dennis Tueart and Dave Watson. One evening we had a cake fight! I'm not a cake eater, but Dennis and Stevie just asked, "Hey what do you think of this cake" and then started pushing it in each other's faces! I think it was just out of boredom though. On tours it's not always easy so you had to make your own entertainment. The first game in the tournament saw us at Ninian Park, again without any Liverpool players. We knew we had to do the best we could before the Liverpool lads came back in, and we did well and got a good win. We always fancied beating Wales and won 3-1.

I kept my place for the next game against Northern Ireland but moved into midfield; I think I was moved to mark Martin O'Neill, but I finished up playing in the centre rather than on the left and Tony Currie went out to mark Martin. We played well and even though we only won 1-0, it was a comfortable win. We travelled to Hampden with the knowledge that we would win the tournament if we won against Scotland; I was named as a substitute, but came on with just over quarter of an hour left to play for Emlyn Hughes who had picked up a knock. It was all hands to the pumps and when Stevie scored with around eight minutes left, the huge terrace was like a wall of silence. The first one to catch him was Emlyn. It just goes to show - beating Scotland at Hampden cures injuries!

It was intimidating playing in front of 88,000. It was

intimidating just going to the ground, driving from the Marine Hotel, with supporters banging on the windows. We were laughing and found it a bit funny; if anything, I suppose it relaxed us as we knew what to expect when we played. Paddy Crerand had asked me for my tickets for the game, and I said he could have them. As we arrived at the game and I went to meet Paddy outside to give him the tickets, he came up with his son Patrick who was wearing an England hat and scarf. I said, "What's that about?!" and Paddy said, "I know, don't ask!". It must have been quite a sight, them both going into the ground, and I must admit it did tickle me. Using a social networking website in later years I talked to Patrick to mention it – and also that his dad still hadn't paid me for the tickets!

Winning the Home Internationals was nice, there was no trophy parade around the ground, just an exchange of handshakes – it was a wonderful feeling to beat them and silence was the most wonderful sound at Hampden Park! The next day we were back on a plane back down to London to prepare for a friendly against Hungary. I came on as a half time substitute for Dave Watson, and played really well in a 4-1 win, before joining up to travel with the United squad to America the following day.

That appearance was the last time I played for England at Wembley. Like I said before, I always felt I would be selected if I kept fit, but soon after that I had further problems with United and I suffered injuries for Leeds. I got into a couple of squads where I was named as substitute yet the uncertainty over my permanent position added to the problem; it wasn't until Allan Clarke gave me a defined position at Leeds that I felt I had a chance of getting back into the squad. When I was called back in for the squad for my final cap it was essentially a "B" squad that travelled to Australia. Bobby Robson was looking after the team but Ron named it and spoke at a do before the game, going through all the players and saying why they had been selected. When he got to me he said, "We've brought Brian because he's had a bad run with injury but I love having him in the squad and I'm glad to have him here with us." I felt then that I still had a chance; but I felt the trip was a long way to go for a week! What with the long journey and suffering jet lag, we were told that we could train if we wanted but if we didn't it didn't matter. I can't sleep on a plane so it was a no-brainer for me, I went to bed.

After waking up, when the team went training I went and had a walk around the pitch but didn't do anything. It was so tiring - we trained the next day on the Sydney Cricket Ground where the match was going to be played. It was lush on the outfield, but rock hard where the centre spot would be. I asked the groundsman if football was actually meant to be played on the pitch, he said yes, and Australian Rules football as well. He said it only took a month to get it ready for the cricket, I thought that was incredible! The stadium was lovely; as a fan of cricket, it was nice to go through and look at all the pictures there. The game itself was a tough old match, we got through it 2-1 in a game that introduced Russell Osman and Terry Butcher, with me coming on as a late substitute for Bryan Robson. We stayed for a couple of days after the game, taking a day on a yacht around Sydney Harbour where I was sat with Bryan. I managed to see more of Sydney than I had done on my previous trip to Australia with United; we got on the yacht at the Opera House, ate a bit of seafood on a day of leisure. The All–Blacks were staying at the same hotel as us at the time; they were due to play Australia in the morning, while we played in the evening. We both won. I remember speaking to them and trying to swap shirts with David Loveridge who was a great half back, but they only got one for the tour, and they still had another game to play.

I hoped that I would get an opportunity to play for my country again; I kept in mind the words of Ron Greenwood, who I respected massively. When I played for Leeds I felt I did well but I do feel – as all players probably do when it doesn't go right – that I suffered from a little bit of mis-management and that my international career suffered as well. I wonder sometimes if I had made the move to West Ham might it have made a difference? With Ron being a former West Ham manager I think the answer is fairly obvious. Leeds turned out to be the wrong move for me on purely football terms but you can't turn the clock back, you can only regret and that is one thing that I do regret.

There are a few things that I take from my international days and a fair few differences from playing for England and my clubs. The intensity of five-a-sides in training was far different and far more competitive. With the clubs it tended to be more for a laugh, but for England, particularly in the early days, it seemed to be a case of taking every opportunity in every single training session to show the manager what you could do. It caused you to up your game, and it might have been nice to have that increased intensity at club level too. It was a good learning curve as it makes you do things quicker, it sharpens you up as others were trying to identify weaknesses in you.

Of the players I was able to play and train with at international level, Kevin Keegan stands out - he was fantastic, unbelievable. The goalkeepers, too - not so much Ray Clemence, as he was so laid back, but Peter Shilton and Joe Corrigan who worked so hard. I had never seen players work so hard in training and it was a real eye opener. Some say you only get out of the game what you put into it, and Kevin Keegan to me made himself into a great player. Ray Clemence was a great keeper, his agility was superb and he was the best I'd played with, but to watch Shilton and Corrigan train to make themselves top goalkeepers was a pleasure.

I played against so many great players, and I don't think any of them made me look a fool. To be on the same pitch as the likes of Johann Cruyff, Jan Neeskens, Rudi Krol, Pele, Rivellino and Zico, to name but a few, was an honour. When I hear people name dropping sometimes, I feel I can do the same! Once I was asked to name a greatest team of players I'd played with and against; I forgot to add Zico and Italian players such as Tardelli, Argentinian players like Ardiles and Passarella. The list is endless, and features many who actually went on to manage their countries too. It's incredible to think at international level I played with and against four players who went on to manage England, Kevin Keegan, Glenn Hoddle and Fabio Capello as well as Peter Taylor on a caretaker basis.

I am proud to have played for England eighteen times. As proud as I was for playing for Park Road Primary School, as proud as I was for representing my home town Barnsley, and as proud as I was playing for Yorkshire. Playing for my country was the pinnacle. There are plenty of quality players out there who have played for their country but not at the highest level – my brother included. It's what everyone wants to do, it's what I wanted on my CV. You only got to say you were "England International" if you were doing the business for your club, and I can't have been doing that badly for United to win 17 caps while I was there. Not every fan loves you, everybody has their own opinions and that's fine but as important as the fans are it's equally important who your manager is. When Tommy Doc managed me at United he got the best out of me and in the early part at England Don Revie gave me the confidence to get good performances out of me. When the manager has confidence in you, there's no better feeling. I gave everything I had to the national team and that I justified myself for every cap I earned; I was never going to leave anything in the dressing room and even if a fan was to criticise me, the one thing they couldn't criticise was my effort.

I gave my all in every game I went into – maybe there were a couple of games, such as the game I played at left midfield, where I might not have played the best. But then, if you were selected it was because of how you had played, and with me being able to play a number of positions, that's why I was trusted in different areas. It was nice to be trusted, and I felt that with both managers for England. I know Don took a lot of abuse subsequently but I can only judge him on what he did for me; he never did me any harm and he was always truthful with me. Ron Greenwood was exactly the same. It's always special to play for your country and for that reason my debut will always stand out as an important memory, but the highlight for me was playing at the Maracana. It was as fantastic to watch teams play in as it was to play in myself. Staying in a hotel on the Copacabana was just a nice bonus!

10. SOUTH AFRICA TO ROCHDALE

A S MENTIONED, I had received a phone call from a fella called John Barr in the April of 1982 who worked with the agent Dennis Roach and he asked if I'd be interested in going on a "rebel tour" to South Africa. It was all hush-hush – we were going to play for six games, and they were trying to get a squad together. It was sponsored by South African Breweries. John asked if I was interested, I said I was, and then the season ended and we went on holiday to Corfu as I'd still not heard any more of it. On our return things started gathering pace quite quickly, and it was arranged that I would fly to Dusseldorf and then to Frankfurt to meet up with some of the lads – former Tottenham Hotspur goalkeeper Milija Alexsic, the ex-Coventry City and Derby County player Barry Powell are two that I really remember, as well as Jimmy Gordon who worked for Brian Clough. From Germany we flew to South Africa and were taken straight up to Sun City for a couple of days where we could unwind and have a couple of games of golf. We flew back to Johannesburg to meet up with the rest of the squad who were coming out. John Barnwell was going to be the manager, and among the players were Ossie Ardiles and Mario Kempes. They came out but they had to go back as their clubs (Tottenham and Valencia, respectively) wouldn't release them to play on the tour. Jimmy Hill and the politician John Carlisle came to support the tour as well – the tour had been shrouded in such secrecy that nobody in the press was aware of it – we had been instructed not to speak to anybody. South Africa were not in FIFA at the time as it was still during Apartheid, and any talk of it beforehand would have caused such a stir.

The day after meeting up with everyone we trained up at the grounds of Witwatersrand University, it was only after getting there that we realised we were six thousand feet above sea level! I'd never been at such altitude and I was wondering, when I was running, why I couldn't breathe. I didn't realise how tough it was going to be but fortunately enough our first game was going to be at sea level. We were kitted out in red jackets and cream pants – all the kits and tracksuits were provided as the Breweries really looked after us well. We went to Cape Town to play the first game at Green Point Stadium, which we won 1-0. I played alongside Dave Watson and got good reports from that game as I did really well; I'd played a lot with Dave for England and had built up a good relationship, but he only featured in that game as his club Stoke City refused to let him play any further part. The day after the game we flew back to Jo'burg and it was arranged that we would go to Soweto to coach kids. Some of them were wonderfully talented with lots of ability. Yet they didn't have any boots – they were playing and training on the Soweto pitches, running around with no boots on, but nonetheless some of them were fantastic. They all had a trick as well; everyone seemed to have one they would be known by.

Our next game was against AmaZulu FC – the same team Manchester United played in their summer tour of 2012. AmaZulu were based in Durban. We again won 1-0 in a very difficult game; played at altitude on a very poor pitch which was hard and bouncy, and AmaZulu had one or two very quick players who made it tough. Before the game we had noticed there was a bit of trouble going on outside; and it seemed as if it was pre-planned as the cameras were with the people doing it. It was a protest against the tour; which I couldn't understand, as we were doing things to help the area and the children such as coaching. We were playing games with the intention of helping football in the country. The police came with guns after the game to allow us to get out safely on the coach, but that wasn't the last time I'd experience trouble. Due to the protest it wasn't certain that the tour would go on but we decided to play the next game, not realising it would be our last.

The game was in Jo'burg again but at Highlands Park FC. Highlands were coached by the former Scottish player Joe Frickleton and he was a real hard taskmaster - he really got his teams going and had a great reputation in South Africa. It was a cracking game, and we equalised in the last minute to secure a 1-1 draw. The Highlands team were comprised of Joe's usual lads and also a couple from Wits University; they made it a really tough game, again at altitude. After the game I was approached by a gentleman by the name of Raymond Hack, who I later discovered was the chairman of Wits University; I cheekily asked if he wanted me to play a few games. He said yeah, and that he would get in touch the next day - he was as good as his word as we met up for lunch and over that we sorted out a contract. The brewery had already informed us that the tour was off, they apologised but said we were not going to play any more games; they paid us up, and offered to take us to Sun City for two nights with 500 RAND which was then approximately £250 as an apology. In the four weeks we were there I earned around £8,500 which in those days was a lot of money. A couple of the lads stayed out for an extra couple of day's holiday and Mick Channon stayed to play at Durban City for a few games. I played three games for Wits, drawing one and winning two and then I flew home to England.

Wondering what I was going to do next, I spoke to Joe Royle who was then manager of Oldham Athletic. He told me there was a contract for me but he couldn't formally offer it to me for a few weeks; it was good money and appealing, I offered to go back to South Africa for a few weeks to keep fit until they were in a position to offer me the deal. He agreed and I ended up staying there for another three months, and I never heard from Joe! I played for Wits again and we had a really good run; we nearly won the league, it went to the last game of the season. We played at Bloemfontein and Durban were at home against Africa Wanderers. The Wanderers were fancied to beat Durban so all we had to do was to go and win; Bloemfontein were near the bottom. It was there I realised just how much some people could cheat! We had two goals disallowed, one where I picked the ball up at the edge of the box, went around two people and put it in the bottom corner, and I was given offside! It was absolutely ridiculous; one of the linesmen hadn't turned up, so they grabbed somebody out of the crowd. We drew, and what made it worse was that Durban got beat, so we lost out by one point in the last game which was really disappointing.

I went to Soweto another couple of times with Wits; we

lost in the Mainstay Cup to Orlando Pirates whose star player was Jomo Sono, who had actually played with my brother when they were both at Toronto Blizzard. Football was a "black run" sport at that time and they would always try and get the Cup Final to be Orlando Pirates against Kaiser Chiefs, so they could have the final at Ellis Park and fill the ground, thereby making lots of money. We got cheated; Jomo fouled me blatantly - a fact I reminded him of afterwards - he just agreed! We played in Soweto against Kaiser Chiefs who had the star player Ace Ntsoelengoe, and we were wondering if we were going to get cheated again. After the first fifteen minutes we were three nil up, they just never got a kick of the ball as we played fantastically. They got a penalty which was always going to happen as soon as anyone went down in the box and Ace scored. We dominated the game and never looked like losing - and with thirty seconds to go, Ace went and chinned our left back. He literally just walked over and hit him. The linesman at that side and referee were both white; the referee went over and said to the linesman, "He hit him then, didn't he?". The linesman replied, "Yes, but he didn't", trying to use common sense, thinking you can't send off the star player in Soweto. The referee didn't listen and sent Ace off. We were lucky that day as it had been raining and there were only twenty thousand there when there would normally be around thirty or forty thousand at least. There were twenty foot high fences around the stands and by now the home crowd were shaking them.

The Chiefs got a free kick about thirty yards out and our keeper let it in on purpose to make it 3-2; he thought it might calm the crowd down, but it didn't. The referee blew the whistle to finish the game and we just wanted to get off the pitch; we were fortunate that the tunnel to the changing rooms was wide, and we had to run right down the middle of it as the crowd were trying to stab us with their umbrellas. We got in the dressing room and we could hear the crowd going crackers outside; hearing bricks hitting the roof and wondering if they were going to get in. In reality they were probably after the referee and not the players, but the referee was coming back on our coach! We stayed in the dressing room for about two hours after the game, waiting for the commotion to die down during which time we heard gunfire. The police had arrived to disperse the crowds and within minutes they burst in the dressing room and told us to get to the coach. Unfortunately someone had tried to set it on fire and nearly every single window had been put through. We were told to get on the floor until we got out of the township; I laid down with my boots over my head and two big rocks (which had been thrown through the window!) by the side of my face, as we drove out with the police escort.

When we finally got to the "white" area we were told we could sit down. One of the lads, Rodney Bush, stood and made a gesture like he was holding a machine gun, and said "One day we'll be back for you bastards". The lads told me about the problems though. Apparently when they played AmaZulu away they'd have to take guns in their bags for protection. At one time they nearly had to use them to protect manager Mike Kenning. To go into a township was incredible; I've never seen anything as horrific, they had shacks instead of houses. At night they would just burn things and there would always be a very low cloud. I went to townships in Soweto, Pretoria,

Durban and Bloemfontein and it was very primitive. It was sad to see people live that way; when you see the appeals on television today, it wasn't any different back then.

I lived in a place called Bedfordview which was about 17 miles outside Jo'burg; there were motorways and lit roads all the way there apart from the last bit which was just darkness. There were traffic lights, but I was told that if I saw traffic lights and it was dark, drive though, even if it was red, as people might attack you. That's what I would do – I never stopped at traffic lights. The car I drove belonged to Raymond's wife, and I put a Kaiser Chiefs sticker in it so that people wouldn't attack the car. The incident on the bus is as scared as I have ever been. I was supposed to go out that night but I stayed in; it took me a few days to get over it. It was a different way of life but it just seemed to be the way it was; on a Monday we'd get the local newspaper to see how many had been killed over the weekend. If it was less than twenty it had been a good weekend. I felt for the people who lived there; one of my friends owned a shop and he had a black lad working for him for just 50 RAND a month.

My friend was living in a detached house, with a double garage and electric doors. We were watching movies on pirate copy that hadn't even been released in England; I remember watching Alien and Rocky 3. We'd watch Match of the Day and the Sunday afternoon football on the Monday at a cinema; it'd be packed with people interested in English football. I would still get recognised; we went to the casino at Sun City for a meal at the restaurant and went to the bar to have a drink, and people would recognise us there. Most of the bar staff were British anyway. Sun City was in Bophuthatswana, which was an area where blacks and whites could mix. Sol Kerzner was the owner, he had the Gary Player golf course there too which had a yearly tournament, the Million Dollar Classic. I was invited to play with Gary there. It was only three holes, but I was invited by the casino staff – Gary Player was playing 18 holes but doing three with different groups. We played three of the hardest holes on the course and he made par on them all with ease. I was never a great golfer; if I was playing a lot I could play up to single figures but I enjoyed it more for the good walk.

Most of our games would be played on a Friday night, and while I was there, the cricket season had just started and they played on Saturdays. One of the players who played for us was Jimmy Cook and he was an opening batsman for South Africa. It's a shame that there was Apartheid because Jimmy was a fabulous player. He went on to play for Somerset in England – I once went down for five days to watch him play against Lancashire, he got two half centuries and a hundred and sixty odd, he must have done it for me being a Yorkshireman! In South Africa Jimmy played for a team called the Pirates and we'd go and watch; it was always a pleasant afternoon sitting on the grass and having a few beers. I went to see Transvaal versus Northern Transvaal, which was essentially Jo'burg versus Pretoria, and saw the great Graeme Pollock get eighty. Transvaal had a very good side, not only Jimmy but also Alvin Kallicharran as well as Graeme. Clive Rice was the local captain where I lived; club cricket was very strong. I was never tempted to play myself but it was great to relax.

We only trained on Tuesdays and Thursdays so we had plenty of time to do different things; I'd play golf quite a bit up at Sun City as I didn't have to pay. I even had my own caddy - Solomon. We had to pick caddies from a cage and I picked Solomon; the first time I played with him, we were playing a game for 10 RAND. I said, "If we win, you can have it." "Right boss, right boss", he replied, he would always call me 'boss'. We played and won the game; I was with Andy Stanton (whose brother Pat had played for Hibernian in Scotland) and we played two lads from the casino. I gave Solomon the ten RAND and he was delighted as it was probably the equivalent of four games for him; he was a great caddy, though. If my ball was in the woods he always found it, if I ever thought it had fallen badly there was always a gap it could get through. I never saw him touch my ball but he was certainly a good caddy!

Every time I played I always got Solomon and looked after him; in the end, I didn't have to think about what to hit, where to putt, he would always get me the right club. He was a good lad and I had many a good time with him on the course. The money I was on at Wits wasn't quite as good as it had been during my first spell in South Africa on the rebel tour but it was still better than I would have been earning in England; and, being out there for the extended time as I was, Maureen came out with Paul and Brian. Where we were living was safe so I wasn't worried about them coming out - it was a nice area, and I knew where was safe to go. A couple of times we went down to the Vaal river where you could go water-skiing or have a barbecue (or 'Braai' as they're known locally). There'd be braii's everywhere, you'd just go and throw your coal on to cook your food. I tried to water ski but couldn't! Maureen was seven months pregnant and everyone looked after us; her hospital trips were organised and everyone made sure she was okay. I've nothing but love for Wits, there were some smashing lads and I had some good times there. I did well there, in fact so well that around a year later I was offered the job of player manager. But despite how well we'd been looked after, my overall perception of South Africa was that I didn't want to raise my family there. It's a shame as it was a beautiful country, but after going to the townships and seeing how things were, it didn't sit right with me. Nor did the prospect of returning to Soweto. I thought, "Do I need this anymore?", and the answer was no.

When I arrived back in England, having not heard from Joe Royle, I decided to speak to the press, and I said that "People who said they were going to get in touch with me haven't." The next day, Joe must have read it, because he rung me and apologised. "Sorry, I should have rung" before adding, "I can't offer you the contract. I didn't realise the chairman was an alcoholic." The chairman had told him to offer me £300 a week and £20,000 as a signing on fee but when Joe went to the board, they told him there was no way they could afford it. I must confess, when I had been offered the deal in the first place it had surprised me that they could afford it.

Two or three weeks after our return, my third son Peter was born. We'd been out for a walk and Maureen said she was ready - we went to the doctors but the nurse said she'd got it wrong. Maureen insisted, saying "It's my third, you know!". The nurse said she'd have a look before saying "Oh blooming hell, you're right!". It happened that quick; the nurse said to me "Get the wedge out (to support her back), give her gas and air and open her legs". I thought, "That's how it started!" So as Peter was being delivered it was just me and the nurse there with Maureen at first. Dr. Hossack had said that he wanted to be there, as he'd been the doctor that delivered Brian and Maureen had had some problems during that pregnancy. The doctor always looked after Maureen and we are to this day very grateful. He used to live just behind us, so whenever we needed him, we could just ring him at home and he would come and help. Maureen always wanted four but after Peter she was told not to have any more. Paul was a nightmare sleeper as a baby and can still live on only five or six hours sleep, but when he was a baby five hours was a godsend! Brian, on the other hand, could sleep for fourteen hours. The other kids would be up and we'd have to go up and shake him to wake him up! He was a fantastic baby for sleep though, particularly when I was a player. I can still hear Paul's little feet running across the landing to come into the bedroom and jump into bed, something that happened very often. And Pete was somewhere in-between; generally very good, but he did have his moments!

I was looking for a club in the North again. The Africa trip was always a short term thing that just happened to go on a bit longer than originally planned; the first part of the trip because I was out of contract (the same as many players who had gone there) and the second part because I was hoping to get fit until a contract materialised back in England. I'd even accepted that I might earn a lower wage, with the thinking that the money earned from the trip to Africa would subsidise me for a while. I was close to signing for Burnley and that wasn't down to my basic wage, it was because of what they were going to put into my pension, I was looking to build that up as much as I could. Maybe that's why they never returned with the concrete offer but even so, the basic wage they did offer me was something I considered an insult, particularly as they would have got me on a free transfer.

I began to apply for jobs in the game as a coach or manager and though I wouldn't necessarily say it upset me, it did bother me that I sent around fifty letters and only got back two replies. Of those replies, I got an interview at Altrincham. I didn't interview very well and I wasn't surprised that I didn't get the job; but the only other club that had the courtesy to reply and thank me for my application was Barnsley. It surprised me that so few clubs had that decency; the least they could have done was send out a bog standard letter even at second class, but I didn't get anything. Perhaps I was struggling because it seemed to be the case that it was very much "Jobs for the boys" and people were looking after each other; it's not too dissimilar these days. I'd love to know what the precise statistic is for managers who get sacked and just walk straight into other jobs; there are managers who haven't won a thing or seem to achieve anything who never have a problem getting work. On some of the letters I wrote, I even offered to work without a contract to save clubs the hassle of paying compensation if it didn't work out. Maybe it was because I'm not a great letter writer. With all the rejections and nothing looking likely to come up, I decided I'd take Christmas off, and resolved to look again in the New Year. I was playing squash and trying to keep myself fit but I always knew I was going to have a problem with my weight. While I was playing I was able to manage it but without a club it was difficult; and perhaps taking Christmas off was the worst thing I could have done, I should have just kept on trying to get a club. The spell in Africa had worked well for my fitness; it didn't half make a difference training at altitude.

For better or worse, I did take Christmas off and soon after I heard a whisper that the Rochdale managers' job might soon become available. I approached the chairman to ask if it was true, if he was going to sack the manager who at the time was Peter Madden. He didn't ask me where the rumour had come from, he just confirmed it. I said, "Well what about me and my brother taking over?" Our James had long since left United and had spells at Crewe, Toronto Blizzard and was currently at Port Vale, and I proposed that he could be manager and I could be player-coach. The chairman suggested a meeting and it was all very cloak and dagger; four directors came around to our house, Maureen and her friend made sandwiches for them. The directors came in, drank all my beer and drank all my whiskey, then said, "We're sacking him next week." I said, "Well you've got another game before then!". They said, "Yeah, we'll let him have that as his last game." We went to the game which was at Halifax; they drew 0-0, and Madden was sacked more or less straight away. We were offered the job the following week but we weren't given a contract; the only benefit was being able to claim expenses. James lived in Alsager so it wasn't so bad having the petrol money paid for, but I would go and watch a lot of games to try and find players. I'd been offered a contract in Hong Kong, but with the Rochdale opportunity, I decided to knock it back.

Rochdale were in the Fourth Division and had a history of finishing around the bottom of the table at a time when that meant having to apply for re-election. We got a couple of players in on loan; I didn't want to be playing, and in truth I wasn't fit enough to. I was hoping to get the remainder of the season out of the way so I could get ready for the following campaign. I wasn't feeling too bad but I was carrying a little bit too much weight. Soon after taking the job we went to play Port Vale and James asked if I would play. I said I wasn't right but he talked me into it. It was a bad decision; I didn't enjoy it, we got stuffed 4-0 and it was embarrassing. The directors weren't pleased and I could understand that as I wasn't fit. After the game we went to friends for something to eat, I spoke to my brother and told him I wanted to pack it in. He tried to talk me around but I stood firm, telling him I was embarrassed about the game, "It shouldn't have happened, I shouldn't have played, I'm finished". During the next week he called me to come down and have a chat, so I did, and he asked me to come back. I said I wasn't going through that again and left the office; he chased me out of the office and down the road, it's probably the only time I've ever got away from him!

A few days later, though, I reneged and went back, as I always knew I would. I resolved to work harder on my fitness and see if I could get playing again. After about a month I looked and felt a lot better, and I played a few games until my old knee problem flared up and I missed the run-in. I was still going to watch games, but in order to get fit I decided I had to find a team that was going to play over the summer and so I organised to go to Finland and a club called Rovaniemen

Palloseura, or RoPs for short. I played for absolute peanuts, around £175 a week plus digs - and Finland was a very expensive place to live, so £175 didn't go very far, especially as I was sending money back home to the family. It was hard work, but I got fit, no thanks to the manager there who was absolutely useless. I went there as a centre half or full back and the first game I was played as a right winger. I did okay, setting up a goal in a win, but it didn't feel right hugging the touchline. The systems were different, we were playing a wide diamond shape, and then in the following game the manager told me to play the front of the diamond. I asked him if that was right - I had to ask through an interpreter as he couldn't speak English - and he confirmed it. I told him it wasn't my position. There was another English lad there, Lee Jenkins who was a Brummie, and he was playing the holding role. Lee was a skilful lad but it would have been better if we'd swapped roles; I didn't understand it.

Yet in the game I ended up doing the worst thing I could have done, score the winner! I called a meeting with the manager, and told the interpreter to tell him that I wasn't playing in my best position. After viewing the games and the set up, I said my best position was sweeper. Even though the lad doing the job was okay, I knew I'd be better, but the manager didn't listen. After a few games that was clear, it just didn't suit me. Then the centre half got injured and I thought that was my chance to move back, but he picked someone else instead. I thought it was going from bad to worse; so then the wife and family came out to join me. It must have been terrible for the lads as it was twenty four hour daylight - not that we didn't have as good a time as we possibly could, living on the arctic circle. We went on a sea plane, and saw reindeers, but then it was like, "There's another reindeer", and it came to pass that it was all ski-jumps and reindeers. They went back home and I still didn't enjoy it; after another run-in with the manager, I wrote a resignation letter and said I wanted to go, but the directors talked me round and so I went to play another game, at HJK Helsinki, starting on the bench as a substitute. I came on in the second half and played fantastically behind the front two; yet afterwards I told the manager I still wanted to go, so it was agreed I would be paid up and then I could leave. There was a local media network called Lapin Kansa that comprised of both the newspaper and television station, and they asked me to go on television and tell people why I was leaving. I obliged; telling them I thought the coach was useless and that I felt they would benefit from having an English coach for the simple reason that it was so disorganised. They must have listened because a couple of years later they went after an English manager. I was in the running, alongside Brian Doyle, the former Exeter player, and Graham Williams, the former West Brom defender. Brian was close to getting it but then I think he suffered a heart attack and so Graham got the job, and did well there. That was my parting shot; I'd done enough to get myself fit for my return to Rochdale. Lapin Kansa threw me a sauna party to say goodbye - it was alcohol free for me, but everyone else enjoyed it!

When I got back and the chairman saw me, he couldn't believe how well I looked, but still didn't give me a contract. I would still go down and help - when James was playing I'd sit on the bench and watch, and pass on my thoughts.

With no guarantee, I decided to start working at the local Beefeater that was called the "Sir Winston Churchill", a nice pub where Jim McCalliog had once worked. The bloke who ran it was called Frank Conroy and he approached me one day. "You're interested in food, why don't you work here?". He said I could train at Rochdale in the morning and then go there in the afternoon, and as I needed the money I agreed. At that point I wasn't even training anyway; I'd go down and help out on the bench at home games, arriving at the ground at around 2pm. Around this time I was offered a deal in Greece at a second division club. The money was good and they offered to put us up in an apartment and the kids in school; but with the contract more or less signed, the move fell through when they rung up saying they'd heard I was injured, but wouldn't tell me who had said that. It was the fittest I'd been in years!

I got a phone call from the Hull City manager Colin Appleton and they asked me if I wanted to go over; I went and played a game for their reserves. Arriving for the next Rochdale home game, I was a bit late to the ground to be on the bench so I decided to go to the bar for a drink. My brother's wife Joan, who I'd always got along with, came and gave me the biggest mouthful ever about how I'd supposedly let my brother down by going to play for Hull; the way I saw it, I'd been to Finland to get fit and when I got back there was no contract for me. Somebody had let somebody down, but I was sure I hadn't done anything wrong. James said it was because the board didn't have any money, but when I went and spoke to the board, they said they'd told James to go and sign me once they'd seen how fit I was. What the truth is,

I still don't know. I didn't watch the game, I went straight home.

After that, James asked me to play against York in the Cup. I'd only played one reserve game for Rochdale and that was against Liverpool "A", where we lost 3-0. He'd wanted me to play the week before against Hereford but I told him, "You're the manager, if you're fit you've got to play. I haven't got a contract, you have." I went on for him when we were losing 3-1 and I changed the game, laying on the equaliser to save the game in a 3-3 draw.

Our next game was against York, who were top of the league. James said he wanted me to start; I repeated my desire for a contract and he said he'd sort it out. We played really well, probably the best Rochdale performance I ever played in, winning 2-0 with me as captain. Afterwards, I was given a contract until the end of the season, but I wasn't even sure if I wanted it. I was really enjoying my time at the Beefeater and learning about catering, Frank and his wife Marie were really good to me. Maureen was working there a couple of days a week too. Frank was fantastic at his job and it was really good fun so I didn't really want to give it up. The 6 month deal on offer from Rochdale wasn't something I was totally sold on, but I signed, and the very first thing I got was a great big bunch of keys so I could open up. I would drop the kids off at school, be the first one at work and be the last to leave. I'd have to organise training; we had to take money with us to pay to use the facilities, otherwise we wouldn't be able to train, although the Trust at Rochdale Council were a fantastic help in getting us places to train. We changed the system and we started to do really well; I was at right back and a lad called Les Chapman was at left back, we played much the same was as I did with Eddie Gray at Leeds in our good spell. My contract was only as a player, but I was assistant manager, coach and scout as well. I enjoyed scouting, even if that wasn't my job.

Following the York game we lost at home to Bristol City, and after that we played at Bury on Boxing Day. We lost 3-1 but played so well; and were able to take many positives away. We were winning 1-0 just before half time when "whack", a player called Joey Jacob went straight over the ball and onto my knee, which was the last thing I needed. After that I was injured and so were a few others, and we were struggling to get players fit for our big game, the Third Round FA Cup tie at home to Telford. James decided to play me at right back as we fielded the strongest side we could; the first ball came to me and I had to kick it out instantly, I could tell my knee wasn't right. We'd started well though, going 1-0 up, but Telford were renowned for giant killings, captained by my old friend Kevin Lewis. One of our centre forwards hit a backpass and it stuck in the mud; they equalised and everything started falling to bits. I wasn't fit, while another defender, Billy Williams, got injured too and we ended up getting beat 4-1 – and four flattered us. Coming back so soon meant I wasn't really fit and I spent too much time at Rochdale Infirmary getting cortisone injections in me for fun.

By now, James was not getting on with the board; he thought they were always reading his mail or talking behind his back. I would always tell him there was only one person he needed to get friendly with and that was Graham Morris; Graham looked after the money. The chairman, David

Kilpatrick, was fine, which is more than can be said for the other two members of the board who I won't even name. Graham and David were the main people at the club and if you were good with Graham he would give you everything they'd got as he had the club's best interests at heart. The previous summer he'd been on holiday and the other three bought Steve Johnstone from Bury for around £15,000. Graham wouldn't have allowed that, and in my opinion he kept Rochdale afloat due to his accounting skills. The club might have had financial help since but to my mind it's people like Graham and David who helped make Rochdale what it is today; unfortunately neither was at the club when they finally got promotion after 41 years in 2010. In fairness, our kid never handled his time there well and he shouldn't have been the manager. I should have been manager and he should have been the coach, but I don't think he would have listened to me. At least if I'd have been manager I could have dealt with the board; and it ended up that James came to an agreement with them and left.

Nothing was said to me about James leaving, but I was invited to the game the following Saturday against Blackpool at home. I was speaking to Sam Ellis, the Blackpool manager, before the game when suddenly I was approached by the secretary and asked to leave the ground. I asked why, and apparently it was because they thought I was telling Sam how we were going to play! I explained I wouldn't do that but I'd known Sam for years; I refused to leave, explaining I'd been invited by the chairman. They left and didn't come back – I watched the game which finished 1-0 to Rochdale and went to the bar afterwards for a drink with Les Chapman who had been made caretaker manager. Les wanted me to stay at the club and I was in two minds when I was summoned into the directors' box.

The two who I won't mention were trying to sack me, David was no help and Graham didn't say anything at all. The meeting went nowhere. I advised them they'd be hearing from my solicitor and afterwards I went to the bar and told Les I didn't think I'd be sticking around as they wanted rid of me. They then called Les in to tell him what had happened, then called me back in after. Graham opened his mouth for the first time, inviting me to his office on 3pm on the Monday. In that meeting he had everything written down - they were going to pay my contract up. I had a lot of time for Graham for doing that and have always got time for a warm handshake with him but I really fell out with the chairman after that. I regret that as he was probably only doing the best for his club. After the 2002 Play-Off Final which Rochdale lost, David was in my local pub, and I sent him a pint over to say bad luck. For the last few years we've got on famously, and I still call him Mr Chairman - something he deserves after his length of service, for the times when they were only pulling in crowds of eight hundred and having to put their hands in their own pockets to make it up to a thousand to make the attendance records look better. People forget or don't realise that these things happen and they're things that the people involved don't go on record to say.

James and myself didn't speak for a few years after the spell at Rochdale. One day in 1989 I got a phone call out of the blue from my sister Joan, who told me James had been around at her house and had suffered a panic attack and was taken to hospital. Joan called me to ask me if I would go and see him, and I said I would – it just so happened that our mother was in a different part of the same hospital at the same time. When we arrived at the hospital, James' wife and his daughter Julie were there – my sister asked if I could go in and see him. They said no, but they would ask him to see if he wanted me to. They didn't even speak to me, but that didn't surprise me. I went to see my mother and after an hour or so went back; they said I was allowed to see him, but all of a sudden they were hugging me when an hour previous they were looking straight through me! Everything seemed to be alright when I saw James, too.

I continued to visit the hospital to see my mother as she had leukaemia but then she suffered a perforated ulcer, so we had to rush over as we knew there could be problems. James picked me up and we stayed at my sister's, visiting the hospital for about five days before she took a turn for the worse. She'd been in and out of hospital for a few months; nonetheless, nothing prepares you for somebody dying and it was still heartbreaking when she passed away.

Sometime in 1992 Paul was enquiring with Mark how the rest of the family were and Mark dropped into conversation that Julie had got married. Maureen and I were out having a meal and when we got back Paul asked us if it was true. I said no, because I'm sure they would have told us. Maureen couldn't let it go so rung them up and asked to speak to James. She asked him bluntly if it was true that Julie had got married and he said yes. "Well, why weren't we invited?"

asked Maureen. James said, "Because we didn't want to", trying to pass it off as only being a small do. He'd fallen out with our sister and said he didn't want to have to invite us and them; when Maureen asked why we hadn't been told – after all, he'd been to see us twice since the apparent wedding – James said it was nothing to do with us. "So you just didn't want us there?", asked Maureen again – James confirmed this. It seemed a strange conversation that Maureen was clearly getting uncomfortable with. She asked him how he could do that and keep contact with us pretending nothing had happened, and he said, "That's life". Maureen told him it might be with his side of the family, but not ours. He said, "If you feel like that, don't bother ringing again".

James had one of my England caps in his possession from a time we'd travelled around the country together; I wrote a letter to him saying that as he didn't want us to be part of his family, would it be okay to have the cap back. The cap was sent back in a jiffy bag without a letter, and that was the last time I heard from him well over twenty years ago.

When I got him the job at Rochdale I went out of my way to do that; I offered him a way out of Port Vale as he was having a particularly tough time with their manager John McGrath when I could have easily taken the manager's job. Such was my desire to work with him and help him out again, I had even decided to give up a lucrative offer in Hong Kong. It was I who was originally asked about for the position at Rochdale; I pushed for Jimmy to get the job, he was interviewed in my front lounge for the job as we entertained the directors.

I was disappointed to not get a contract without really

having to fight for it; I was disappointed to be confronted by James' wife for apparently letting him down - particularly in the knowledge that he was only in the role because of me - and I was disappointed that he just left Rochdale without telling me. I can't understand why anyone could have been upset with me for simply wanting a contract! I'd looked after my brother, I had a responsibility to myself, my wife and sons too.

I had watched him play for the school, the town, the county, for Leeds youth, the first team at Leeds... as a younger brother I idolised him and for everything to end the way it has is very disappointing. Playing with my brother is something I wanted and to play in an FA Cup Final and win it with him is the stuff that dreams are made of; and it made my mother so proud as well. And despite what happened, it doesn't sour my mind or memories of him as a footballer as I keep the two separate. We were as close as brothers and families can and should be; I was asked to be godfather to his children, and we'd go and visit them and baby-sit for them regularly.

It wasn't so much that we weren't invited to the wedding; that would have been fine, as long as we'd have been told. He had fallen out with my sister, not me - I might not have been happy about it, but I would have accepted it. To find out about six months after the event when we had continued to receive birthday cards and Christmas cards that had his daughter's name and no mention that she was married; the pretence, the charade, the devious and dishonest way in which he did it was really hurtful. I had never been like that with him.

In all of this, if he was to sit down and reflect on what happened, he could ask himself if he thinks I would do the same, then I think honestly he would know that I wouldn't. Years after we lost contact, when my son Paul got married, I still invited my sister even though I didn't invite James. He made the decision to not be part of my life; so I'm just going along with it. James' response has been "that's life", as if he wasn't bothered, as if he was happy with his life the way it was and the way that environment is set up. If that's what he wants, then that's fine, but it will be him who has to live with it. He's dismissive because he knows he's in the wrong; it's his way of dealing with it, he won't apologise and I don't ever expect him to.

I'm always asked "how's your brother?" I'm sure he is asked the same question. There's only so long that you can give a non-answer answer, and though it has been extremely difficult to put on record - for my family as well as me - I feel that it is right for me to document as it is something that happened; and it might put an end to the questions. I'm sure he's not happy with how things are but he hasn't rung and that's his choice. The only thing I would say is that he's missed out on my three wonderful, great lads growing up, as well as my grandchildren. It all started with me getting James the Rochdale job, and in some ways I wish I never had now. I still talk to my sister, who has since moved to Germany, and occasionally she tells me that James has said we should let bygones be bygones, but I feel he is just saying it for her benefit as my phone has never rung.

In that final meeting with Graham Morris, he said the reason one or two of them weren't happy with me is because they'd heard that I was going to take over the pub "The Elephant and Castle" which is about a mile away from the ground. I hadn't, but I did know somebody in the industry called Tony Whelan who worked for Thwaites. I'd heard that the landlord and landlady of a pub called "The Hare and Hounds" which was opposite the Winston Churchill, were leaving and by this time I'd had enough of football. My relationship with my brother wasn't at its best, our wives weren't speaking either. I hadn't enjoyed the best of ends at Rochdale and it was only afterwards that I realised how hard it must have been for them, trying to do their best, right down to people telling you to turn the light off if you left a room in order to save money. I really do feel for the Rochdale supporters; they're a loyal lot, they don't come and go like City fans! They have a good away following, too. As a football club, I've got a lot of time for Rochdale, even if I can't really say I look back on my time there with great fondness. After getting my brother the job there I felt I should have been looked after better, and I felt I should have had a contract from the start. At times I felt I was used, so it wasn't a happy time and not an ideal way to end my playing career. I was getting phone calls to play here and there; Gerry Francis wanted me to go and play at Exeter, but I didn't want to move. There was interest from Witton Albion and other places but I wasn't really interested in continuing my playing career any longer.

What had done for my top level career was going to South Africa for the second time. I'd only gone back as Joe Royle had told me about the Oldham chance – then, knowing it had gone, instead of coming back fighting fit and looking for a club, taking the Christmas period off was the worst thing I could have done. When Rochdale came around I had barely trained for six weeks; it was essentially a few wrong decisions, primarily based around not keeping myself fit when I needed to, that really marked the end of my playing career. I was prone to putting weight on anyway; I was about a stone overweight, but I seemed to be able to do that without much difficulty at all. The Port Vale disaster when I'd just started at Rochdale showed how unfit I was and even though the Finland trip did wonders for me I knew my career at the top level was over anyway, probably due to my decision to go to South Africa in the first place. I was in a difficult position as there were no worthwhile offers from English clubs, I was out of contract and the money on offer for a relatively short stint was too appealing for a player out of work to turn down. There were a number of decisions I had to make in a relatively short space of time, which was made more difficult by the fact my wife was pregnant.

Though some players in my era might have struggled to come to terms with a sudden departure from the game and an entrance into the "real world", I had already served my apprenticeship (so to speak) by working at the Beefeater while I was still at Rochdale. And when the interview for the Hare and Hounds came along, I went to it and got the job.

11. LIFE AFTER FOOTBALL

BEFORE MAUREEN AND I could become publicans, we had to attend a course at the Thwaites Brewery in Blackburn - they had a pub at the front called Daniel's. You had to go into the cellar and tap a barrel; of course I was a natural as I'd done it since I was a thirteen. Clearly impressed, we got the job no problem. We took over at the Hare and Hounds in 1984 and it was fine to begin with; Stevie Coppell came up with his wife Jane to pull the first pint and spend a few hours with us which was nice. Everything was running fine with the pub when out of the blue the following March I got a phone call asking me if I wanted to go and play in Malta for Hibernian. They wanted me to play every two weeks for a fee of £300 per appearance; I had a few friends over there from a few holidays we'd had there previously, so I agreed and it was arranged for me to stay in a five star hotel. Prior to the first game I met the chairman and he took me for a meal and told me I couldn't play as my registration hadn't gone through. They took me to the game which was in a newly built stadium; the standard was very poor and I was wondering how I was expected to make it better. I flew back to England the next day, and was told to come back two weeks later which I did, arriving on the Friday night in time for the game on the Saturday.

On arriving, I was told that the game was cancelled

because of a referee's strike but that the game would be played on Sunday. That Saturday night I went to my friend Jozan's house; his brother Norman was part of the committee on the Maltese FA. We had a Chinese and they asked me if I was going to have a drink; I said I couldn't as we were playing the next day. Norman said, "You're not playing tomorrow, I'll tell you now." So I had a glass of wine! True to what I'd been told, the game was cancelled. I'd heard nothing from the club and I was due to fly back on the Sunday but it hadn't been arranged. Jozan came and picked me up to take me to the hotel he was running and let me stay there on the Sunday night. He took me to Michael Zammit Tabona who ran the Fortuna Hotel where we had stayed the first year we went in 1977; Michael used to charter all of the planes back to England. It was arranged that I would fly back to Birmingham and someone would pick me up and take me back to Rochdale. Michael got me home but the club did nothing to help; I thought it couldn't go on that way, particularly as the brewery didn't know either and didn't give me their permission to go away. The club rung up again and I refused to go back; I said I hadn't got a penny from them and I was ending up out of pocket. That was the last time I actually thought of playing. If it had happened, it would have been great, as would have been the potential move to Greece a year previously.

As it turned out we stayed at the Hare for just over twelve months. The kids were young; one day we were really busy, and Maureen had to come down to the bar when she was in the middle of bathing Pete, who was still only three. Pete turned the hot tap on and scolded himself while we were downstairs - we began to realise we couldn't run a pub with three young kids. I got a written warning in the post, too, for adulterated beer, which meant they thought I was watering it down or adding stuff in that shouldn't be in. I rung to ask them and they said it had been tested by a chemist; I said I'd never done anything of the sort, and that I would appeal. In the appeal meeting it transpired that the beer had been adulterated because I was sending the barrels back too late, which influenced the beer. I won the appeal, but decided to give them a month's notice. It was hard work. The only time you're not working in a pub is when you're asleep, you're working as soon as you're awake. The clientele were good, we never had any trouble, so parts of the job were pleasing – as was the catering side, but even then, I was promised a new kitchen and it took them six months to build it, which was ridiculous as that was the main appeal in the first place.

Maureen and I decided to move back into the cottages after leaving the pub, while we looked for something else to do together; we'd been renting them out to make the wages up to make it bearable. We bought a sweet shop in Rochdale in 1987; we took good money, the profit margin wasn't fantastic but it gave us a good living for two or three years. We'd split the shifts between us and it worked well to begin with – we weren't earning thousands but we were surviving. The Post Office across the road decided to start selling sweets and business just dropped a little bit – I got a phone call from the bank manager and he called the money in. He gave me a week to find the money I owed, or they would take the house off me. It was the biggest shock of my life. I had to re-mortgage the house, which was the only thing I'd left football with, and we suffered a real cashflow problem. I tried some pub relief jobs but it didn't help; we sold as much of the shop stock as we could, and I still had to pay the lease up until it was ready to move on. We ended up with a fifth of what we originally paid out, and we ended up losing around £40,000. My sister started paying our household bills because we were in such a bad situation; we were getting around in a small Fiat car which the kids had to push start just so they could get to school!

It was difficult for me to find work, particularly as I'd only ever really done one thing. Frank Conroy, who had run the Beefeater, would have given me a job but he moved to York. We put the house up for sale as we were trying to downsize. Maureen got a job working for Hitachi; which kept us ticking over. I was waiting on my pension, which was due when I was 35. We sold the house and moved into the village in Norden – I never liked the house we moved into, but we made the best out of a bad time, and in fact Peter now owns that house so he must have liked it! One day Maureen said that Hitachi were looking for people to come into the office and call people for £100 a week; I went in and did that over Christmas and was invited to return in the new year. As is typical with these sort of companies, they had to downsize and when they did it was last in, first out. Fair do's to them, they offered me a position in the warehouse, which was actually on more money, and I accepted. The majority of lads were good, there was only one who wasn't a nice fella who just happened to be a City fan. I did my stacker truck licence, and was enjoying it. I would take overtime when it was offered, but I couldn't see myself getting a career there. I had an illness and was off for two weeks; on my return they called me in, told me they had to get rid of someone and it was me. I'm sure the City bloke had a lot to do with it, as I was a far better worker than the majority there. I left gracefully – by this time Maureen had left, so I didn't really want to be there anyway.

I started to look in newspapers for vacancies, from the *Rochdale Observer* to the *Manchester Evening News*. There was an advert for front of house of a new club in Manchester, which I didn't get. Soon after that I got a phone call from the same company, the Noble brothers who were renowned for their amusements businesses. They called me into their building at Piccadilly (it was situated where the old Woolworths was before it burned down in 1979); I didn't realise that the third and fourth floors above the nightclub housed a snooker club. I met the general manager and the area manager and they created a PR job for me. I was to go around companies organising snooker competitions for their employees, where we would do the parties and put food on for them. Everything was going well, but then they sacked the manager. I wondered what would happen, but then they offered me the manager's job, taking me from £10,000 to £15,000 a year. The facilities were immaculate; there were 65 tables and plenty of cues, it really was a fantastic place with no expense spared. The main table was the 1985 table which Dennis Taylor won the World Championship on; Stephen Hendry would use the table to practice on before he won the Championship. Alex Higgins came in too – we used to try and put the big names on the main table as much as possible.

There was a balcony upstairs overlooking the table where the regulars could just watch – Stephen Hendry in particular was fantastic to watch. Steve Davis would come in and practice but he wouldn't go on the championship table as he didn't want to ruin it because he never had his cue.

Many years ago, with Frank, we once went to Alex Higgins' house and he had a snooker table there. His cue, his pride and joy, was just thrown in the middle of it, whereas everyone would always put theirs away in a box. But that was Alex. I remember going to see him in the last Championships to be played outside of the Crucible with my nephew Alan Stevenson (who, coincidentally, was also on the books at United) at the Forum in Manchester. Alex was walking around with a glass of milk trying to impress the sponsors. He was a big United fan and got us the tickets; he used to go to United games too. He once called me up at quarter to three asking for two tickets! We sorted it, and after the game he was stood there with a pint in the players' lounge. He was a character. There's an old place in Salford, the Potters Bar, not far from the Cliff – one day Alex picked me up and said he fancied a game of snooker. I'd had a light training session at United and it wasn't even 12pm. We got in there and there was only one person in playing – Alex asked me if I fancied a pint. I said, "It's not even midday, you've got to let the yard arm get past!" So I got a coffee and the bloke who was in asked us if we fancied a game. Alex accepted the invitation and the fella set the balls up, he tossed a coin saying, "Heads or tails?" Alex went tails, it was heads. The bloke said, "I'll break. Do you fancy a little flutter on it?". Alex said yeah, and the bloke put fifty quid down. The bloke broke off, Alex cleared up and scored 139. The fella set the balls back up and asked if he fancied another game. Alex said "Yeah, that's fine, same bet?". "Yes", said the bloke, "but can you give me a bit of a start?". "Piss off", said Alex, "I haven't seen you play yet!"

He was a real character Alex. One of the last times I saw him was in the Winston Churchill after he'd split up with his wife. Being able to see those players was the one aspect of the job I really liked, being able to have a couple of pints with the likes of Steve Davis, and having Stephen Hendry come and practice in match conditions were perks of the job. Stephen was a lovely lad. I enjoyed being a manager; I was a lot more laid back than the previous one, as I wanted everyone to have a smile on their face. The best night we had there was when we were the only place to get a four o'clock drink licence for the Mike Tyson/Frank Bruno fight. We put tournaments on, the general manager organised televisions to be around everywhere, and we took over £10,000. There was no trouble and everything went like clockwork but then that kind of return was expected every week; the area manager then left as he didn't like the way things were being run. The new area manager was called Brendan - another City fan, and he was horrendous! When checking on things I had on my to-do list, if there were things I hadn't had time to do, he'd say, "The boss won't be pleased". I said, "Well, you're not helping!", to which he replied, "You'd better decide if you want to keep working here". As I put my hand on his tie, struggling to refrain myself from strangling him, I said he had better start being more civil to people. He was lucky that I never hit him - I wanted to so badly, one for being an absolute arsehole of an area manager, and two for being a blue bastard! It was so hard to work for him; I ended up going on the sick for two weeks as the doctor said I was too stressed to work. I got a phone call from Brendan who wanted to meet me, so we ended up meeting at a service station. The very first words he said to me were "It's not working, is it?". I said no – we just couldn't work together. He agreed to pay me a month's wages, which was fine, and then he asked if I wanted a lift home. As we got to the village, I asked him to let me out, and I told him in no uncertain terms where to go.

Perhaps it's no coincidence that some of my better times were associated with sport. Away from football, I played charity cricket a few times in the late 70's and early 80's for a team called Robinson's in Rochdale who I got involved with through a policeman I knew from playing squash. Even when we got the pub, a local team used to ask if they could use our pub because we didn't open for the evening until 5pm. They said, "Sometimes we finish early". I thought, "Well what kind of league is this?" They played at a tiny ground which was lethal – they kept knocking on the door at half past four saying the game was finished, but they hadn't started while two o'clock! The wicket was so bad that the games didn't last long. They asked me to come and play for them, and after some resistance I accepted and had some good fun. I didn't bowl anymore, or not as much, I liked batting. It was enjoyable, and they were a good bunch of lads, but it was always going to be short term.

Later I got involved with Norden Cricket Club, who'd been going for a few years and had joined the Central Lancashire League in 1981. There was a big difference in standard; I could probably have managed it if I'd tried harder. I got involved with the cricketing side; the running of the club didn't particularly bother me, so I got involved in the selection. Luckily enough the first year I was on it, we won the league. We had Gus Logie, the West Indian professional, who had a great season but we also had some good amateurs but because I wasn't involved on the committee, I wasn't allowed to be on the selection committee the year after. I just didn't want to be involved with the running; I'd organise sportsman dinners and help them sell tickets by trying to get speakers for them, but it was hard work. Not being permitted to be involved with selection I began to start playing again, turning out for the second team. The captain Bob Dearden had dropped to the second team to look after the kids, and knew that with me he had someone who was going to try and get kids ready for the first team.

I was never known as a 'slogger', I was more like a Geoff Boycott, front foot down the wicket, don't let them see anything, straight bat and wait for a bad ball. One particular game we played local rivals Heywood at home – this was the big one. Heywood had a massive ground and Norden's is a nice tight little ground; it seemed to be below them to come and play us, which was the attitude of a lad for them called David Fayre who was always rubbishing Norden. He'd come over every Friday to see Bob but he got that much abuse he stopped coming in! I don't think anybody missed him. In this game they were on 192 and on Norden that wasn't a particularly good score. We didn't start off very well; the first four got into double figures but never went on. Ian Schofield came in and I was batting seven; then it went to eight, then nine. By this time we were seven down there was me and Schoey as the last two. Schoey was a big hitter, I was a bit of a push and nudge man, and after about twenty balls I was on eleven. Schoey got out and then Ian Butterworth came in, and he never stuck around, he either smacked it or got out. I said to him, "Four overs to go, we want forty-four." Eleven an over at a ground like Norden doesn't sound a problem if you've got plenty of wickets but we only had two wickets and we thought it'd be a struggle. The first ball I hit for four, and the next three I hit for six - and the lad I hit for the three sixes already had six wickets. I said to Butty, "Let's just push them around and get them around the other end".

By this time, we'd halved the score. He pushed one, I did the same, then we both did the same again. Then Butty had a great big yahoo and got out. We were left with 18 to win and Steven Thorpe came in; he pushed the last ball and told me to run. I said, "Look, two overs to go, I think I can get them from this end". Heywood brought on Craig Irvine who was an experienced first team bowler. I knew straight away he was going to bowl a slow one as he was noted for it. I hit him for six, and then he dropped it short. My favourite shot was the pull, so I did it and Steven Thorpe came running over and said, "Take your time, we've won it". I said "Ok" but I was so pumped up that it didn't matter where he was going to put it, I was going to hit it for six. I did, straight into the gardens of the houses that back on to the ground, and I didn't realise it until a long time after but I hit a woman on the arm! We won the game, and it had been so totally unlike me, that I couldn't stop laughing. We were sat in the changing room afterwards, me and Bob Dearden - I said, "I can't believe I've done that." He said, "Neither can I." Apparently, the first team game at Heywood had been rained off, and people had mentioned what had happened in our game, and while they were in the dressing room, the "Greenhoff" chant was going up. I wish someone had videoed the game; I bet I didn't hit seven sixes in my cricket career other than in that game. It was picked up by the local paper in Heywood, but not in Rochdale for some reason. I played for the second team for about three years before I finally decided to retire, primarily because I didn't want to keep a kid from getting his chance. I was only in my early forties but there were too many older players and too many good players coming through.

Meanwhile, I'd maintained my interest in football, mainly watching local pub sides play. I'd get asked for my opinion and to get involved, but I'd just go and watch and add my two penneth. I hope that my being there helped to improve a couple of the players; I'm sure it did on one, a lad called Stevie Cunningham, who I used to call "Flicker". It used to really, really, piss him off. Every time a ball came to him he'd be flicking it, so I'd say, "Get hold of it Flicker!". Even when he'd get hold of it before passing it, I'd say, "That's better, Flicker!". He told me years later that his son went playing football, and one of the first things his son did was flick the ball – Stevie said, "You can stop that flicking!"

My mate Birdie played for Whitworth Valley, so I would go and watch him with his dad Albie. They always had nice pies there. Being there week in and week out, we'd always get asked our opinions. The manager there was Mick Blood and his heart and soul was in Whitworth – he offered to stand down to allow me to be the manager. I said you can

stand down, but you have to be my number two. I didn't
know the league, but I offered to bring some players in. We
formed a very good team. There was a nice little set up there
and it seemed like a good bunch of people to work with;
they worked hard, which is something you don't always see
at amateur clubs. We trained one day a week in the gym at
the local school – Mick would take it as he trained them hard,
and sometimes after he'd take them running up the quarries
to keep them fit. Mick and I would dovetail well together; if
I wanted to give somebody a bollocking, he was always good
to give it, and if he wanted to have a rant I'd let him do it. If I
was to have a go I'd do it sparingly, and Mick was quite happy
with that. When approaching training it was important to
remember that it was an amateur side and some of them had
been working on the Saturday morning. But what I wanted
the players to do first and foremost was to enjoy it, which was
something I'd always been taught at United, to work hard
and work for each other.

One of the favourite things I'd say was "If your mate
was in trouble, would you run across the road to help him?"
in an attempt to instil a discipline where they would help
their team-mates. There was a very successful Sunday side
locally called the Cock and Magpie, and I got a few lads from
there to play for us alongside the people who had been at
Whitworth for a while. I made a lad called Mark Kirkham
the captain – he was a big honest lad but to be fair he lacked
discipline; I thought giving him the captaincy might calm
him down a bit and it did. He was one of these lads who
would react to going 1-0 down in the first five minutes by
wanting to go and play centre forward when he was a centre

half; I changed that and said that we must keep our shape. If we were losing with ten minutes to go, then I might put him up front, but never too early. He was a cracking captain for me in my time there. The first five or six weeks were very difficult; being in charge of an amateur side that had players who played in Saturday and Sunday teams, suspensions were picked up quite easily and we had a big backlog from the end of the previous season, so for those first few weeks I never had a full squad available. I only had about thirteen players but I knew once we had those available we'd be okay; and so it proved, as with my full complement we won 25 out of the next 26 games, drawing the other. The credit goes to the lads because they were a great bunch and they developed a will to win; some of the victories were incredible. We even won a game 6-5; I sent a lad on with two minutes to go and told him to go and get the winner, and he did! He wasn't even in my original thirteen but he wanted to play for me, and was a good lad, so we took him along.

There were a few United fans there who wanted to play for me but in fairness there were probably more Leeds fans who were playing there – they didn't call me boss or anything like that, in fact they probably called me other things, but we all had a laugh. I tried to make it more organised, taking tea into the dressing room before the game and telling them to stop smoking before, getting them not to just throw their kit down and to help the people who would be coming to wash it. These were just small things that I was taught as a kid and that Tommy Cav used to hate; such as boots on the floor. Things that didn't require much effort but might make a difference in attitude; for example, Tommy Cav used to

want us to tuck our shirts in, and that's something I passed on
- "Look smart, play smart".

As well as Mark, we had the best amateur centre forward
I'd seen, a lad called John Burgoyne. He really did miss his
way as a youngster because he was a fabulous player; we had a
left back called Andy Taylor who would play further forward
than Patrice Evra when we were winning! I tried to drum
it into him that he had to defend as well even if we were
winning 5-0, and tried to keep him from crossing the halfway
line - trying to instil the pride of winning 5-0 instead of 5-1
because of a daft mistake. The team spirit was great and it was
a real shame that we finished runners up in the league and the
cup; but it was still a lovely time.

The following season I let a couple of lads go which was
probably the wrong decision in hindsight, but there were a
couple of young lads coming through - my eldest lad Paul
was looking like he should be in, as well as a few others who
I had a lot of faith in and who would be good players for
Whitworth if I could keep them there. Paul did really well in
a season that was all about surviving as we'd been promoted;
we did it comfortably, but we still had to be careful. I could
never get the players I wanted to win the Manchester Premier
League because there were teams who were paying players
and we couldn't afford to do that. After that season I tried
to have a word with a few older players to get us a bit more
experience and improve; it was difficult as it was easy for
them to earn £20 playing elsewhere. Nonetheless, we had a
good pre-season, upping the training to two sessions a week
- on Tuesdays, where we worked hard, and Thursdays would
be ball work on the pitch. We ended up getting as many

on the Thursday as we did on the Tuesday and it was some commitment from the lads to come twice a week. Sadly that wasn't matched by the committee, we'd turn up and the nets and posts wouldn't be up or the grass wouldn't be cut; eventually I told them that our ambitions were obviously not the same. I suggested they got somebody else as I wasn't prepared to put the effort in when it wasn't being matched; maybe it was time for me to move on anyway as it wasn't easy. I even got a phone call one Saturday morning from a lad who said he couldn't play because he had to go and book his holidays!

It was hard work; when we got it right it was very enjoyable but it was frustrating as well. I got offered a job at Bacup Borough who paid their players, but it wasn't the right club for me. I went for a job in a higher league at Rossendale when I was manager at Whitworth but I didn't get the job because I refused to poach any of the Whitworth players during the season – I wouldn't have done that. I realised that if I wanted to manage I'd want to do it at a level where they paid decent money to players but those jobs were difficult to come by as they normally went to lads who had played in the leagues for years and rightly so. For me to go in it would have been a learning curve, and I couldn't see that working for me. I really enjoyed my time at Whitworth and it made me think that in hindsight I wish I'd have taken the Rochdale job myself. The biggest problem was working with the board due to the lack of money available; James couldn't get on with them but I did. The row with them that triggered my departure was the only one I had with them; after I left I must have applied for nearly fifty jobs as a coach or manager over the next few years, I even offered to work without a contract.

Paul left Whitworth too and he joined Chadderton Town, and as always with my kids I'd go and support him. All of the boys played school football – Paul played at Bamford, Pete and Brian played at Norden, and they all went to Oulder Hill and played football there. Paul and Pete both played for their town team but Brian got more interested in cricket, and was probably better at that than football. Paul and Pete would train but Brian just wanted to play instead of practicing; he could play though. He was a good swing bowler and he could bat a bit too. Paul had played for Norden juniors but we took him away from there because the parents were horrendous – we'd be watching a game and the parents would be wanting to fight with the opposing parents! So we took Paul to Boundary Park and that was very well run. One of the first things we were told was not to get involved shouting from the sidelines, and we were fine with that. It was a delight to go to the games and be relaxed.

Paul was substitute every week and we were thinking of leaving because he wasn't getting a game (and to be fair, they had a good team - five signed for Oldham and two signed for Blackburn from the side Paul was in during the last year before the academies kicked in). After Christmas Paul got into the side and stayed in, and he enjoyed it, so in the following years it seemed a natural progression for him to go to Chadderton. He knew a few of the lads, but even though they were in the North West Counties league they weren't paying him any money. I went along to support him and just as I'd experienced before, they tried to get me involved so I did, offering advice on what to change around for them and the manager went along with it. At the end of the season they offered me the job; I was undecided but they gave it to someone else anyway. I wasn't that disappointed as it seemed like a lot of hard work for no reward – I had already given a lot of my time away for no reward and it was getting to the stage where I thought I wanted a bit more, particularly as at this time we'd just endured the rough spell with the shop and the money we owed.

I still watched amateur football, sometimes to see old mates play, but I gradually spent more time watching cricket. Brian started playing for Norden in the third team and graduated into the second; with watching Brian in the summer and Paul and Pete in the winter, my year was mapped out. But there was nothing better when it was a lovely day than to go and watch the cricket. Things did turn a bit sour at Norden; I'm a typical Yorkshireman and say what I think, and I'd often be asked questions which they didn't like the answer to. I don't know what they expected me to do or say, but I upset one or two people through being honest and they never spoke to me after. I got the blame for one or two things that went wrong; there was a benefit game involving Gus Logie which I had a lot of input into, and during the game someone reacted badly to a point I made – it got back to other people who thought I was trying to stir. It ended up that I got on fine with the person I'd disagreed with but those who had picked up the Chinese whisper part of it wouldn't speak to me – I'd have a spell of over a year where people would go quiet when I walked in, but so much time has passed that I am not particularly bothered about setting the record straight – it's the responsibility of others to tell the truth, though it should be left in the past. Over the last fifteen years I've probably only been back a dozen times, though when I do I'm treated like a long lost brother, even by people who didn't want anything to do with me, but I'm not two faced like some. Those things happen; I wasn't the first, and I won't be the last, but it was a shame as I worked so hard while I was there.

Brian left Norden and went to play at Fieldhouse Cricket Club, playing in the seconds and being named man of the match as they won the Cup Final after batting superbly. He'd have been a lot better as a cricketer if he'd had practiced; but that was the same with everything! All of the lads are United fans when it comes to football; Pete has never known any different, although Paul and Brian would come and watch me at Leeds and followed them because of me. I used to go to the players reunion do's, and meet up with Sir Matt and a few of the old lads. I took one of my mates to one of them and he got six autographs from the 1948 side, which was one of his favourite teams and he was absolutely delighted. Another year my neighbour got Sir Matt's autograph and he was over the moon. I'd always get the most pleasure at the reunion dinners when I got to meet up with people I'd come through the first team with – Bill Fairhurst, Tommy O'Neill and Eric Young came one year. I was so pleased to see them, people I cleaned the floors and toilets with. Drew Harris and Damien Ferguson came over from Ireland, Gordon Hill would turn up, Gary Bailey came over once with a lad called Greg who played left back with me when I was at Wits and it was so nice to see him. Some of the big stars would be there and it would be nice to say hello but my big pleasure came from seeing my mates. I once went with some people I knew to watch United play Derby, and I bumped into Jimmy Fleming – I'd not seen him for around twenty years. He looked over and said, "Brian...", to which I exclaimed, "Jimmy!". He said in shock, "You remember me?", I said, "Remember you? I'd never forget you!". He was a great lad, but he must have thought because I'd played a lot more, I might have forgotten them. But they were my mates.

By this stage I started work at Lindop Sports Suppliers, repping in the North of England. It was hard work as some sports brands and outlets such as JJB were coming into prominence and everyone was fighting for business; the last thing I needed with all that was to work for Chadderton with no reward. I enjoyed working at Lindop because it was all sports related; though in some shops the people there didn't even know about sports. As long as I walked out with an order, it was worth standing and having a chat – I was on basic wage and commission and it was the commission I was after! The reunion dinners at the club changed from Friday nights to Sunday, and then that made it almost impossible to attend. On Mondays I'd always have a long trip repping; so I stopped going to them, and after I finished working at Lindop I just heard nothing from the club to start attending again. I worked for Lindop for 11 years, until I was 50 before embarking on another big move.

12. BACK HOME

AFTER OUR MONEY TROUBLES we never got the opportunity to have a proper holiday. The lads and Maureen would go to Anglesey to stay with Maureen's sisters while I would stay at home and work, but in 1994 we finally saved up enough money to go away on holiday together. Paul didn't come as he was at the age where he wanted to go with his mates; so we went away with Brian and Pete to Son Parc in Menorca. Out there, we met a man called Peter Morgan who was a big United fan I'd known for a few years. He had a house out there and he took us out for a trip in his car to a place called Addaia where his daughters were running eight apartments all around a pool. We had a look at them and Peter said if we wanted, we could book them with him – and we did that for the next three years. We got to know the local restaurant owners, who were all really nice despite being Leeds fans! We got on really well with everyone, and I would play cricket with Bri to relax.

All of the family went in 1998, and we really enjoyed ourselves. By then I had started working for MUTV so although we would still go to Menorca every year, we'd only go for a week and it wouldn't be as a "main" holiday. On our 25th wedding anniversary we decided to go on a cruise of Barbados and the Caribbean; we couldn't sort that out, so we ended up going to St. Petersburg and sailed from Tampa to the Gulf of Mexico and New Orleans. We had a fantastic time, and the following year we went on a cruise around the Mediterranean. The base was in Majorca, but we still had to go to Menorca for a week's holiday. With my 50th birthday approaching, I decided I wanted to have it there. So the lads and their girlfriends came out and we booked a six bedroom villa; we had a great time and we started to seriously consider the idea of making a go of living out there. We wanted to go and work, and just see what happened. I told Lindop that I would leave in February of 2003, to go out to Menorca in March by myself and try and sort out everything so that Maureen could join me and start work. I stopped with a friend, Sean, for a few weeks and then rented an apartment for a month until I found another one that Maureen and I could move into. She came out in April; I'd found her a job working behind the bar in the local restaurant but still hadn't got one for myself. I decided to go working on the cars for a lad called Tony Perkins. I did about two or three weeks but I couldn't get enough work - we'd taken 20,000 Euros out with us.

By my fiftieth birthday we were finally able to clear the debt that we'd had since the problems with the shop. But I still needed work, and when I bumped into Dave who ran Bar Pins where Maureen was working, I asked if he was alright because he looked a bit down, and he said his mother wasn't so well back in Gloucestershire. He asked how I was and I said how I was struggling, and he said, "Come and work for me, I'll sort some hours out for you". It was working nights, which I didn't really want, but as they say beggars can't be choosers; one of the girls who worked at the bar fell out with Dave, and so Maureen worked two nights on 8pm while 10pm. It was a busy restaurant but we did okay; we earned enough money to last us the winter, as we were to work six months and have six months off. We earned 5,000 Euros in tips but we were working without a contract, so we got offered one for the following year. That meant we were able to work the six months and claim dole for the following six – the money we were earning in the summer was enough to help us with rent in the winter. I started to run the quiz night, too – we were essentially living off the tips in the summer and saving the wages; we were able to live off the dole money, so we were saving money while we were there, which is something we never thought would happen. So the first week in November, we signed on, and we went on holiday to Gran Canaria – living in Menorca, and going on holiday!

It wasn't as if they were the best people to work for in the restaurant but it was busy and the staff were good; the chef was as mad as a hatter, and the girls Elaine, Lesley and Jackie were all good girls but very strong willed and not shy in telling you if they thought something was wrong. We worked there for a few years but then I left because I fancied doing something else; I went to another restaurant opened by a friend called Bruce who we'd met out there. We got it going well, until one day the chef threw a wobbler – and when he threw one, you had to stand back because he was crazy. I left because I hadn't gone to work there with a nutcase! I went back to Bar Pins and I started doing the breakfast and lunchtime cooking from 9am-3pm, and then the preparation for the evening chef. I absolutely loved it, doing the soups and the sauces, lasagnes and fish cakes – it was great as it was something

I really enjoyed doing. We would be visited by old friends
from Barnsley; Steve Thomas, John Michael Hobson, and I
know Arnie came over once but we just didn't get a chance
to get together. Every April the Roses Cricket Club came
over from Barnsley; we'd always go to the cricket at Menorca
Cricket Club whenever we went, and it would always be the
same team every year.

Going back many years, I used to have a drink with a
fella called Norman Brooks on a Sunday night. We'd play
squash and have a couple of drinks together. He always got
his cards out, and would tell a story that he would call a trick.
It fascinated me; it was really fantastic, he used every card in
the pack. We'd gather as many people as we could around,
and I'd make him do the trick every week. One day I asked
him if I could try it, I did but it didn't work - so I got a pack,
and practiced it over and over again. I showed Norman and
he said, "Watching that now, I could learn it from you!" You
never tell the same story twice with it even though the gist
of it is the same.

In Menorca, one day there was a fella on a table in the
restaurant doing card tricks. He was very good, there must
have been half a dozen of us, but then everyone started asking
him if I could do mine; he refused as he didn't want anyone else
playing with his cards. I said fair enough, I could understand
that if he was a serious magician. But he changed his mind
and gave me his cards. I set the table up, went away and came
back, during which time he had put a coat on which had a
badge which read "Magic Circle". I thought "No pressure
there then!".

I did the story, and the people he was with applauded it

even though he didn't. He said to me, "That's the best version of that trick that I've ever seen". I call it a story rather than a trick, but I thought he must have never seen it before. Brian booked him into a restaurant where the man wanted to go as he was going there the same night; the man was called Arthur MacTier. Brian met him and his wife the same night and he was doing tricks again, and afterwards he asked Brian for my address. He wrote to me asking if he could put "my" card story into a book he was doing. I replied, apologising and saying that I couldn't as I'd promised Norman I'd only pass it through the family. The next time I saw Arthur, he was on Countdown! I've shown the same story countless times; I did it once on a jumbo jet with Bobby Robson gathering everyone around to see it, I played with the Lord Taverners in Paris once and Nicholas Parsons was getting everyone to come and watch my story. I did it on the back of the yacht going round Sydney Harbour; I still love it, it's fun and requires a bit of sharpness. I tried to teach it to Paul but whether he can do it, I'm not sure.

Our time in Menorca finished sadly though when Dave died and Lynne, who was his wife, didn't want to work and although I don't know exactly what happened, she left without paying us two months wages. With that, we decided to come back to England. We had to fly back to Spain a few times, once to go to court to try and get our money back. We got paid from the Spanish Government, as they do that and then go after the culprit. To this day I'm not sure if they ever did catch up with her but it would be nice if they did because there were one or two of the girls who were in a desperate mess and they did not deserve that after working for them for around twelve years. It was an extra shame as Lynne's mother was good friends with Maureen but they also fell out. It wasn't a nice ending, and left a sour taste in the mouth. We still go back to Addaia and we get invited out but Maureen finds it difficult; fortunately, my son Paul has moved out there in the meantime and lives around 30km away from Addaia – there's enough to do where he lives so we're happy.

Paul came with a friend to stay with us in the May after we moved there; they had a night out in Mahon, and he met a Spanish girl named Fara. In 2008, they got married – she is a lovely girl with a big heart who wants the best for Paul, she is really good for him and he is good for her. We asked Brian and Peter if they wanted to come and live with us – they both said no, but we were a bit shocked when Bri said no as we half expected him to say yes. They stayed behind, and Pete and Brian lived in our house. I didn't leave them in the lurch; I paid some of the bills, and then Brian moved out. Pete met his partner Joanne and she moved in, and it wasn't long until they decided to buy it. When we decided to move back, we moved into Paul's old house, which he was renting out. Brian got a job in Chester and met a girl called Louise; they had my first grandson, a little boy called Jack in March 2008, and moved to Bromley in 2010. Pete had a little boy named James in 2011. It was strange; all the boys were living in the same village when we left to live in Menorca, and when we returned, Paul had moved out to Menorca, Brian was in London and Pete was in the village! They all make the effort to meet up and spend time together; Brian and Pete will go to Paul's, and Paul comes over twice a year at least. They're a good bunch of lads, I love them to bits – if their kids turn out as good as they have, they'll be very happy. They've all got hearts of gold and I can't speak highly enough of them - I'm so proud of them. Our grandkids are fantastic, but the big difference with them and my kids is that I can give them back! They bring a smile to my face - unfortunately for the first months after Jack was born, we were in Menorca, and we were only back for about six months before Brian moved to Bromley. It's great whenever we get to see him; he always used to be more like "Granddad, Granddad" but these days it's more like "Grandma, Grandma"! He's a credit to his mum and dad, as is James, who we see a lot more of. I get a lot of pleasure from them both.

My sister has been married fifty-odd years, my brother forty odd years and Maureen and myself have been married almost forty years too. I hope our boys look at us and that we're inspirations to them in their own relationships; you've got to have a strong person behind you. After all, Maureen brought the kids up. I was playing football, enjoying myself. In later years I'd take the kids to play football and pick them up from school but Maureen had the hard tasks. Part of the reason we went to Menorca was to get a better quality of life which Maureen deserved so much after working so hard. It shows the strength of our relationship that after thirty years we still wanted to go away together and keep spending all of our time together. We enjoy each other's company; she knows me inside out. I do my best around the house - well, I cook and that's about it!

13. LOOKING BACK

SINCE I'VE BEEN BACK it's been difficult to find something to do. I did have thoughts about scouting but in the time after I retired from playing and was coaching Whitworth, scouts were on peanuts; at Rochdale I would scout both players and opposition teams, and though I have often thought about it I feel I've reached the point where instead of watching every game I'll now just watch teams I'm interested in; I watch United, I enjoy watching Real Madrid and Barcelona, but I'll also enjoy watching cricket and rugby too. I started playing football as a child and after having such a long attachment with the game, I didn't want to be tied to it any more, I wanted to be able to choose what I wanted to do. Before we left for Menorca I was involved with United for both MUTV and on the corporate side before games; I enjoyed both, although I probably enjoyed the phone-ins more. I enjoy interacting with supporters whereas sometimes with doing the corporate I might not be able to go into the stadium and watch the game live. If I was in the South Stand I might be able to sneak in the Press Box, otherwise I'd have to watch it on one of the televisions. Following my return I've not yet been involved with the club, though I do get asked a lot by supporters and people about Liverpool due to the Cup Final in 1977.

If I was to say which question I get asked most, it would

probably be "What's your favourite game", and it would have to be that final, because we won something. It must be hard for someone to have played for Manchester United and not win anything; I was there for eleven years, winning the Second Division in the Lancashire League, the Second Division of the Football League and the FA Cup, and it was the final that stands out. It was special because we'd lost the year before and we were playing Liverpool who were the best team at the time. The memory of purposefully soaking everything up, after being at the club for nine years and finally having something to show for it. We got a plaque for winning the Second Division and I don't know where that is; nor could I tell you where the trophy for the "B" team is. But I could tell you where my FA Cup winner's medal is!

Apart from that one specific memory that stands out, I look back on my early days at the club with a special fondness. Being there at the club and having experiences like being paid fifty pence to clean Paddy Crerand's shoes – I'm sure he won't remember it! – and I would enjoy going in on a Sunday and cleaning the boots, because the first team players might be around and that was what you wanted in order to feel part of it more. You were aspiring to be these people and it was exciting to be near them.

Even the troubles – my sinus, my appendix and breaking my leg – I battled through those tough times with my mates at the club. Likewise with Sammy, when he had a car crash as a kid, I'd pick him up and take him around. When he was homesick I looked after him. When you come through together, there's more of a bond than there is with people who sign. I got on well with Gordon Hill, Stevie Coppell,

Panch... there were some I didn't socialise with, but I felt then and still feel now a strong affinity to the lads I came through with. It's still a source of confusion to me why Eric Young never made it. I wanted to ask Wilf McGuinness once why I made it and Eric didn't; what made me different to the rest that made me the last one to leave. I don't know the answer, and I never saw myself as a better player than any of them. I used to look up to Eric Young and wanted to be as good as him. When he left at 19, I thought, what chance have I got? Perhaps breaking my leg when I did actually helped me; I'm certain that the help of Bill Foulkes did. The arrival of Tommy Doc helped me. That combination of events enabled me to stay there longer than anybody else.

The 1992 Youth Team that came through together were a special lot and that happens rarely; United have been fortunate that they've had it happen a few times. Some clubs don't even get a team like that once. Whenever United sign a group of lads there's an expectation that they can break through. When I signed there was Tommy O'Neill, Eric, Kevin Lewis and Bobby Lomas who all played for England schoolboys who you thought would definitely make it. Tommy arrived with his reputation for giving kids chances and I watched a few of them, kids younger than me, making their debuts in the Anglo-Italian Cup - I was thinking at some stages that I would be gone. Not only did I think I was behind the likes of Eric, but kids younger than me like Paul Jones were getting a chance and I was nearly twenty.

That full pre-season that I got really helped; it was a make or break season for me but getting as fit as I possibly could gave me a great chance. It was just a matter of getting that opportunity to prove myself after running the practice matches – and Bill Foulkes' help in getting me fit was something I consider extremely influential to my success. He was a fitness fanatic and he taught me that I had to put the effort in; we didn't have the facilities to help remedial work so Bill's assistance was ahead of its time. Physically, Bill had a major influence on preparing me for the rigours of a career at Manchester United but mentally there is no question who was my biggest influence; and that is the Doc. He could get to me, he knew what buttons to press with me. He was somebody I needed; somebody who had faith in me, who wanted me to play for him, who appreciated my love for the club. He didn't rush me in, he gave me every chance to prove myself. He gave me confidence; he knew when to give me a pat on the back or a quiet word in my ear. He knew I liked the easy life, so he knew when to push me, like the time he sent me off to play with England when I could have stayed behind and missed out. I did want to have a quiet life but then you couldn't do that when you were living in Manchester and playing for Manchester United.

When I lived in Barnsley, I didn't have to walk more than twenty metres from my front door before I would see someone playing football. In cricket season, they'd be playing cricket, even games like tennis and skittles on summer days. I'm still a huge fan of Manchester United who are still very much my team; I watch every game. And in the summer, when we go to Menorca, I enjoy nothing more than going to the local cricket club.

How does the old saying go? The more things change, the more things stay the same.

ARNIE SIDEBOTTOM

Brian and I were at school together, at Racecommon Road in Barnsley - we were good friends, and he was a talented player at school at both football and cricket. He was far better than me at football! He could have been a cricketer; he was a really good player for Barnsley boys.

A year after he signed for United I was spotted by a scout and joined him at Old Trafford; with Brian and I being two Barnsley lads, and knowing each other well, he really helped me settle in by taking me out and showing me around. Though I didn't play many times, I can remember lining up with Brian to play at Anfield; we had George Best in our side and were against Toshack and Keegan... what a fantastic experience for two lads from Barnsley!

It was a surprise but a honour when I was asked to Brian's best man for his wedding to Maureen - it was top drawer and I was really pleased, Maureen is fantastic and a lovely lady too.

Brian was an absolute top player, a top professional who always gave 100% in every single game. What a player, and as a friend, what a great lad. Down to earth, a typical Barnsley and Yorkshire character who called a spade a spade - Brian is a really top bloke, and was a fantastic player.

GORDON HILL

When I signed for Manchester United, Brian was the first to greet me at training. He was living a couple of houses away from Jim Holton, another nice person, (who was taken too early in his life – God rest his soul) who I became friends with as well – both welcomed me to United.

I can also remember going round to Brian's house to have some lunch and meet his wife. He said that it was a nice place to live and showed me around. That, I will never forget, and the reason I never forgot was Big Jim lived a couple of houses away and had just broken his leg and had it in plaster, and then drove his car through the back of his garage having got his plastered leg stuck on the throttle!!

I had the pleasure of playing with Brian, and he was the same as a player, always willing to help and support you. I could always count on him to back me up in a game and also tell me off if I did something stupid. He worked well with Martin, and those two was our main central defence men – they would have a never say die attitude and could always be depended on, Martin was cool headed and Brian was the enforcer which relayed into the rest of the team.

Like the Boss TD used to say to them, "The ball may pass by you, the man may pass by you... but not both together". He should have played longer at the club but alas, he became another casualty of Dave Sexton and got moved on.

Of course Brian went on to gain international recognition which said a lot for him and his honest playing ability. As a person I would just say that I got on very well with him, and liked him. I have not seen Brian for a few years and after we finished we kept in touch at reunions and such, but I moved away and have not seen him since – I would just like to say, thanks for being a friend Brian. My door is always open.

STATISTICS

1. INTERNATIONAL APPEARANCES

2. ENGLISH CLUB CAREER

INTERNATIONAL APPEARANCES

1.   v WALES (Ninian Park, 8th May 1976)
Home Championship Match. Started. Won 1-0
2.   v NORTHERN IRELAND (Wembley, 11th May 1976)
Home Championship Match. Started. Won 4-0
3.   v REPUBLIC OF IRELAND
(Wembley, 8th September 1976)
Friendly Match. Started. Drew 1-1
4.   v FINLAND (Wembley, 13th October 1976)
World Cup Qualifier. Started. Won 2-1
5.   v ITALY (Stadio Olimpico, 17th November 1976)
World Cup Qualifier. Started. Lost 0-2
6.   v HOLLAND (Wembley, 9th February 1977)
Friendly Match. Started, substituted after 40 minutes. Lost 0-2
7.   v NORTHERN IRELAND (Windsor Park, 28th May
1977) Home Championship Match. Started. Won 2-1
8.   v WALES (Wembley, 31st May 1977)
Home Championship Match. Started. Lost 0-1
9.   v SCOTLAND (Wembley, 4th June 1977)
Home Championship Match.
Started, substituted after 57 minutes. Lost 1-2
10.   v BRAZIL (Estadio do Maracana 8th June 1977)
Friendly Match. Started. Drew 0-0
11.   v ARGENTINA (La Bombonera, 12th June 1977)
Friendly Match. Started, substituted at half time. Drew 0-0
12.   v URUGUAY (Estadio Centenario, 15th June 1977)
Friendly Match. Started. Drew 0-0
13.   v BRAZIL (Wembley, 19th April 1978)
Friendly Match. Started. Drew 1-1
14.   v WALES (Ninian Park, 13th May 1978)
Home Championship Match. Started. Won 3-1

15.   v NORTHERN IRELAND (Wembley, 16th May 1978)
Home Championship Match. Started. Won 1-0
16.   v SCOTLAND (Hampden Park, 20th May 1978)
*Home Championship Match. Substituted on for Emlyn Hughes, 73 mins.
Won 1-0*
17.   v HUNGARY (Wembley, 24th May 1978)
Friendly Match. Substituted on for Dave Watson, half time. Won 4-1
18.   v AUSTRALIA (Sydney Cricket Ground, 31st May 1980)
Friendly Match. Substituted on for Bryan Robson, 88 minutes. Won
2-1

ENGLAND STATISTICS

Caps : 18
Starts : 15
Goals : 0
Won : 9
Drew: 5
Lost : 4
Minutes played in competitive matches : 794
Total minutes played for England : 1286

CLUB CAREER

MANCHESTER UNITED - 1973-74 TO 1978-79

LEEDS UNITED - 1979-80 TO 1981-82

SUMMARY

SEASON	TEAM	APPEARANCES	GOALS
1973/74	Man Utd	36	3
1974/75	Man Utd	39 (2)	4
1975/76	Man Utd	40	0
1976/77	Man Utd	40	3
1977/78	Man Utd	31	1
1978/79	Man Utd	32 (1)	2
1979/80	Leeds	22 (2)	0
1980/81	Leeds	36	1
1981/82	Leeds	10 (2)	0

MANCHESTER UNITED

1973-74

Date	Opponent	Competition	Result	Venue	Scorers
Sat 08 Sep	Ipswich Town	League	L 1-2	Portman Road	Trevor Anderson 89'
Sat 22 Sep	Leeds United	League	D 0-0	Elland Road	
Sat 29 Sep	LIVERPOOL	League	D 0-0	Old Trafford	
Sat 06 Oct	Wolverhampton Wanderers	League	L 1-2	Molineux	Sammy McIlroy
Mon 08 Oct	MIDDLESBROUGH	League Cup	L 0-1	Old Trafford	
Sat 13 Oct	DERBY COUNTY	League	L 0-1	Old Trafford	
Sat 20 Oct	BIRMINGHAM CITY	League	W 1-0	Old Trafford	Alex Stepney (pen)
Sat 27 Oct	Burnley	League	D 0-0	Turf Moor	
Sat 03 Nov	CHELSEA	League	D 2-2	Old Trafford	Trevor Young 88', Brian Greenhoff 90'
Sat 10 Nov	Tottenham Hotspur	League	L 1-2	White Hart Lane	George Best 12'
Sat 17 Nov	Newcastle United	League	L 2-3	St. James Park	Lou Macari, George Graham 43'
Sat 24 Nov	NORWICH CITY	League	D 0-0	Old Trafford	
Sat 08 Dec	SOUTHAMPTON	League	D 0-0	Old Trafford	
Sat 15 Dec	COVENTRY CITY	League	L 2-3	Old Trafford	George Best 47', Willie Morgan 72'
Sat 22 Dec	Liverpool	League	L 0-2	Anfield	
Wed 26 Dec	SHEFFIELD UNITED	League	L 1-2	Old Trafford	Lou Macari
Sat 29 Dec	IPSWICH TOWN	League	W 2-0	Old Trafford	Sammy McIlroy 77', Lou Macari 80'
Tue 01 Jan	Queens Park Rangers	League	L 0-3	Loftus Road	
Sat 05 Jan	PLYMOUTH ARGYLE	F.A. Cup	W 1-0	Old Trafford	Macari
Sat 12 Jan	West Ham United	League	L 1-2	Boleyn Ground	Sammy McIlroy 67'
Sat 19 Jan	ARSENAL	League	D 1-1	Old Trafford	Steve James 50'
Sat 26 Jan	IPSWICH TOWN	F.A. Cup	L 0-1	Old Trafford	
Sat 02 Feb	Coventry City	League	L 0-1	Highfield Road	
Sat 09 Feb	LEEDS UNITED	League	L 0-2	Old Trafford	
Sat 16 Feb	Derby County	League	D 2-2	Baseball Ground	Stewart Houston, Brian Greenhoff
Sat 23 Feb	WOLVERHAMPTON WANDERERS	League	D 0-0	Old Trafford	
Sat 02 Mar	Sheffield United	League	W 1-0	Bramall Lane	Lou Macari 35'
Wed 13 Mar	Manchester City	League	D 0-0	Maine Road	
Sat 16 Mar	Birmingham City	League	L 0-1	St. Andrews	
Sat 23 Mar	TOTTENHAM HOTSPUR	League	L 0-1	Old Trafford	
Sat 30 Mar	Chelsea	League	W 3-1	Stamford Bridge	Willie Morgan 7', Gerry Daly 60', Sammy McIlroy 67'
Wed 03 Apr	BURNLEY	League	D 3-3	Old Trafford	Sammy McIlroy, Alex Forsyth, Jim Holton
Sat 06 Apr	Norwich City	League	W 2-0	Carrow Road	Lou Macari 65', Brian Greenhoff 86'
Sat 13 Apr	NEWCASTLE UNITED	League	W 1-0	Old Trafford	Jim McCalliog
Mon 15 Apr	EVERTON	League	W 3-0	Old Trafford	Jim McCalliog x2, Stewart Houston
Sat 20 Apr	Southampton	League	D 1-1	The Dell	Jim McCalliog (pen)
Tue 23 Apr	Everton	League	L 0-1	Goodison Park	
Sat 27 Apr	MANCHESTER CITY	League	L 0-1	Old Trafford	
Mon 29 Apr	Stoke City	League	L 0-1	Victoria Ground	

1974-75

Sat 17 Aug	Orient	A	League	W 2-0	Brisbane Road	Willie Morgan, Stewart Houston
Sat 24 Aug	MILLWALL	H	League	W 4-0	Old Trafford	Gerry Daly x3 (2 pens), Stuart Pearson
Wed 28 Aug	PORTSMOUTH	H	League	W 2-1	Old Trafford	Gerry Daly (pen), Sammy McIlroy
Sat 31 Aug	Cardiff City	A	League	W 1-0	Ninian Park	Gerry Daly (pen)
Sat 07 Sep	NOTTINGHAM FOREST	H	League	D 2-2	Old Trafford	Brian Greenhoff, Sammy McIlroy
Wed 11 Sep	CHARLTON ATHLETIC	H	League Cup	W 5-1	Old Trafford	Macari (2), Houston, McIlroy, own goal
Sat 14 Sep	West Bromwich Albion	A	League	D 1-1	The Hawthorns	Stuart Pearson
Mon 16 Sep	Millwall	A	League	W 1-0	The Den (old)	Gerry Daly (pen)
Sat 21 Sep	BRISTOL ROVERS	H	League	W 2-0	Old Trafford	Brian Greenhoff, Frankie Prince (o.g.)
Wed 25 Sep	BOLTON WANDERERS	H	League	W 3-0	Old Trafford	Lou Macari, Stewart Houston, McAllister (o.g.)
Sat 28 Sep	Norwich City	A	League	L 0-2	Carrow Road	
Sat 05 Oct	Fulham	A	League	W 2-1	Craven Cottage	Stuart Pearson x2
Wed 09 Oct	MANCHESTER CITY	H	League Cup	W 1-0	Old Trafford	Daly
Sat 12 Oct	NOTTS. COUNTY	H	League	W 1-0	Old Trafford	Sammy McIlroy
Tue 15 Oct	Portsmouth	A	League	D 0-0	Fratton Park	
Sat 19 Oct	Blackpool	A	League	W 3-0	Bloomfield Road	Alex Forsyth 22', Lou Macari 60', Jim McCalliog 72'
Sat 26 Oct	SOUTHAMPTON	H	League	W 1-0	Old Trafford	Stuart Pearson
Sat 02 Nov	OXFORD UNITED	H	League	W 4-0	Old Trafford	Stuart Pearson 9', 32', 45', Lou Macari 24'
Sat 09 Nov	Bristol City	A	League	L 0-1	Ashton Gate	
Wed 13 Nov	BURNLEY	H	League Cup	W 3-2	Old Trafford	Macari (2), Morgan
Sat 16 Nov	ASTON VILLA	H	League	W 2-1	Old Trafford	Gerry Daly 2', 69' (pen)
Sat 23 Nov	Hull City	A	League	L 0-2	Boothferry Park	
Sat 30 Nov	SUNDERLAND	H	League	W 3-2	Old Trafford	Stuart Pearson 11', Willie Morgan 55', Sammy McIlroy 61'
Wed 04 Dec	Middlesbrough	A	League Cup	D 0-0	Ayresome Park	
Sat 07 Dec	Sheffield Wednesday	A	League	D 4-4	Hillsborough	Stewart Houston 7', Lou Macari 53', 85', Stuart Pearson 63'
Sat 14 Dec	ORIENT	H	League	D 0-0	Old Trafford	
Wed 18 Dec	MIDDLESBROUGH	H	League Cup	W 3-0	Old Trafford	Macari, McIlroy, Pearson
Sat 21 Dec	York City	A	League	W 1-0	Bootham Crescent	Stuart Pearson 18'
Thu 26 Dec	WEST BROMWICH ALBION	H	League	W 2-1	Old Trafford	Sammy McIlroy 5', Gerry Daly 63' (pen)
Sat 28 Dec	Oldham Athletic	A	League	L 0-1	Boundary Park	
Sat 04 Jan	WALSALL	H	F.A. Cup	D 0-0	Old Trafford	
Tue 07 Jan	Walsall	A	F.A. Cup	L 2-3	Fellows Park	Daly, McIlroy
			after extra time			
Sat 11 Jan	SHEFFIELD WEDNESDAY	H	League	W 2-0	Old Trafford	Jim McCalliog 22' (pen), 50'
Wed 15 Jan	NORWICH CITY	H	League Cup	D 2-2	Old Trafford	Macari (2)
Sat 18 Jan	Sunderland	A	League	D 0-0	Roker Park	
Wed 22 Jan	Norwich City	A	League Cup	L 0-1	Carrow Road	
			Norwich City won 3-2 on aggregate			
Sat 01 Feb	BRISTOL CITY	H	League	L 0-1	Old Trafford	
Sat 08 Feb	Oxford United	A	League	L 0-1	Manor Ground	
Sat 15 Feb	HULL CITY	H	League	W 2-0	Old Trafford	Stewart Houston 2', Stuart Pearson 45'
Sat 22 Feb	Aston Villa	A	League	L 0-2	Villa Park	
Sat 01 Mar	CARDIFF CITY	H	League	W 4-0	Old Trafford	Stewart Houston 59', Stuart Pearson 62', Sammy McIlroy 85', Lou Macari 88'
Sat 08 Mar	Bolton Wanderers	A	League	W 1-0	Burnden Park	Stuart Pearson 29'
Sat 15 Mar	NORWICH CITY	H	League	D 1-1	Old Trafford	Stuart Pearson 50'
Sat 22 Mar	Nottingham Forest	A	League	W 1-0	City Ground	Gerry Daly 35'
Fri 28 Mar	Bristol Rovers	A	League	D 1-1	Eastville Stadium	Lou Macari 35'
Sat 29 Mar	YORK CITY	H	League	W 2-1	Old Trafford	Willie Morgan 74', Lou Macari 86'
Mon 31 Mar	OLDHAM ATHLETIC	H	League	W 3-2	Old Trafford	Sammy McIlroy 23', Lou Macari, Steve Coppell
Sat 05 Apr	Southampton	A	League	W 1-0	The Dell	Lou Macari 76'
Sat 12 Apr	FULHAM	H	League	W 1-0	Old Trafford	Gerry Daly 20'
Sat 19 Apr	Notts. County	A	League	D 2-2	Meadow Lane	Stewart Houston 12', Brian Greenhoff 40'
Sat 26 Apr	BLACKPOOL	H	League	W 4-0	Old Trafford	Stuart Pearson 20', 54', Lou Macari 78', Brian Greenhoff 82'

1975-76

Sat 16 Aug	Wolverhampton Wanderers	A	League	W 2-0	Molineux	Lou Macari 73', 79'
Tue 19 Aug	Birmingham City	A	League	W 2-0	St. Andrews	Sammy McIlroy 47', 82'
Sat 23 Aug	SHEFFIELD UNITED	H	League	W 5-1	Old Trafford	Stuart Pearson 11', 40', Badger (o.g.) 38', Gerry Daly 64', Sammy McIlroy 84'
Wed 27 Aug	COVENTRY CITY	H	League	D 1-1	Old Trafford	Stuart Pearson 23'
Sat 30 Aug	Stoke City	A	League	W 1-0	Victoria Ground	Dodd (o.g.) 15'
Sat 06 Sep	TOTTENHAM HOTSPUR	H	League	W 3-2	Old Trafford	John Pratt (o.g.) 26', Gerry Daly 45', 47' (pen)
Wed 10 Sep	BRENTFORD	H	League Cup	W 2-1	Old Trafford	Macari, McIlroy
Sat 20 Sep	IPSWICH TOWN	H	League	W 1-0	Old Trafford	Stewart Houston 28'
Wed 24 Sep	Derby County	A	League	L 1-2	Baseball Ground	Gerry Daly 82'
Sat 27 Sep	Manchester City	A	League	D 2-2	Maine Road	David McCreery 29', Lou Macari 31'
Sat 04 Oct	LEICESTER CITY	H	League	D 0-0	Old Trafford	
Wed 08 Oct	Aston Villa	A	League Cup	W 2-1	Villa Park	Coppell, Macari
Sat 11 Oct	Leeds United	A	League	W 2-1	Elland Road	Sammy McIlroy 30', 55'
Sat 18 Oct	ARSENAL	H	League	W 3-1	Old Trafford	Steve Coppell 35', 68', Stuart Pearson 48'
Sat 25 Oct	West Ham United	A	League	L 1-2	Boleyn Ground	Lou Macari 55'
Sat 01 Nov	NORWICH CITY	H	League	W 1-0	Old Trafford	Stuart Pearson 79'
Sat 08 Nov	Liverpool	A	League	L 1-3	Anfield	Steve Coppell 52'
Wed 12 Nov	Manchester City	A	League Cup	L 0-4	Maine Road	
Sat 15 Nov	ASTON VILLA	H	League	W 2-0	Old Trafford	Steve Coppell 15', Sammy McIlroy 55'
Sat 22 Nov	Arsenal	A	League	L 1-3	Highbury	Stuart Pearson 58'
Sat 29 Nov	NEWCASTLE UNITED	H	League	W 1-0	Old Trafford	Gerry Daly 68'
Sat 06 Dec	Middlesbrough	A	League	D 0-0	Ayresome Park	
Sat 13 Dec	Sheffield United	A	League	W 4-1	Bramall Lane	Stuart Pearson 3', 74', Gordon Hill 31', Lou Macari 87'
Sat 20 Dec	WOLVERHAMPTON WANDERERS	H	League	W 1-0	Old Trafford	Gordon Hill 90'
Tue 23 Dec	Everton	A	League	D 1-1	Goodison Park	Lou Macari 26'
Sat 27 Dec	BURNLEY	H	League	W 2-1	Old Trafford	Sammy McIlroy 51', Lou Macari 80'
Sat 03 Jan	OXFORD UNITED	H	F.A. Cup	W 2-1	Old Trafford	Daly (2)
Sat 10 Jan	QUEENS PARK RANGERS	H	League	W 2-1	Old Trafford	Gordon Hill 15', Sammy McIlroy 57'
Sat 17 Jan	Tottenham Hotspur	A	League	D 1-1	White Hart Lane	Gordon Hill 4'
Sat 24 Jan	PETERBOROUGH UNITED	H	F.A. Cup	W 3-1	Old Trafford	Forsyth, Hill, McIlroy
Sat 31 Jan	BIRMINGHAM CITY	H	League	W 3-1	Old Trafford	Alex Forsyth 36', Lou Macari 43', Sammy McIlroy 88'
Sat 07 Feb	Coventry City	A	League	D 1-1	Highfield Road	Lou Macari 82'
Sat 14 Feb	Leicester City	A	F.A. Cup	W 2-1	Filbert Street	Daly, Macari
Wed 18 Feb	LIVERPOOL	H	League	D 0-0	Old Trafford	
Sat 21 Feb	Aston Villa	A	League	L 1-2	Villa Park	Lou Macari 44'
Wed 25 Feb	DERBY COUNTY	H	League	D 1-1	Old Trafford	Stuart Pearson 27'
Sat 28 Feb	WEST HAM UNITED	H	League	W 4-0	Old Trafford	Alex Forsyth 49', Lou Macari 56', David McCreery 76', Stuart Pearson 88'
Sat 06 Mar	WOLVERHAMPTON WANDERERS	H	F.A. Cup	D 1-1	Old Trafford	Daly
Tue 09 Mar	Wolverhampton Wanderers	A	F.A. Cup	W 3-2	Molineux	Greenhoff, McIlroy, Pearson
			after extra time, 90 minutes			
Sat 13 Mar	LEEDS UNITED	H	League	W 3-2	Old Trafford	Stewart Houston 3', Stuart Pearson 42', Gerry Daly 61'
Wed 17 Mar	Norwich City	A	League	D 1-1	Carrow Road	Gordon Hill 9'
Sat 20 Mar	Newcastle United	A	League	W 4-3	St. James Park	Stuart Pearson 12', 58', John Bird (o.g.) 15', Pat Howard (o.g.) 49'
Sat 27 Mar	MIDDLESBROUGH	H	League	W 3-0	Old Trafford	Gerry Daly 60' (pen), David McCreery 65', Gordon Hill 70'
Sat 03 Apr	Derby County	Neu	F.A. Cup	W 2-0	Hillsborough	Hill (2)
			played at Hillsborough			
Sat 10 Apr	Ipswich Town	A	League	L 0-3	Portman Road	
Sat 17 Apr	EVERTON	H	League	W 2-1	Old Trafford	Roger Kenyon (o.g.) 56', David McCreery 69'
Mon 19 Apr	Burnley	A	League	W 1-0	Turf Moor	Lou Macari 57'
Wed 21 Apr	STOKE CITY	H	League	L 0-1	Old Trafford	
Sat 24 Apr	Leicester City	A	League	L 1-2	Filbert Street	Peter Coyne 57'
Sat 01 May	Southampton	Neu	F.A. Cup	L 0-1	Wembley (old)	
			played at Wembley			

1976-77

Date	Opponent	H/A	Competition	Result	Venue	Scorers
Sat 21 Aug	BIRMINGHAM CITY	H	League	D 2-2	Old Trafford	Coppell, Pearson
Tue 24 Aug	Coventry City	A	League	W 2-0	Highfield Road	Macari, Hill
Sat 28 Aug	Derby County	A	League	D 0-0	Baseball Ground	
Wed 01 Sep	TRANMERE ROVERS	H	League Cup	W 5-0	Old Trafford	Daly (2), Hill, Macari, Pearson
Sat 04 Sep	TOTTENHAM HOTSPUR	H	League	L 2-3	Old Trafford	Coppell, Pearson
Sat 11 Sep	Newcastle United	A	League	D 2-2	St. James Park	Pearson, Greenhoff
Wed 15 Sep	Ajax Amsterdam	A	UEFA Cup	L 0-1		
Sat 18 Sep	MIDDLESBROUGH	H	League	W 2-0	Old Trafford	Pearson, McAndrew (o.g.)
Wed 22 Sep	SUNDERLAND	H	League Cup	D 2-2	Old Trafford	Pearson, own goal
Sat 25 Sep	Manchester City	A	League	W 3-1	Maine Road	Daly, Coppell, McCreery
Wed 29 Sep	AJAX AMSTERDAM	H	UEFA Cup	W 2-0	Old Trafford	Macari, McIlroy

Manchester United won 2-1 on aggregate

Date	Opponent	H/A	Competition	Result	Venue	Scorers
Sat 02 Oct	Leeds United	A	League	W 2-0	Elland Road	Daly, Coppell
Mon 04 Oct	Sunderland	A	League Cup	D 2-2	Roker Park	Daly, Greenhoff (B)
after extra time						
Wed 06 Oct	SUNDERLAND	H	League Cup	W 1-0	Old Trafford	Greenhoff (B)
Sat 16 Oct	West Bromwich Albion	A	League	L 0-4	The Hawthorns	
Wed 20 Oct	JUVENTUS	H	UEFA Cup	W 1-0	Old Trafford	Hill
Sat 23 Oct	NORWICH CITY	H	League	D 2-2	Old Trafford	Daly 38' (pen), Hill 42'
Wed 27 Oct	NEWCASTLE UNITED	H	League Cup	W 7-2	Old Trafford	Hill (3), Nicholl, Pearson, Houston, Coppell
Sat 30 Oct	IPSWICH TOWN	H	League	L 0-1	Old Trafford	
Wed 03 Nov	Juventus	A	UEFA Cup	L 0-3		

Juventus won 3-1 on aggregate

Date	Opponent	H/A	Competition	Result	Venue	Scorers
Sat 06 Nov	Aston Villa	A	League	L 2-3	Villa Park	Pearson, Hill
Wed 10 Nov	SUNDERLAND	H	League	D 3-3	Old Trafford	Greenhoff (B), Pearson, Hill
Sat 20 Nov	Leicester City	A	League	D 1-1	Filbert Street	Daly (pen)
Sat 27 Nov	WEST HAM UNITED	H	League	L 0-2	Old Trafford	
Wed 01 Dec	EVERTON	H	League Cup	L 0-3	Old Trafford	
Sat 18 Dec	Arsenal	A	League	L 1-3	Highbury	McIlroy
Mon 27 Dec	EVERTON	H	League	W 4-0	Old Trafford	Greenhoff (J), Pearson, Macari, Hill
Sat 01 Jan	ASTON VILLA	H	League	W 2-0	Old Trafford	Pearson (2)
Mon 03 Jan	Ipswich Town	A	League	L 1-2	Portman Road	Pearson
Sat 08 Jan	WALSALL	H	F.A. Cup	W 1-0	Old Trafford	Hill
Sat 15 Jan	COVENTRY CITY	H	League	W 2-0	Old Trafford	Macari (2)
Wed 19 Jan	BRISTOL CITY	H	League	W 2-1	Old Trafford	Pearson, Greenhoff
Sat 22 Jan	Birmingham City	A	League	W 3-2	St. Andrews	Houston, Greenhoff, Pearson
Sat 29 Jan	QUEENS PARK RANGERS	H	F.A. Cup	W 1-0	Old Trafford	Macari
Sat 05 Feb	DERBY COUNTY	H	League	W 3-1	Old Trafford	Houston, Macari, Powell (o.g.)
Sat 12 Feb	Tottenham Hotspur	A	League	W 3-1	White Hart Lane	McIlroy, Macari, Hill
Wed 16 Feb	LIVERPOOL	H	League	D 0-0	Old Trafford	
Sat 19 Feb	NEWCASTLE UNITED	H	League	W 3-1	Old Trafford	Greenhoff (3)
Sat 26 Feb	Southampton	A	F.A. Cup	D 2-2	The Dell	Hill, Macari
Sat 05 Mar	MANCHESTER CITY	H	League	W 3-1	Old Trafford	Pearson, Hill, Coppell
Tue 08 Mar	SOUTHAMPTON	H	F.A. Cup	W 2-1	Old Trafford	Greenhoff (J) (2)
Sat 12 Mar	LEEDS UNITED	H	League	W 1-0	Old Trafford	Cherry (o.g.)
Sat 19 Mar	ASTON VILLA	H	F.A. Cup	W 2-1	Old Trafford	Houston, Macari
Sat 02 Apr	Norwich City	A	League	L 1-2	Carrow Road	Powell 57' (o.g.)
Tue 05 Apr	Everton	A	League	W 2-1	Goodison Park	Hill (2)
Sat 09 Apr	STOKE CITY	H	League	W 3-0	Old Trafford	Houston, Macari, Pearson
Mon 11 Apr	Sunderland	A	League	L 1-2	Roker Park	Hill (pen)
Sat 16 Apr	LEICESTER CITY	H	League	D 1-1	Old Trafford	Greenhoff (J)
Tue 19 Apr	Queens Park Rangers	A	League	L 0-4	Loftus Road	
Sat 23 Apr	Leeds United	Neu	F.A. Cup	W 2-1	Hillsborough	Coppell, Greenhoff (J)
					played at Hillsborough	
Tue 26 Apr	Middlesbrough	A	League	L 0-3	Ayresome Park	
Sat 30 Apr	QUEENS PARK RANGERS	H	League	W 1-0	Old Trafford	Macari
Tue 03 May	Liverpool	A	League	L 0-1	Anfield	
Sat 07 May	Bristol City	A	League	D 1-1	Ashton Gate	Greenhoff (J) (pen)
Wed 11 May	Stoke City	A	League	D 3-3	Victoria Ground	Hill (2), McCreery
Sat 14 May	ARSENAL	H	League	W 3-2	Old Trafford	Greenhoff (J), Macari, Hill
Mon 16 May	West Ham United	A	League	L 2-4	Boleyn Ground	Hill, Pearson
Sat 21 May	Liverpool	Neu	F.A. Cup	W 2-1	Wembley (old)	Greenhoff (J), Pearson

1977-78

Sat 13 Aug	Liverpool	Neu	Ch. Shield	D 0-0	Wembley (old)	

shield shared; played at Wembley

Sat 20 Aug	Birmingham City	A	League	W 4-1	St. Andrews	Lou Macari x3, Gordon Hill
Wed 24 Aug	COVENTRY CITY	H	League	W 2-1	Old Trafford	Gordon Hill (pen), David McCreery
Sat 27 Aug	IPSWICH TOWN	H	League	D 0-0	Old Trafford	
Tue 30 Aug	Arsenal	A	League Cup	L 2-3	Highbury	McCreery, Pearson
Wed 14 Sep	St. Etienne	A	C.W.C.	D 1-1		
Sat 17 Sep	CHELSEA	H	League	L 0-1	Old Trafford	
Sat 24 Sep	Leeds United	A	League	D 1-1	Elland Road	Hill
Sat 01 Oct	LIVERPOOL	H	League	W 2-0	Old Trafford	McIlroy, Macari
Wed 05 Oct	ST. ETIENNE	H	C.W.C.	W 2-0	Old Trafford	Coppell, Pearson

Manchester United won 3-1 on aggregate

Sat 08 Oct	Middlesbrough	A	League	L 1-2	Ayresome Park	Coppell
Sat 12 Nov	Nottingham Forest	A	League	L 1-2	City Ground	Pearson
Sat 19 Nov	NORWICH CITY	H	League	W 1-0	Old Trafford	Pearson 73'
Sat 26 Nov	Queens Park Rangers	A	League	D 2-2	Loftus Road	Hill 43', 87'
Sat 03 Dec	WOLVERHAMPTON WANDERERS	H	League	W 3-1	Old Trafford	McIlroy 12', Greenhoff (J) 37', Pearson 83'
Sat 10 Dec	West Ham United	A	League	L 1-2	Boleyn Ground	McGrath 10'
Sat 17 Dec	NOTTINGHAM FOREST	H	League	L 0-4	Old Trafford	
Mon 26 Dec	Everton	A	League	W 6-2	Goodison Park	McIlroy, Coppell, Greenhoff (J), Macari (2), Hill
Tue 27 Dec	LEICESTER CITY	H	League	W 3-1	Old Trafford	Greenhoff (J), Coppell, Hill
Sat 31 Dec	Coventry City	A	League	L 0-3	Highfield Road	
Mon 02 Jan	BIRMINGHAM CITY	H	League	L 1-2	Old Trafford	Greenhoff (J)
Sat 07 Jan	Carlisle United	A	F.A. Cup	D 1-1	Brunton Park	Macari
Wed 11 Jan	CARLISLE UNITED	H	F.A. Cup	W 4-2	Old Trafford	Macari (2), Pearson (2)
Sat 14 Jan	Ipswich Town	A	League	W 2-1	Portman Road	McIlroy 11', Pearson
Sat 21 Jan	DERBY COUNTY	H	League	W 4-0	Old Trafford	Hill 6', 28' (pen), Pearson 70', Buchan 88'
Sat 28 Jan	WEST BROMWICH ALBION	H	F.A. Cup	D 1-1	Old Trafford	Coppell
Wed 01 Feb	West Bromwich Albion	A	F.A. Cup	L 2-3	The Hawthorns	Hill, Pearson

after extra time, 90 minutes

Wed 08 Feb	BRISTOL CITY	H	League	D 1-1	Old Trafford	Hill (pen)
Sat 11 Feb	Chelsea	A	League	D 2-2	Stamford Bridge	McIlroy 52', Hill 90' (pen)
Wed 01 Mar	LEEDS UNITED	H	League	L 0-1	Old Trafford	
Sat 04 Mar	MIDDLESBROUGH	H	League	D 0-0	Old Trafford	
Sat 11 Mar	Newcastle United	A	League	D 2-2	St. James Park	Jordan 27', Hill
Wed 15 Mar	MANCHESTER CITY	H	League	D 2-2	Old Trafford	Hill (2 pens)
Sat 18 Mar	WEST BROMWICH ALBION	H	League	D 1-1	Old Trafford	McQueen
Sat 25 Mar	Leicester City	A	League	W 3-2	Filbert Street	Pearson, Hill, Greenhoff (J)
Mon 27 Mar	EVERTON	H	League	L 1-2	Old Trafford	Hill (pen)
Wed 29 Mar	ASTON VILLA	H	League	D 1-1	Old Trafford	McIlroy
Sat 01 Apr	Arsenal	A	League	L 1-3	Highbury	Jordan
Sat 08 Apr	QUEENS PARK RANGERS	H	League	W 3-1	Old Trafford	Pearson x2 (1 pen), Grimes
Sat 15 Apr	Norwich City	A	League	W 3-1	Carrow Road	Jordan 67', McIlroy 69', Coppell 78'
Sat 22 Apr	WEST HAM UNITED	H	League	W 3-0	Old Trafford	Grimes (pen), McIlroy, Pearson
Tue 25 Apr	Bristol City	A	League	W 1-0	Ashton Gate	Pearson
Sat 29 Apr	Wolverhampton Wanderers	A	League	L 1-2	Molineux	Greenhoff (B)

1978-79

Sat 19 Aug	BIRMINGHAM CITY	H	League	W 1-0	Old Trafford	Jordan 70'
Wed 23 Aug	Leeds United	A	League	W 3-2	Elland Road	McIlroy, McQueen, Macari 82'
Sat 26 Aug	Ipswich Town	A	League	L 0-3	Portman Road	
Wed 30 Aug	Stockport County	A	League Cup	W 3-2	Edgeley Park	Greenhoff (J), Jordan, McIlroy
Sat 02 Sep	EVERTON	H	League	D 1-1	Old Trafford	Buchan 90'
Sat 09 Sep	Queens Park Rangers	A	League	D 1-1	Loftus Road	Greenhoff (J) 87'
Sat 16 Sep	NOTTINGHAM FOREST	H	League	D 1-1	Old Trafford	Greenhoff (J) 66'
Sat 23 Sep	Arsenal	A	League	D 1-1	Highbury	Coppell
Sat 30 Sep	MANCHESTER CITY	H	League	W 1-0	Old Trafford	Jordan 89'
Wed 04 Oct	WATFORD	H	League Cup	L 1-2	Old Trafford	Jordan
Sat 21 Oct	BRISTOL CITY	H	League	L 1-3	Old Trafford	Greenhoff (J) 70'
Sat 28 Oct	Wolverhampton Wanderers	A	League	W 4-2	Molineux	Greenhoff (J) 21', 28', Brian Greenhoff 30', Joe Jordan 52'
Sat 04 Nov	SOUTHAMPTON	H	League	D 1-1	Old Trafford	Greenhoff (J) 30'
Sat 11 Nov	Birmingham City	A	League	L 1-5	St. Andrews	Jordan 13'
Sat 18 Nov	IPSWICH TOWN	H	League	W 2-0	Old Trafford	Coppell 7', Greenhoff (J) 85'
Tue 21 Nov	Everton	A	League	L 0-3	Goodison Park	
Sat 25 Nov	Chelsea	A	League	W 1-0	Stamford Bridge	Greenhoff (J) 68'
Sat 09 Dec	Derby County	A	League	W 3-1	Baseball Ground	Ritchie (2) Greenhoff (J)
Sat 16 Dec	TOTTENHAM HOTSPUR	H	League	W 2-0	Old Trafford	McIlroy, Ritchie
Fri 22 Dec	Bolton Wanderers	A	League	L 0-3	Burnden Park	
Tue 26 Dec	LIVERPOOL	H	League	L 0-3	Old Trafford	
Sat 30 Dec	WEST BROMWICH ALBION	H	League	L 3-5	Old Trafford	Greenhoff (B) 21', McQueen, Sammy McIlroy
Mon 15 Jan	CHELSEA	H	F.A. Cup	W 3-0	Old Trafford	Coppell, Greenhoff (J), Grimes
Wed 31 Jan	Fulham	A	F.A. Cup	D 1-1	Craven Cottage	Greenhoff (J)
Sat 03 Feb	ARSENAL	H	League	L 0-2	Old Trafford	
Sat 10 Feb	Manchester City	A	League	W 3-0	Maine Road	Coppell 22', 35', Ritchie 69'
Mon 12 Feb	FULHAM	H	F.A. Cup	W 1-0	Old Trafford	Greenhoff (J)
Tue 20 Feb	Colchester United	A	F.A. Cup	W 1-0	Layer Road	Greenhoff (J)
Sat 24 Feb	ASTON VILLA	H	League	D 1-1	Old Trafford	Greenhoff (J) (pen)
Wed 28 Feb	QUEENS PARK RANGERS	H	League	W 2-0	Old Trafford	Greenhoff (J), Steve Coppell
Tue 20 Mar	Coventry City	A	League	L 3-4	Highfield Road	Coppell 36', 89', McIlroy 64'
Sat 24 Mar	LEEDS UNITED	H	League	W 4-1	Old Trafford	Ritchie ??, 18', 79', Thomas 20'
Tue 27 Mar	Middlesbrough	A	League	D 2-2	Ayresome Park	McQueen, Coppell 51'
Sat 31 Mar	Liverpool	Neu	F.A. Cup	D 2-2	Maine Road	Greenhoff (B), Jordan
					played at Maine Road	
Sat 14 Apr	Liverpool	A	League	L 0-2	Anfield	
Mon 16 Apr	COVENTRY CITY	H	League	D 0-0	Old Trafford	
Wed 18 Apr	Nottingham Forest	A	League	D 1-1	City Ground	Jordan
Sat 21 Apr	Tottenham Hotspur	A	League	D 1-1	White Hart Lane	McQueen
Sat 05 May	West Bromwich Albion	A	League	L 0-1	The Hawthorns	
Mon 07 May	WOLVERHAMPTON WANDERERS	H	League	W 3-2	Old Trafford	Ritchie, Coppell x2

LEEDS UNITED

1979-80

Date	Opponent	H/A	Competition	Result	Ground	Scorers	Attendance
Sat 18 Aug	Bristol City	A	League	D 2-2	Ashton Gate	Curtis (2)	22,845
Wed 22 Aug	EVERTON	H	League	W 2-0	Elland Road	Hird, Harris	30,000
Sat 25 Aug	Norwich City	A	League	L 1-2	Carrow Road	Hart	18,444
Wed 29 Aug	ARSENAL	H	League Cup	D 1-1	Elland Road	Stevenson (pen)	23,421
Sat 01 Sep	ARSENAL	H	League	D 1-1	Elland Road	Hart	23,245
Tue 04 Sep	Arsenal	A	League Cup	L 0-7	Highbury		35,129
Arsenal won 8-1 on aggregate							
Sat 08 Sep	Nottingham Forest	A	League	D 0-0	City Ground		26,914
Sat 15 Sep	LIVERPOOL	H	League	D 1-1	Elland Road	Curtis	39,779
Wed 19 Sep	Valletta	A	UEFA Cup	W 4-0		Hart, Graham (3)	18,000
Sat 22 Sep	Bolton Wanderers	A	League	D 1-1	Burnden Park	E.Gray (pen)	21,724
Sat 29 Sep	MANCHESTER CITY	H	League	L 1-2	Elland Road	Hankin	29,592
Wed 03 Oct	VALLETTA	H	UEFA Cup	W 3-0	Elland Road	Hart, Curtis, Hankin	13,682
Leeds United won 7-0 on aggregate							
Sat 06 Oct	IPSWICH TOWN	H	League	W 2-1	Elland Road	Cherry, Hird (pen)	19,342
Sat 13 Oct	Brighton & Hove Albion	A	League	D 0-0	Goldstone Ground		27,002
Sat 20 Oct	TOTTENHAM HOTSPUR	H	League	L 1-2	Elland Road	Hankin	25,203
Wed 24 Oct	University Craiova	A	UEFA Cup	L 0-2			40,000
Sat 27 Oct	Southampton	A	League	W 2-1	The Dell	Curtis, Entwistle	23,259
Sat 03 Nov	BRISTOL CITY	H	League	L 1-3	Elland Road	E.Gray	17,376
Wed 07 Nov	UNIVERSITY CRAIOVA	H	UEFA Cup	L 0-2	Elland Road		14,438
University Craiova won 4-0 on aggregate							
Sat 10 Nov	Coventry City	A	League	L 0-3	Highfield Road		19,402
Tue 13 Nov	Everton	A	League	L 1-5	Goodison Park	Hird	23,000
Sat 17 Nov	WEST BROMWICH ALBION	H	League	W 1-0	Elland Road	Connor	17,481
Sat 24 Nov	Aston Villa	A	League	D 0-0	Villa Park		29,736
Sat 01 Dec	CRYSTAL PALACE	H	League	W 1-0	Elland Road	Hird	21,330
Sat 08 Dec	Manchester United	A	League	D 1-1	Old Trafford	Connor	57,478
Sat 15 Dec	WOLVERHAMPTON WANDERERS	H	League	W 3-0	Elland Road	Connor, Graham, Hamson	21,227
Fri 21 Dec	Stoke City	A	League	W 2-0	Victoria Ground	Connor, Harris	16,878
Wed 26 Dec	Middlesbrough	A	League	L 1-3	Ayresome Park	Entwistle	23,259
Sat 29 Dec	NORWICH CITY	H	League	D 2-2	Elland Road	Hird, Hankin	23,493
Tue 01 Jan	DERBY COUNTY	H	League	W 1-0	Elland Road	Hird	24,271
Sat 05 Jan	NOTTINGHAM FOREST	H	F.A. Cup	L 1-4	Elland Road	OG	35,945
Sat 12 Jan	Arsenal	A	League	W 1-0	Highbury	Connor	32,799
Sat 19 Jan	NOTTINGHAM FOREST	H	League	L 1-2	Elland Road	Connor	29,816
Sat 09 Feb	BOLTON WANDERERS	H	League	D 2-2	Elland Road	Graham, Hird (pen)	16,428
Sat 16 Feb	Manchester City	A	League	D 1-1	Maine Road	Graham	34,392
Sat 23 Feb	BRIGHTON & HOVE ALBION	H	League	D 1-1	Elland Road	Flynn	17,216
Sat 01 Mar	Tottenham Hotspur	A	League	L 1-2	White Hart Lane	Chandler	35,331
Sat 08 Mar	SOUTHAMPTON	H	League	W 2-0	Elland Road	Hart, Parlane	21,169
Fri 14 Mar	Ipswich Town	A	League	L 0-1	Portman Road		23,140
Wed 19 Mar	Liverpool	A	League	L 0-3	Anfield		37,008
Sat 22 Mar	COVENTRY CITY	H	League	D 0-0	Elland Road		16,967
Sat 29 Mar	West Bromwich Albion	A	League	L 1-2	The Hawthorns	Chandler	18,898
Wed 02 Apr	MIDDLESBROUGH	H	League	W 2-0	Elland Road	Flynn, Cherry	17,906
Sat 05 Apr	Derby County	A	League	L 0-2	Baseball Ground		22,745
Tue 08 Apr	STOKE CITY	H	League	W 3-0	Elland Road	Harris (2), Parlane	15,541
Sat 12 Apr	Crystal Palace	A	League	L 0-1	Selhurst Park		25,318
Sat 19 Apr	ASTON VILLA	H	League	D 0-0	Elland Road		15,840
Sat 26 Apr	Wolverhampton Wanderers	A	League	L 1-3	Molineux	Flynn	22,746
Sat 03 May	MANCHESTER UNITED	H	League	W 2-0	Elland Road	Parlane, Hird (pen)	39,625

1980-81

Date	Opponent	H/A	Competition	Result	Venue	Scorers	Attendance
Sat 16 Aug	ASTON VILLA	H	League	L 1-2	Elland Road	Stevenson (pen)	23,401
Tue 19 Aug	Middlesbrough	A	League	L 0-3	Ayresome Park		19,470
Sat 23 Aug	Norwich City	A	League	W 3-2	Carrow Road	Hart, Connor, Graham	17,890
Wed 27 Aug	Aston Villa	A	League Cup	L 0-1	Villa Park		24,238
Sat 30 Aug	LEICESTER CITY	H	League	L 1-2	Elland Road	Hart	18,530
Wed 03 Sep	ASTON VILLA	H	League Cup	L 1-3	Elland Road	Graham	12,236
	Aston Villa won 4-1 on aggregate						12,729
Sat 06 Sep	Stoke City	A	League	L 0-3	Victoria Ground		21,947
Sat 13 Sep	TOTTENHAM HOTSPUR	H	League	D 0-0	Elland Road		32,539
Sat 20 Sep	MANCHESTER UNITED	H	League	D 0-0	Elland Road		29,619
Sat 27 Sep	Sunderland	A	League	L 1-4	Roker Park	Parlane	24,087
Sat 04 Oct	Ipswich Town	A	League	D 1-1	Portman Road	Sabella	19,134
Wed 08 Oct	MANCHESTER CITY	H	League	W 1-0	Elland Road	Harris	25,601
Sat 11 Oct	EVERTON	H	League	W 1-0	Elland Road	Curtis	20,699
Sat 18 Oct	Wolverhampton Wanderers	A	League	L 1-2	Molineux	Connor	25,033
Wed 22 Oct	Nottingham Forest	A	League	L 1-2	City Ground	Harris	19,208
Sat 25 Oct	CRYSTAL PALACE	H	League	W 1-0	Elland Road	Connor	13,970
Sat 01 Nov	Coventry City	A	League	L 1-2	Highfield Road	Connor	20,855
Sat 08 Nov	ARSENAL	H	League	L 0-5	Elland Road		17,382
Wed 12 Nov	MIDDLESBROUGH	H	League	W 2-1	Elland Road	Hird (2, 1 pen)	29,106
Sat 15 Nov	Aston Villa	A	League	D 1-1	Villa Park	Sabella	20,278
Sat 22 Nov	Southampton	A	League	L 1-2	The Dell	Graham	14,333
Sat 29 Nov	BRIGHTON & HOVE ALBION	H	League	W 1-0	Elland Road	Harris	17,771
Sat 06 Dec	West Bromwich Albion	A	League	W 2-1	The Hawthorns	Graham, Harris	21,882
Sat 13 Dec	NOTTINGHAM FOREST	H	League	W 1-0	Elland Road	Greenhoff	31,866
Sat 20 Dec	Manchester City	A	League	L 0-1	Maine Road		19,214
Fri 26 Dec	BIRMINGHAM CITY	H	League	D 0-0	Elland Road		44,086
Sat 27 Dec	Liverpool	A	League	D 0-0	Anfield		24,523
Sat 03 Jan	COVENTRY CITY	H	F.A. Cup	D 1-1	Elland Road	Hird (pen)	22,057
Tue 06 Jan	Coventry City	A	F.A. Cup	L 0-1	Highfield Road		21,007
Sat 10 Jan	SOUTHAMPTON	H	League	L 0-3	Elland Road		16,094
Sat 17 Jan	Leicester City	A	League	W 1-0	Filbert Street	Hart	15,836
Sat 31 Jan	NORWICH CITY	H	League	W 1-0	Elland Road	Harris	32,372
Sat 07 Feb	Tottenham Hotspur	A	League	D 1-1	White Hart Lane	Harris	16,530
Sat 14 Feb	STOKE CITY	H	League	L 1-3	Elland Road	Flynn	23,236
Sat 21 Feb	SUNDERLAND	H	League	W 1-0	Elland Road	Harris	45,733
Sat 28 Feb	Manchester United	A	League	W 1-0	Old Trafford	Flynn	23,014
Sat 14 Mar	Everton	A	League	W 2-1	Goodison Park	Harris, Parlane	19,252
Sat 21 Mar	WOLVERHAMPTON WANDERERS	H	League	L 1-3	Elland Road	Harris	15,053
Sat 28 Mar	Crystal Palace	A	League	W 1-0	Selhurst Park	Parlane	26,462
Tue 31 Mar	IPSWICH TOWN	H	League	W 3-0	Elland Road	Hart, Hird, Harris	15,882
Sat 04 Apr	COVENTRY CITY	H	League	W 3-0	Elland Road	Flynn, Parlane, Stevenson	29,339
Sat 11 Apr	Arsenal	A	League	D 0-0	Highbury		39,206
Sat 18 Apr	LIVERPOOL	H	League	D 0-0	Elland Road		14,505
Tue 21 Apr	Birmingham City	A	League	W 2-0	St. Andrews	Parlane, Hird (pen)	27,577
Sat 02 May	Brighton & Hove Albion	A	League	L 0-2	Goldstone Ground		17,218
Wed 06 May	WEST BROMWICH ALBION	H	League	D 0-0	Elland Road		15,840

1981-82

Date	Opponent	Competition	Result	Scorers	Attendance
Aug-29	Swansea City (A)	Division One	1-5 (L)	Parlane	23,489
Sep-02	Everton (H)	Division One	1-1 (D)	Graham	26,502
Sep-05	Wolverhampton Wanderers (H)	Division One	3-0 (W)	Graham (3)	20,216
Sep-12	Coventry City (A)	Division One	0-4 (L)		13,065
Sep-19	Arsenal (H)	Division One	0-0 (D)		21,410
Sep-23	Manchester City (A)	Division One	0-4 (L)		35,077
Sep-26	Ipswich Town (A)	Division One	1-2 (L)	Barnes	22,319
Sep-30	Manchester United (A)	Division One	0-1 (L)		47,019
Oct-03	Aston Villa (H)	Division One	1-1 (D)	Balcombe	21,065
Oct-07	Ipswich Town (H)	FL Cup R2 1L	0-1 (L)		16,994
Oct-10	Liverpool (A)	Division One	0-3 (L)		35,840
Oct-17	West Bromwich Albion (H)	Division One	3-1 (W)	Cherry, Connor, Graham	19,164
Oct-24	Sunderland (H)	Division One	1-0 (W)	E.Gray	25,220
Oct-27	Ipswich Town (A)	FL Cup R2 2L	0-3 (L)		16,494
Oct-31	Nottingham Forest (A)	Division One	1-2 (L)	Butterworth	25,272
Nov-07	Notts County (H)	Division One	1-0 (W)	Butterworth	19,552
Nov-21	Southampton (A)	Division One	0-4 (L)		21,127
Nov-28	West Ham United (H)	Division One	3-3 (D)	Cherry, Graham, Hird (pen)	25,637
Dec-05	Stoke City (A)	Division One	2-1 (W)	Graham, Hamson	13,901
Dec-12	Tottenham Hotspur (H)	Division One	0-0 (D)		28,780
Jan-02	Wolverhampton Wanderers (A)	FA Cup R3	3-1 (W)	Hird, Hamson, E. Gray	20,923
Jan-16	Swansea City (H)	Division One	2-0 (W)	Stevenson, Butterworth	18,700
Jan-28	Tottenham Hotspur (A)	FA Cup R4	0-1 (L)		46,126
Jan-30	Arsenal (A)	Division One	0-1 (L)		22,408
Feb-06	Coventry City (H)	Division One	0-0 (D)		16,385
Feb-20	Ipswich Town (H)	Division One	0-2 (L)		20,287
Feb-27	Liverpool (H)	Division One	0-2 (L)		33,689
Mar-02	Brighton & Hove Albion (A)	Division One	0-1 (L)		12,857
Mar-10	Manchester City (H)	Division One	0-1 (L)		20,797
Mar-13	Sunderland (A)	Division One	1-0 (W)	Worthington	20,285
Mar-16	Wolverhampton Wanderers (A)	Division One	0-1 (L)		11,729
Mar-20	Nottingham Forest (H)	Division One	1-1 (D)	Worthington (pen)	18,036
Mar-27	Notts County (A)	Division One	1-2 (L)	Worthington	13,316
Apr-03	Manchester United (H)	Division One	0-0 (D)		31,118
Apr-06	Middlesbrough (A)	Division One	0-0 (D)		15,494
Apr-10	Birmingham City (A)	Division One	1-0 (W)	Hart	14,497
Apr-13	Middlesbrough (H)	Division One	1-1 (D)	Parlane	20,458
Apr-17	Southampton (H)	Division One	1-3 (L)	Worthington	21,353
Apr-24	West Ham United (A)	Division One	3-4 (L)	Flynn, Connor, Graham	24,748
Apr-28	Aston Villa (A)	Division One	4-1 (W)	Connor, Graham, Worthington (2)	20,566
May-01	Stoke City (H)	Division One	0-0 (D)		17,775
May-04	Everton (A)	Division One	0-1 (L)		17,137
May-08	Tottenham Hotspur (A)	Division One	1-2 (L)	Worthington	35,020
May-12	Birmingham City (H)	Division One	3-3 (D)	Connor, Worthington, (2, 1pen)	18,583
May-15	Brighton & Hove Albion (H)	Division One	2-1 (W)	Hird, Hamson	19,831
May-18	West Bromwich Albion (A)	Division One	0-2 (L)		23,118

INDEX

Kirkham, Mark 221
Krol, Rudi 95, 180
Ladley, Geoff 151, 159
Lancaster, Joe 37
Law, Denis 33, 39, 51, 114
League Cup Final (1968) 1, 13
Lewis, Kevin 18, 22, 201
Lindsay, Maurice 143
Logie, Gus 218
Lomas, Bobby 18, 22
Lorimer, Peter 44
Loveridge, Dave 179
Lukic, John 146, 159
Lyall, John 138, 139, 143

Macari, Lou ix, 49, 50, 56, 64, 73,
    80, 100, 105
MacTier, Arthur 233
Madden, Peter 195
Madeley, Paul 92, 146, 167
Marjason, Jack 156, 159
Marsh, Rodney 129
Matthews, Sir Stanley 14
McCalliog, Jim 51, 57, 62, 84, 199
McCreery, David 41, 61, 91, 101
McDermott, Terry 103
McDowell, John 53
McGhee, Frank 83
McGrath, John 205
McGuinness, Wilf 20, 31, 238
McHugh, Dr 27, 37
McIlroy, Sammy xiii, 19, 27, 32,
    41, 42, 50, 56, 68, 69, 81, 91,
    102
McMenemy, Lawrie x, 116
McQueen, Gordon 125, 126, 132,
    148

Merrington, Dave 140, 143, 149
Miller, Ronnie 33
Millwall 59
Montgomery, Jim 96
Moore, Bobby 92
Morgan, Michael 19
Morgan, Willie 44, 49, 50, 61, 62,
    63, 67
Morris, Graham 201, 208
Mortenson, Stan 14
Muller, Gerd 137
Murphy, Barry 150
Murphy, Jimmy 25, 30, 38
MUTV 229, 236

Neal, Phil 103, 105
Neeskens, Jan 180
Nicholl, Jimmy 41, 104, 105, 135
Nicholson, Bill ix
Noble Brothers, The 214
Norden CC 217, 227
Ntsoelengoe, Ace 187

O'Farrell, Frank 31, 34, 114
O'Neill, Martin 176
O'Neill, Tommy 25, 33, 227
Ogley, Alan 6
Osgood, Peter 84
Osman, Russell 178
Osmond–Clarke, Sir 122

Park, Tony 136
Parkinson, Keith 151
Pauline, Jaack 29
Pearson, Stuart 55, 56, 79, 93, 104,
    119, 139, 163, 238
Pegg, David 14